THAILAND
in the 90s
(Revised Edition)

Published by the National Identity Board
Office of the Prime Minister
Kingdom of Thailand
1995

CONTENTS

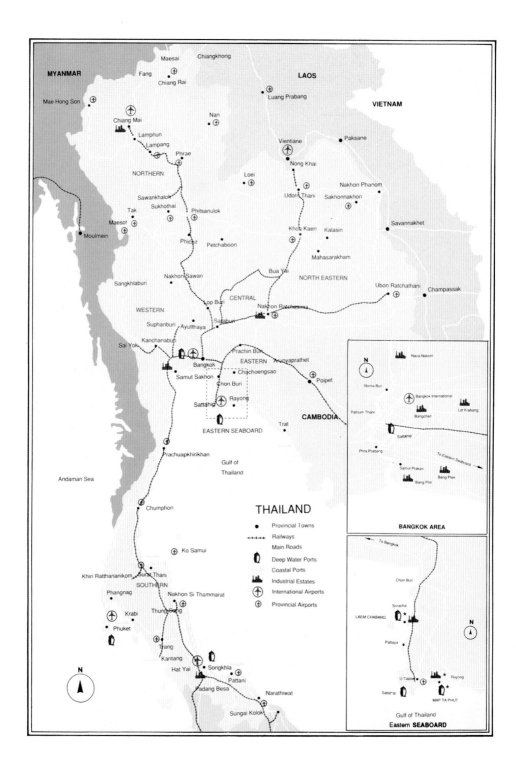

THAILAND

- Provincial Towns
- ┼┼┼┼┼ Railways
  Main Roads
- Deep Water Ports
- Coastal Ports
- Industrial Estates
- ⊕ International Airports
- ⊕ Provincial Airports

BANGKOK AREA

Eastern SEABOARD

THAILAND AT A GLANCE

Historical Background

There are conflicting opinions as to the origins of the Thais. Three decades ago it could be said with presumed certainty that the Thais originated in northwestern Szechuan in China about 4,500 years ago and later migrated down to their present homeland. However, this theory has been altered by the discovery of remarkable prehistoric artifacts in the village of Ban Chiang in the Nong Han District of Udon Thani Province in the Northeast. These include evidence of bronze metallurgy going back 3,500 years, as well as other indications of a far more sophisticated culture than any previously suspected by archaeologists. It now appears that the Thais might have originated here in Thailand and later scattered to various parts of Asia, including some parts of China.

The prehistoric painted pottery unearthed at Ban Chiang testifies to the fact that the Northeast of present Thailand has been inhabited since about 4,000 years ago.

A prehistoric rock painting in Ubon Ratchathani Province.

"Siam" is the name by which the country was known to the world until 1939 and again between 1945 and 1949. On May 11, 1949, an official proclamation changed the name of the country to "Prathet Thai", or "Thailand", by which it has since been known. The word "Thai" means "free", and therefore "Thailand" means "Land of the Free".

Geography

Situated in the heart of the Southeast Asian mainland and covering an area of 513,115 sq. km., from North 5° 30" to 21° and from East 97° 30" to 105° 30", Thailand borders the Lao People's Domocratic Republic and Myanmar to the north, Cambodia and the Gulf of Thailand to the east, Myanmar and the Indian Ocean to the west, and Malaysia to the south. Thailand has maximum dimensions of about 2,500 km. north to south and 1,250 km. east to west, with a coastline of approximately 1,840 km. on the Gulf of Thailand and 865 km. along the Indian Ocean.

Topography

Thailand is divided into four natural regions: (1) the North, (2) the Central Plain, or Chao Phraya River Basin, (3) the Northeast, or the Korat Plateau, and (4) the South, or Southern Peninsula.

The North is a mountainous region comprising natural forests, ridges and deep, narrow, alluvial valleys. The leading city of this region is Chiang Mai.

Central Thailand, the basin of the Chao Phraya River, is a lush, fertile valley. It is the richest and most extensive rice-producing area in the country and has often been called the "Rice Bowl of Asia". Bangkok, the capital of Thailand, is located in this region.

The Northeast region, or the Korat Plateau, is an arid region characterized by a rolling surface and undulating hills. Harsh climatic conditions often result in this region being subjected to floods and droughts.

Mexican sunflowers in bloom in a mountainous province of the North.

A vast stretch of rice paddy field is a common sight in the Central Plain.

The Southern region is hilly to mountainous, with thick virgin forests and rich deposits of minerals and ores. This region is the centre for the production of rubber and the cultivation of other tropical crops.

Climate

Thailand is a warm and rather humid tropical country. The climate is monsoonal, marked by a pronounced rainy season lasting from about May to September and a relatively dry season for the remainder of the year. Temperatures are highest in March and April and lowest in December and January. The average temperature is 23.7°c to 32.5°c.

The serenity of a southern island out of monsoon season.

Population

The population of Thailand is approximately 58.5 million (1994), with an annual growth rate of approximately 1.3 percent. The population includes ethnic Chinese, Malays, Cambodians, Vietnamese, Indians, and others. Immigration is controlled by a quota system.

Religion

Buddhism, the national religion, is the professed faith of 95 percent of the population. Islam, Christianity, Hinduism and others are embraced by the rest of the population. There is absolute religious freedom. The King of Thailand, under the constitution and in practice, is patron of all major religions embraced by the people.

The Walking Buddha centre the Buddha's precincts or Phuttha Monthon (Buddha Mandala) in Nakhon Pathom Province.

Language

The official national language, spoken by almost 100 percent of the population, is Thai. It is a tonal language, uninflected, and predominantly monosyllabic. Most polysyllabic words in the vocabulary have been borrowed, mainly from Khmer, Pali or Sanskrit. Dialects are spoken in rural areas. Other languages are Chinese and Malay. English, a mandatory subject in public schools, is widely spoken and understood, particularly in Bangkok and other major cities.

The Government House.

Government

Thailand is governed by a constitutional monarchy with a parliamentarian form of government. The Bangkok Metropolitan

Administration is administered by an elected governor and is divided into 38 districts. The country is divided into 76 provinces, each administered by an appointed governor, which are sub-divided into districts, sub-districts, *tambons* (groups of villages), and villages.

Economy

GDP (1994) at current prices was approximately 3,602 billion baht or US$ 142.94 billion. Total merchandise export for 1994 amounted to approximately 1,102.5 billion baht or US$ 43.75 billion and merchandise import was approximately 1,343 billion baht or US$ 53.29 billion.

Flag

Thailand's national flag, ceremoniously raised each morning and evening at 08.00 hrs and lowered at 18.00 hrs in every town and village, is composed of five horizontal bands of red, white, and blue. Outer bands of red representing the nation enclose equal inner bands of white evoking religion. The blue band, occupying the central one-third of the total area, symbolizes the monarchy. The harmony of design expresses the complimentary nature of these three pillars of the Thai nation.

This tri-coloured flag, first introduced by King Vajiravudh (Rama VI) in 1917, succeeded an earlier design which placed a white elephant on a red background.

National Anthem

The national anthem is played on all ceremonial occasions of national importance and while the national flag is being raised and lowered. Its music was composed in 1932 by Professor Phra Jenduriyang, while the lyrics,

as presently constituted, were written in 1939 by Colonel Luang Saranuprabhandh. A literal translation is as follows:

Thailand is the unity of Thai blood and body.

The whole country belongs to the Thai people, maintaining thus far for the Thai.

All Thais intend to unite together.

Thais love peace, but do not fear to fight.

They will never let anyone threaten their independence.

They will sacrifice every drop of their blood to contribute to the nation, will serve their country with pride and prestige-full of victory. *Chai Yo* (CHEERS).

Royal Anthem

The royal Thai anthem, acclaiming the Chakravatin ideal King Bhumibol Adulyadej embodies, is played during state occasions and public meetings– sports events, cinema shows, concerts, etc. Unlike other anthems whose lyrics often archaic or obsolete, the sentiments expressed in the royal Thai anthem precisely mirror the feelings of the Thai people towards their King. An English translation may be found in the section on the monarchy.

National Symbols

The Thai national and royal symbol is the Garuda, a mythical half-bird half-human figure (steed of the Hindu god Vishnu) that adorns King Bhumibol Adulyadej's scepter and royal standard. Many ministries and departments have incorporated the Garuda into their insignias. Moreover, the Garuda is signification of "By Royal Appointment" and is awarded, at the personal discretion of His Majesty the King, as a sign of royal approval to companies that have rendered outstanding economic and charitable services to Thailand. Such an award is rarely bestowed and is considered a great honour.

National Colours

Thailand has no official national colours, although the use of red, white, and blue, inspired by the colours of the Thai flag, are used by Thai international sporting teams, as well as on other appropriate occasions.

General Prem Tinsulanonda, Statesman and Privy Counsellor in traditional dress.

National Dress

Although there is no official national dress, the traditional dress has been adopted as the unofficial national costume and can be seen on both formal and informal occasions. For women, it is a full length **pasin** — a rectangular piece of cloth worn like a skirt or sarong — generally made of Thai silk. The **pasin** can be of any colour and generally has contrasting bands around the hem. It is worn with a long-sleeved silk blouse. On formal occasions a sash may be worn across the breast from the left shoulder to the right part of the waist. For men, the traditional dress is trousers with a **"sua phra ratchathan"**, a short-sleeved shirt (long-sleeved for formal occasions) with a high collarless neck. On formal occasions, a cummerbund is tied around the waist.

National Day

December 5, the birthday of His Majesty King Bhumibol Adulyadej, is the Thai national day. It is a public holiday.

His Majesty the King's birthday is celebrated nationwide.

Public Holidays

Most national holidays and festivals are of religious nature and serve to evoke a sense of devotion to the monarchy, the religion, and the nation. Some are celebrated by the lunar calendar and thus vary in date from year to year, while others are celebrated according to the solar calendar.

HISTORICAL SETTING

The Earliest Inhabitants

The area which is now Thailand has been populated ever since the dawn of civilization in Asia. The first humans in this region were hunter-gatherers whose way of life was based on hunting wild animals and gathering whatever grew wild in the woods and the hills. Later on man learnt to modify nature, growing cereals such as rice and breeding livestock. Rice-growing communities sprang up. Metal casting and pottery making also became highly-developed skills as these prehistoric settlements prospered. Cast bronze technology in the northeastern Thailand area dates from around 2000 B.C., making the prehistoric settlements in Thailand just as technologically advanced as those of India and China.

Since the 1960's, archaeological excavations in various parts of Thailand have unearthed many interesting and important sites, a large number of which are prehistoric. There are several Stone Age settlements, the most notable among them being Ban Kao in Kanchanaburi Province, Non Nok Tha in Khon Kaen Province, and Ban Chiang in Udon Thani Province.

(Facing page) Prehistoric pottery unearthed in situ at Ban Chiang, Udon Thani Province.

A prehistoric riverside rock painting in Ubon Ratchathani Province reflecting the environment among which the painter(s) lived.

The spectacular finds at Ban Chiang include bronze utensils and ornaments, painted pottery, and bimetallic (bronze and iron) weapons. Ban Chiang was apparently settled as far back as 6,000 years ago and was continually inhabited for some 4,000 years. It was an agricultural community, with skilled metal workers and potters. Artistically, the glory of Ban Chiang is the large amount of painted pottery found at the site. The most graceful shapes and intricate designs can be found on pottery dating back to the 300 B.C. - 200 A.D. period. The people who lived in Ban Chiang comprised only one among many prehistoric communities in Thailand, which makes Thailand one of the cradles of Asian civilization and an area which was inhabited for thousands of years before the emergence of the first Thai state.

Mon and Khmer Dominance

From the 9th to the 11th century A.D., the area which is now central and western Thailand was occupied by a Mon civilization called Dvaravati. The Mon race, who shared the same linguistic lineage as the Khmers, were later to settle in southern Burma. Little is known about the political or social "empire" of Dvaravati, but it seems quite likely that there were in fact several Mon states sharing a common culture, rather than a monolithic "empire" with a capital city. Important Dvaravati sites in Thailand include Nakhon Pathom, Khu Bua, Phong Tuk, and Lawo (Lopburi). Some superb bas-reliefs, sculptures, and archaeological remains survive from this obscure period of history.

A Hindu shrine, the stone sanctuary of Phanom Rung in Buri Ram Province stands as a monument to ancient Khmer dominance over northeastern Thailand.

Dvaravati was an "Indianized" culture, Theravada Buddhism being the dominant religion. Theravada Buddhism was to remain the major religion in this area for the next millennium, co-existing with animism, Hinduism, and Mahayana Buddhism. The ideas and philosophy of Theravada Buddhism inspired much of

Dvaravati art and sculpture, whose forms were also based on Indian prototypes.

By the 11th-12th centuries, Mon dominance over central Thailand had been replaced by the power of the ever-expanding Khmer empire to the east. The capital of this empire was the great city of Angkor, and the Khmer rulers were masters of a tightly-organized society with remarkable capacities for territorial and cultural expansion. The Khmers also success-fully controlled most of the trade routes in the Thailand-Indochina region. Khmer territories stretched well into the area that is present-day Thailand, covering the northeastern region, much of the centre, and coming as far west as Kanchanaburi Province. The Khmer built stone temples in the northeast, some of which have been restored to their former glory, notably those at Phimai and Phanom Rung. Stone

sculptures and lintels depicting Hindu gods, stone Buddha images in the distinctive Khmer style, and bronze statuary, some of great beauty, are other vestiges of Khmer cultural dominance. Politically, however, the Khmers probably did not control the whole of this area directly but exercised power through vassals and governors.

The *"Reclining Visnu"* lintel at Prasat Hin Phanom Rung.

The Chao Phraya River Basin had always been an area with an ethnic mix: Mons, Khmers, and Lawas. Towards the end of the 13th century, Khmer power in this area waned and new kingdoms, dominated by the Thai race, sprang up. They had been influenced by Khmer rule and culture, but spectacular legacies from his ancestors is his fleet of this new race come from?

The Emergence of the Thais

The origin of the Thai (or Tai) race is shrouded in mystery. Many theories and hypothesis have been put forward, some more convincing than others.

One theory is that the Thai race emigrated southwards into Southeast Asia from the Altai mountain range in northwestern China-Mongolia. Since archaeological, ethnographic, and linguistic researches do not bear this out, the theory now has few champions. Another unconvincing hypothesis contends that the Thai, having migrated from Sichuan province in central China, founded a kingdom in southern China called Nanchao, from whence they were driven further south by the all-conquering Mongol ruler Kubilai (Kublai Khan) in 1253, into Indochina and present-day Thailand. This theory is not very tenable because Nanchao was not a Thai-dominated kingdom, and it appears too that Thai had emigrated into the area that is now Thailand well before 1253.

A third theory propounds that the Thais were originally of Austronesian, rather than Mongoloid, stock and had migrated northwards from the Malay Archipelago. The most convincing theory, however, is that which relies largely on linguistic evidence. From research done in the southern Chinese provinces of Kwangtung, Kwangsi, and Yunnan, where the Thai language is still spoken, the proponents of this theory maintain that the Thais migrated southward from these provinces.

The fifth, and latest, hypothesis claims that archaeological and anthropological evidence prove that Thailand has been inhabited continuously even since prehistoric times. Ethnic groups mixed with each other until it was difficult to tell them apart. Animism, material culture, and folklore, however, point to a continuity in the settlement of this area. This hypothesis has been cogently put forward by its proponents, but it sidesteps too conveniently the issue of Thai migration by maintaining that the Thai have been here all along, the present-day Thai nation being but a mixture of various races.

The controversy over the origin of the Thais shows no sign of abating, and further research is needed before we can draw any definite conclusions. What is beyond dispute, however, is that by the 13th century the Thais had become a force to be reckoned within mainland Southeast Asia, and Thai princes ruled over states as far apart as Lanna, Suphannaphum (Suphanburi), Nakhon Si Thammarat, and Sukhothai.

Sukhothai (13th - 15th Centuries)

The state that is still regarded by Thai historical tradition as the "first Thai kingdom" was Sukhothai. There were, in fact, contemporaneous Thai states such as Lanna and Phayao, both in present-day northern Thailand, but the Thai historical imagination has been most stirred by Sukhothai. Even today, the evocative ruins of Sukhothai and its twin city Si Satchanalai conjure up images of material prosperity, artistic greatness, and serene Buddhist piety. Indeed, Sukhothai is remembered as much for its art and architecture as for its political achievements.

The Standing Buddha of Sukhothai has stood here for centuries since the kingdom reached its zenith of prosperity.

Sukhothai began life as a chiefdom under the sway of the Khmer empire: the oldest monuments in the city were built in the Khmer style or else show clear Khmer influence. During the first half of the 13th century the Thai rulers of Sukhothai threw off the Khmer yoke and set up an independent Thai kingdom. One of the victorious Thai chieftains became the first king of Sukhothai, with the name of Si Inthrathit (Sri Indraditya). Sukhothai's power and influence expanded in all directions by conquest (the Khmer were driven southwards), by a farsighted network of marriage alliances with the ruling families of other Thai states, and by the use of a common religion, Theravada Buddhism, to cement relations with other states.

Si Inthrathit's son and successor was King Ramkhamhaeng, undoubtedly the most famous and dynamic monarch ever to rule the Sukhothai kingdom. Much of what we know about Sukhothai in the 13th century derives from King Ramkhamhaeng's stone inscription of 1292. The inscription is problematic, but it is considered to be a seminal source of Sukhothai history as well as a masterpiece of Thai literature. It eloquently extols the benevolence of King Ramkhamhaeng's rule, the power and prosperity of Sukhothai. The king was accessible to his people. For example, he had a bell hung in front of a palace gate so

Sukhothai, as its name suggests, means "the Dawn of Happiness".

that any subject with a grievance could ring it and ask
for justice:

"King Ramkhamhaeng, the ruler of the kingdom,
hears the call; he goes and questions the man, examines
the case, and decides it justly for him. So the people of
… Sukhothai praise him."

According to the inscription, the king did not
levy road tolls or taxes on merchandise. His liberality was
such that he did not tax his subjects' inheritance at all.
Such a paternalistic and benevolent style of kingship has
caused posterity to regard the Sukhothai kingdom's
heyday as a "golden age" in Thai history.

Even allowing for some hyperbole in King
Ramkhamhaeng's inscription, it is probably true that
Sukhothai was prosperous and well-governed. Its economy
was self-sufficient, small-scale, and agricultural. The
Thai people's basic diet was the same as that of many
other people in Southeast Asia, consisting of rice and fish
as staple foods. Both, according to King Ramkhamhaeng's
inscription were plentiful:

"In the time of King Ramkhamhaeng this land of
Sukhothai is thriving. There are fish in the water and
rice in the fields."

King Ramkhamhaeng the
Great, the inventor of the
Thai script.

Sukhothai may have been self-sufficient as far as food was concerned, but its prosperity also depended on commerce. During the Sukhothai period glazed ceramic wares known as "sangkhalok" were produced in great quantities at the kilns of Sukhothai and Si Satchanalai and exported regularly to other countries in the South China Sea area, specimens having been found in Indonesia and the Philippines. Sukhothai also traded with China through the traditional Chinese tributary system: the Thai king was content to send tribute to the Chinese emperor and be classified as a vassal, in return for permission to sell Thai goods and buy Chinese products.

(Facing page) Ancient remains of Sukhothai architecture were restored and the whole area was established as Sukhothai Historical Park.

Although animistic beliefs remained potent in Sukhothai, King Ramkhamhaeng and his successors were all devout Buddhist rulers who made merit on a large scale. The major cities of the Sukhothai kingdom were therefore full of monasteries, many of which were splendid examples of Thai Buddhist architecture. Sukhothai adopted the Ceylonese school of Theravada Buddhism, beginning with King Ramkhamhaeng's invitation to Ceylonese monks to come over and purify Buddhism in his kingdom. This Ceylonese influence manifested itself not only in matters of doctrine but also in religious architecture. The bell-shaped stupa, so familiar in Thai religious architecture, was derived from Ceylonese models. Sukhothai style Buddha images are distinctive for their elegance and stylized beauty, and Sukhothai's artists introduced the graceful form of the "walking Buddha" into Buddhist sculpture.

Sukhothai's cultural importance in Thai history also derives from the fact that the Thai script evolved into a definite form during King Ramkhamhaeng's time, taking as its models the ancient Mon and Khmer scripts. Indeed, this remarkable king is credited with having invented the Thai script.

King Si Inthrathit and King Ramkhamhaeng were both warrior kings and extended their territories far and wide. Their successors, however, could not maintain such a far-flung empire. Some of these later kings were more remarkable for their religious piety and extensive building activities than for their warlike exploits. An example of this type of Buddhist ruler was King Mahathammaracha Lithai, believed to have been the compiler of the Tribhumikatha, an early Thai book on the Buddhist universe or cosmos. The political decline of Sukhothai was, however, not wholly owing to deficiencies in leadership. Rather it resulted from the emergence of strong Thai states further south, whose political and economic power began to challenge Sukhothai during the latter half of the 14th century. These southern states, especially Ayutthaya, were able to deny Sukhothai access to the area.

The Sukhothai kingdom did not die a quick death. Its decline lasted from the mid-14th until the 15th century. In 1378, the Ayutthaya King Borommaracha I subdued Sukhothai's frontier city of Chakangrao (Kamphaengphet), and henceforth Sukhothai became a tributary state of Ayutthaya. Sukhothai later attempted to break loose from Ayutthaya but with no real success, until in the 15th century it was incorporated into the Ayutthaya kingdom as a province. The focus of Thai history and politics now moved to the central plains of present-day Thailand, where Ayutthaya was establishing itself as a centralized state, its power outstripping not only Sukhothai but also other neighbouring states such as Suphannaphum and Lawo (Lopburi).

The Kingdom of Ayutthaya (1350 - 1767)

For 417 years the kingdom of Ayutthaya was the dominant power in the fertile Menam or Chao Phraya Basin. Its capital was Ayutthaya, an island-city situated at the confluence of three rivers, the Chao Phraya, the Pasak, and the Lopburi, which grew into one of Asia's most renowned metropolises, inviting comparison with great European cities such as Paris. The city must indeed have looked majestic, filled as it was with hundreds of monasteries and criss-crossed with several canals and waterways which served as roads.

An ancient community had existed in the Ayutthaya area well before 1350, the year of its official "founding" by King Ramathibodi I (Uthong). The huge Buddha image at Wat Phananchoeng, just outside the island-city, was cast over twenty years before King Ramathibodi I moved his residence to the city area in 1350. It is easy to see why the Ayutthaya area was settled prior to this date since the site offered a variety of geographical and economic advantages. Not only is Ayutthaya at the confluence of three rivers, plus some canals, but its proximity to the sea also gave its inhabitants an irresistible stimulus to engage in maritime trade. The rice fields in the immediate environs flooded each year during the rainy season, rendering the city virtually impregnable for several months annually. These fields, of course, had an even more vital function, that of feeding a relatively large population in the Ayutthaya region. Rice grown in these plants yielded a surplus large enough to be exported regularly to various countries in Asia.

Ruins of the three pagodas at Wat Phra Si Sanphet grace the vast compound of Phra Nakhon Si Ayutthaya Historical Park.

Ayutthaya's first king, Ramathibodi I, was both a warrior and a lawmaker. Some old laws codified in 1805 by the first Bangkok king date from this much earlier reign. King Ramathibodi I and his immediate successors expanded Ayutthaya's territory, especially northward towards Sukhothai and eastward towards the Khmer capital of Angkor. By the 15th century, Ayutthaya had established a firm hegemony over most of the northern and central Thai states, though attempts to conquer Lanna failed. Ayutthaya also captured Angkor on at least one occasion but was unable to hold on to it for long. The Ayutthaya kingdom thus changed, during the 15th century, from being a small state *primus inter pares* among similar states in central Thailand into an increasingly centralized kingdom wielding tight control over a core area of territory, as well as having looser authority over a string of tributary states.

The greater size of Ayutthaya's territory, as compared with that of Sukhothai, meant that the method of government could not remain the same as during the days of King Ramkhamhaeng. The paternalistic and benevolent Buddhist kingship of Sukhothai would not have worked in Ayutthaya. The king of the latter therefore created a complex administrative system allied to a hierarchical social system. This administrative system dating from the reign of King Trailok, or Borommatrailokanat (1448-1488), was to evolve into the modern Thai bureaucracy. The Ayutthayan bureaucracy contained a hierarchy of ranked and titled officials, all of whom had varying amounts of "honour marks" (*sakdina*).

Thai society during the Ayutthaya period also became strictly hierarchical. There were, roughly, three classes of people, with the king at the very apex of the structure. At the bottom of the social scale, and the most numerous, were the commoners (freemen or *phrai*) and the slaves. Above the commoners were the officials or "nobles" (*khunnang*), while at the top of the scale were the princes (*chao*). The one classless sector of Thai society was the Buddhist monkhood, or *sangha*, into which all classes of Thai men could be ordained. The monkhood was the institution which could weld together all the different social classes, the Buddhist monasteries being the centre of all Thai communities both urban and agricultural.

The Ayutthayan kings were not only Buddhist kings who ruled according to the dhamma (dharma), but they were also *devaraja*, god-kings whose sacred power was associated with the Hindu, gods Indra and Vishnu. To many Western observers, the kings of Ayutthaya were treated as if they were gods. The French Abbe de Choisy, who came to Ayutthaya in 1685, wrote that, "the king has absolute power. He is truly the god of the Siamese: no-one dares to utter his name." Another 17th century writer, the Dutchman Van Vliet, remarked that the king of Siam was "honoured and worshipped by his subjects more than a god."

The Ayutthaya period was early Thai history's great era of international trade. Ayutthaya's role as a port made it one of Southeast Asia's richest emporia. The port of Ayutthaya was an entrepôt, an international market place where goods from the Far East could be bought or bartered in exchange for merchandise from the Malay/Indonesian Archipelago, India, or Persia, not to mention local wares or produce from Ayutthaya's vast hinterland. The trading world of the Indian Ocean was accessible to Ayutthaya through its possession, for much of its 417-year history, of the seaport of Mergui on the Bay of Bengal. This port in Tenasserim province was linked to the capital by a wild but ancient and frequently used overland trade route.

Throughout its long history, Ayutthaya had a thriving commerce in "forest produce," principally sapanwood (a wood which produces reddish dye), eaglewood (an aromatic wood), benzoin (a type of incense), gumlac (used as wax), and deerhides (much in demand in Japan). Elephant teeth and rhinoceros horns were also highly valued exports, but the former was a strict royal monopoly and the latter relatively rare, especially compared with deerhides. Ayutthaya also sold provisions such as rice and dried fish to other Southeast Asian states. The range of minerals found in the kingdom was limited, but tin from Phuket ("Junkceylon")

Like a blood-vessel, river has
played an important role in
the Thai daily life since the
old days. Several foreign
settlements back in
Ayutthaya period were also
situated on the riverside.

and Nakhon Si Thammarat ("Ligor") was much sought
after by both Asian and European traders.

The Chinese, with their large and versatile junks,
were the traders who had the most regular and sustained
contact with Ayutthaya. The Ayutthaya kings, in order
to conduct a steady and profitable trade with Ming and
Manchu China, from the 14th to the 18th centuries,
entered willingly into a tributary relationship with the
Chinese emperors. The Thais recognized Chinese
suzerainty and China's preeminent position in Asia in
return for Chinese political sanction and, even more
desirable, Chinese luxury goods. Muslim merchants
came from India and further West to sell their highly-
prized clothes both to Thais and to other foreign traders.
So dominant were Chinese and Muslim merchants in
Ayutthaya that an old Thai law dating back to the 15th
century divides the Thai king's foreign trade department
into two: a Chinese section and a Muslim section.
Chinese, Indians, and later on Japanese and Persians all
settled in Ayutthaya, the Thai kings welcoming their
presence and granting them complete freedom of
worship. Several of these foreigners became important
court officials.

Containing merchandise from all corners of Asia, the thriving markets of Ayutthaya attracted traders from Europe. The Portuguese were the first to arrive, in 1511, at the time when Albuquerque was attempting to conquer Melaka (Malacca). They concluded their first treaty with Ayutthaya in 1516, receiving permission to settle in Ayutthaya and other Thai ports in return for supplying guns and ammunition to the Thai king. Portugal's powerful neighbour Spain was the next European nation to arrive in Ayutthaya, towards the end of the 16th century. The early 17th century saw the arrival of two

northern European East India Companies: the Dutch (V.O.C.) and the British. The Dutch East India Company played a vital role in Ayutthaya's foreign trade from 1605 until 1765, succeeding in obtaining from the Thai kings a deerhide export monopoly as well as one of all the tin sold at Nakhon Si Thammarat. The Dutch sold Thai sapanwood and deerhides for good profits in Japan during Japan's exclusion period, after 1635.

The French first arrived in 1662, during the reign of Ayutthaya's most outward-looking and cosmopolitan

ruler. King Narai (1656-1688). French missionaries and merchants came to the capital, and during the 1680's splendid embassies were exchanged between King Narai and King Louis XIV. The French tried to convert King Narai to Christianity and also attempted to gain a foothold in the Thai kingdom when, in 1687, they sent troops to garrison Bangkok and Mergui. When a succession conflict broke out in 1688 an anti-French official seized power, drove out the French garrisons, and executed King Narai's Greek favourite Constantine Phaulkon, who had been championing the French cause. After 1688, Ayutthaya had less contact with Western nations, but there was no policy of national exclusion. Indeed, there was increased trading contact with China after 1683, and there was continued trade with the Dutch, the Indians, and various neighbouring countries.

Ayutthaya's relations with its neighbours were not always cordial. Wars were fought against Cambodia, Lanna, Lanchang (Laos), Pattani, and above all, Burma, Ayutthaya's powerful neighbour to the west. Burmese power waxed and waned in cycles according to their administrative efficiency in the control of manpower. Whenever Burma was in an expansionist phase, Ayutthaya suffered. In 1569, King Bayinnaung captured Ayutthaya, thus initiating over a decade's subjection to the Burmese. One of the greatest Thai military leaders, Prince (later King) Naresuan, then emerged to declare Ayutthaya's independence and to defeat the Burmese in several battles and skirmishes, culminating in the victory of Nong Sarai, when he killed the Burmese Crown Prince in combat on elephant back.

During the 18th century Burma again adopted an expansionist policy. The kings of the Alaunghphaya Dynasty were intent on subduing the Ayutthaya kingdom, then in its cultural and artistic prime. During the 1760's, the Burmese armies inflicted severe defeats on the Thais, who had been somewhat too fortunate and complacent in having enjoyed over a century of comparative peace. In April 1767, after a 15-month seige, Ayutthaya finally succumbed to the Burmese, who sacked and burnt the city, thus putting an end to one of

the most politically glorious and culturally influential epochs in Thai history.

King Taksin: Warfare and National Revival (1767-1782)

After the shattering defeat which had culminated in Ayutthaya's destruction, the death and capture of thousands of Thais by the victorious Burmese, and the dispersal of several potential Thai leaders, the situation seemed hopeless. It was a time of darkness and of troubles for the Thai nation. Members of the old royal family of Ayutthaya had died, escaped, or been captured by the Burmese and many rival claimants for the throne emerged, based in different areas of the country. But out of this national catastrophe emerged yet another saviour of the Thai state: the half-Chinese general Phraya Taksin, former governor of Tak. Within a few years this determined warrior had defeated not only all his rivals but also the Burmese invaders and had set himself up as king.

A mural painting in the ordination hall of Wat Suwandaram, Ayutthaya, depicts the glorious victory of King Naresuan in the traditional single combat on elephant back.

Since Ayutthaya had been so completely devastated. King Taksin chose to establish his capital at Thon Buri (across the river from Bangkok). Although a small town, Thon Buri was strategically situated near the mouth of the Chao Phraya River and therefore suitable as a seaport. The Thais needed weapons, and one way of acquiring them was through trade. Besides, foreign trade was also needed to bolster the Thai economy, which had suffered extensively during the war with Burma (now Myanmar). Chinese and Chinese-Thai traders helped revive the economy by engaging in maritime trade with neighbouring states, with China, and with some European nations.

The equestrian statue of King Taksin the Great in Thon Buri, Bangkok.

King Taksin's prowess as a general and as an inspirational leader meant that all attempts by the Burmese to reconquer Siam failed. The rallying of the Thai nation during a time of crisis was King Taksin's greatest achievement. However, he was also interested in cultural revival, in literature and the arts. He was deeply religious and studied meditation to an advanced level. The stress and strain of such much fighting and the responsibility of rebuilding a centralized Thai state took their toll on the king. Following an internal political conflict in 1782. King Taksin's fellow general Chao Phraya Chakri was chosen king. King Taksin's achievements have caused posterity to bestow on him the epithet "the Great".

King Rama I, the founder of the Royal House of Chakri and the present capital, Bangkok, also known as "Krung Thep" or the City of Angel.

King Rama I and the Reconstruction of the Thai State (1782-1809)

The new king, Phraphutthayotfa Chulalok, or Rama I, was like King Taksin a great general. He was also an accomplished statesman, a lawmaker, a poet, and a devout Buddhist. His reign has been called a "reconstruction" of the Thai state and Thai culture, using Ayutthaya as a model but at the same time not slavishly imitating all things Ayutthaya. He was the monarch who established Bangkok as the capital of Thailand and was also the founder of the Royal House of Chakri, of which the ruling monarch, King Bhumibol Adulyadej, is the ninth king. The significance of his reign in Thai history is therefore manifold.

King Rama I was intent on the firm re-establishment of the Buddhist monkhood, allying church to state and purifying the doctrine. The Tripitaka, or Buddhist scriptures, were re-edited in a definitive text by a grand council of learned men convened by the king in 1788-9. This concern with codification and textual

Kotmai tra samduang or the Three Seals Code.

accuracy was also apparent in the collation and editing of laws both old and new which resulted in one of the major achievements of his reign: the "Three Seals Code" or *Kotmai tra samduang*. This too was the work of a panel of experts assembled by the king.

King Rama I consistently explained all his reforms and actions in a rational way. This aspect of his reign has been interpreted as a major change in the intellectual outlook of the Thai elite, or a re-orientation of the Thai world-view.

The organization of Thai society during the early Bangkok period was not fundamentally different from that of the late Ayutthaya period. Emphasis was still placed on manpower and on an extensive system of political and social patronage. The officials' main duty was still to provide the crown with corvée labour and to provide patronage to the commoners.

The Burmese remained a threat to the Thai kingdom during this reign, launching several attacks on Thai territory. King Rama I was ably assisted by his brother and other generals in defeating the Burmese in 1785 and 1786, when the Burmese tried to invade Siam. King Rama I not only drove out these invading armies but also launched a bold counter-attack as retaliation, invading Tavoy in Lower Burma. During this reign, Chiang Mai was added to the Thai kingdom, and the Malay states of Kedah, Perlis, Kelantan, and Trengganu all sent tribute to King Rama I. The recovery of the Thai state's place and prestige in the region was one of King Rama I's major achievements.

The most long-lasting creation of King Rama I was perhaps the city of Bangkok (Rattanakosin). Before 1782, it was just a small trading community, but the first king transformed it into a thriving, cosmopolitan city based on Ayutthaya's example. He had a canal dug to make it an island-city and it contained Mon, Lao, Chinese, and Thai communities similar to Ayutthaya. He also had several Ayutthaya-style monasteries built in and around the city.

Mural painting at the Temple of the Emerald Buddha depicting a scene from the Ramakian.

King Rama I was indeed, a great builder-king. He endeavoured to model his new palace closely on the Royal Palace at Ayutthaya and in doing so helped create one of Bangkok's enduring glories: the Grand Palace with its resplendent royal chapel, the Temple of the Emerald Buddha. King Rama I also completely rebuilt an old monastery, Wat Photharam, and had it renamed Wat Phra Chetuphon, which became not only an exemplar of classical Thai architecture but also a famous place of learning.

The cosmopolitan outlook of the Thais during King Rama I's reign was also reflected in the arts of the period. Both painting and literature during the early Bangkok period showed a keen awareness of other cultures, though Thai traditional forms and conventions were adhered to, King Rama I's reconstruction of the Thai state and Thai culture was so comprehensive that it extended also to literature. The king and his court poets composed new versions of the Ramakian (the Thai version of the Indian Ramayana epic) and the Inao (based on the Javanese Panji story).

King Rama II and His Sons

King Rama I's son Phra Phutthaloetla Naphalai, or Rama II, acceded to the throne peacefully and was fortunate to have inherited the crown during a time of stability. His reign was especially remarkable for the heights attained by Thai poetry, particularly in the works of the King himself and of Sunthon Phu, one of the court poets. King Rama II was a man gifted with an all-round artistic talent: he had a hand in the carving of Wat Suthat's *vihara* door-panels, considered to be the supreme masterpiece of Thai woodcarving.

At the end of King Rama II's reign, two princes were in contention for the succession. Prince Chetsadabodin was lesser in rank than Prince Mongkut, but he was older, had greater experience of government, and had a wider power base. In a celebrated example of Thai crisis power management. Prince Mongkut (who had just entered the monkhood) remained monk for the whole of his brother's reign (1824-1851). The avoidance of an open struggle between the princes worked out well for both the country and for the Royal House. While King Rama III ruled firmly and with wisdom, his half-brother was accumulating experience which was to prove invaluable to him during his years as king. The priest-prince Mongkut was able to travel extensively, to see for himself how

The statue of King Rama II.

King Rama III.

Westerners as depicted in a mural painting.

ordinary Thais lived, and to the lay the foundations for a reform of the Buddhist clergy. In the late 1830's he had set up what was to become the Thammayut sect or order (*dhammayutika nikaya*), an order of monks which became stronger under royal patronage. To this very day the royal family of Thailand is still closely associated with the Thammayut order.

The Growing Challenge of the West (1821-1868)

The major characteristic of Thai history during the 19th and 20th centuries may be summed up by the phrase "the challenge of the West." The reigns of King Rama II and his two sons, Rama III and Rama IV, marked the first stage in the Thai kingdom's dealings with the West during the Age of Imperialism.

During the Ayutthaya period, the Thais had more often than not chosen just how they wanted to deal with foreign countries, European states included. By the 19th century this freedom of choice became more and more constricted. The West had undergone a momentous change during the Industrial Revolution, and western technology and economy had begun to outstrip those of Asian and African nations. This fact was not readily apparent to the Asians of the early 19th century, but it became alarmingly obvious as the century wore on and several erstwhile proud kingdoms fell under the sway of the western powers. The early 19th century was a time when the Napoleonic Wars were preoccupying all the major European powers, but once the British had gained their victory in Europe, they resumed their quest for additional commerce and territory in Asia.

King Rama III may have been "conservative" in outlook, striving hard to uphold Buddhism (he built or repaired many monasteries), and refusing to acknowledge the claims of Western powers to increased shares in the Thai trade, but he was above all a shrewd ruler. He was justifiably wary of Western ambitions in Southeast Asia, but he was tolerant enough to come to an agreement with Burney, as well as to allow Christian missionaries to work in the kingdom.

King Mongkut.

One of the men most intellectually stimulated by the Western missionaries was Prince Mongkut. The priest-prince had an inquiring mind, a philosophical nature, and a voracious appetite for new knowledge. He learnt Latin from the French Catholic bishop Jean-Baptiste Pallegoix and English from the American Protestant missionary Jesse Caswell. Prince Mongkut's intellectual interests were wide-ranging; not only did he study the Buddhist Pali scriptures but also Western astronomy, mathematics, science, geography, and culture. His wide knowledge of the West helped him to deal with Britain, France, and other powers when he reigned as King of Siam (1851-1868).

King Mongkut was the first Chakri king to embark seriously on reform based on Western models. This did not mean wholesale structural change, since King Mongkut did not wish to undermine his own status and power as a traditional and absolute ruler. He concentrated on the technological and organizational aspects of reform. During this reign, there were road building, canal digging, ship-building, a reorganization of the Thai army and administration, and the minting of

money to meet the demands of a growing money economy. The King employed Western experts and advisers at the court and in the administration. One of his employees at court was the English governess Anna H. Leonowens, whose books on Siam have resulted in several misunderstandings concerning King Mongkut's character and reign. Far from being the strutting "noble savage" figure portrayed by Hollywood in the musical "The King and I." King Mongkut was a scholarly, conscientious, and humane monarch who ruled at a difficult time in Thai history.

The Reign and Reforms of King Chulalongkorn (1868-1910)

The reforms and foreign policy of King Mongkut were carried on by his son and successor, King Chulalongkorn (Rama V), who came to the throne a frail youth of 16 and died one of Siam's most loved and revered kings, after a remarkable reign of 42 years. Indeed, modern Thailand may be said to be a product of the comprehensive and progressive reforms of his reign, for these touched almost every aspect of Thai life.

King Chulalongkorn faced the Western world

with a positive, eager attitude: eager to learn about Western ideas and inventions, positively working towards Western-style "progress" while at the same time resisting Western rule. He was the first Thai king to travel abroad; he went to the Dutch and British colonial territories in Java, Malaya, Burma, and India, and also made two extended trips to Europe towards the end of his reign. He did not just travel as an observer or tourist but worked hard during his trips to further Thai interests. For instance, during one of his European sojourns he obtained support from Tsar Nicholas II of Russia and the German Kaiser Wilhelm II to put Siam in a stronger international position, no longer dominated by Britain and France.

The King also travelled within his own country. He was passionately interested in his subjects' welfare and was intent on the monarchy assuming a more visible role in society. He wanted to see at first-hand how his subjects lived and went outside his palace

often, sometimes incognito. His progressive outlook led him, in what was his first official act, to forbid prostration in the royal presence. He considered that such prostration was humiliating to the subject and apt to engender arrogance in the ruler. Influenced by Buddhist morality and Western examples, he gradually abolished both the corvée system and the institution of slavery, a momentous and positive change for Thai society.

During this reign, Siam's communications system was revolutionized. Post and telegraph services were introduced and a railway network was built. Such advances enabled the central government to improve its control over outlying provinces. One of the central issues

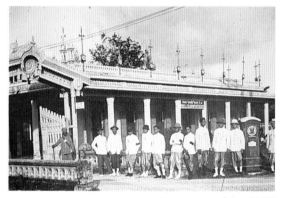

of King Chulalongkorn's reign was the imposition of central authority over the more distant parts of the kingdom. The King initiated extensive reforms of the administration, both in the provinces and in Bangkok. Western-style ministries were set up, replacing older, traditional administrative bodies. The old units which were remodelled according to the Western pattern were those of the Interior, of War, of Foreign Affairs, of Finance, of Agriculture, of the Palace, and of Local Administration. Completely new ministries were also created, such as the ministries of Justice, of Public Instruction, and of Public Works. This new ministerial system of government was inaugurated in 1892.

King Chulalongkorn's contribution to education was also to prove of great significance to modern Thailand. During this reign "public instruction" or education became more secular than ever before in Thai history. Secular schools were established in the 1880's aimed at producing the educated men necessary for the smooth functioning of a centralized administration. One of the pressing issues of the reign was the necessity to prove to the Western colonial powers that Siam had become a "modern" and "progressive" country: the problem, however, was that the King and his advisers had very little time in which to do so.

The King was eager to send Thais abroad for their education partly because the country needed skills and knowledge from the West and partly because the Thai students abroad could come into direct contact with Europe's elite. Conversely, the King also hired several

Westerners to act as advisers to the Thai government in various fields, among them the Belgian Rolin-Jacquemyns (a "General Adviser" whose special knowledge was in jurisprudence) and the British Financial Advisers H. Rivett-Carnac and W.J.F. Williamson. Such policies were deemed to be essential for Siam's survival as a sovereign state and its progress to modernity.

Thai foreign policy during King Chulalongkorn's long reign was a series of precarious balancing acts, playing off one Western power against another, and trying to maintain both sovereignty and territorial integrity. Siam's heartland had to be preserved at all costs, even to the extent of conceding to Britain and France some peripheral territories whenever the pressure became too intense.

Even Siam's subtle and supple foreign policy was not always enough to offset the appetite for territory. In 1893, Siam ceded all territories on the east ("left") bank of the Mekong River to France, then building up its Indochinese empire. In 1904, the Thais had to cede all territories on the west bank of the Mekong to France.

Rail transport was introduced into Thailand during the reign of King Chulalongkorn.

The Thai government wanted to put an end to the clauses concerning extra-territoriality, land tax, and trade duties in the treaties concluded with Western countries during King Mongkut's reign. In return for the mitigation of treaty disabilities, the Thais had to cede several territories. For example, in 1907 the Khmer provinces of Siem Reap, Battambang, and Sisophon were ceded to France in return for French withdrawal from the eastern Thai province of Chanthaburi and the abandon-

The equestrian statue of King Chulalongkorn.

ment of French extraterritorial claims over their "protected persons" (mostly Asian and therefore not properly French at all). In 1909, Siam gave up its claims to the Malay states of Kedah, Perlis, Kelantan, and Trengganu, all of which became British protectorates. This cession of territory was again agreed to by Siam in return for a lessening of certain treaty disabilities. It was fortunate indeed for the Thai kingdom that Britain and France had agreed in 1896 to keep Siam as a "buffer zone" between British and French territorial possessions in Southeast Asia.

King Chulalongkorn kept Siam an independent sovereign state in spite of all these crises, and all the while he strove to uphold Thai cultural, artistic, and religious values. The Thammayut order of monks founded by King Mongkut thrived during this reign, extending its influence from Bangkok to the provinces.

When King Chulalongkorn died in 1910 a new Siam had come into being. The Thai kingdom was now a more centralized, bureaucratic state partly modelled on Western examples. It was also a society without slaves, with a ruling class that was partly Westernized in outlook

and much more aware of what was going on in Europe and America. Technologically, too, there had been many advances: there were now railroads and trams, postage stamps and telegraphs.

With so many achievements to his credit, and a charisma that was enhanced by his longevity, it was no wonder that the Thai people grieved long and genuinely for King Chulalongkorn when he died. October 23, the date of his death, is still a national holiday, in honour of one of Siam's greatest and most beloved kings.

Nationalism and Constitution (1910-1932)

King Chulalongkorn's son and successor Vajiravudh (Rama VI) was the first Thai king to have been educated abroad, in his case at Harrow School and Oxford University in England. King Vajiravudh (r. 1910-1925) was notable for his accomplishments as a poet, dramatist (in both English and Thai), and polemicist. He was a convinced nationalist and was the first person to try to instil a Western-style nationalistic

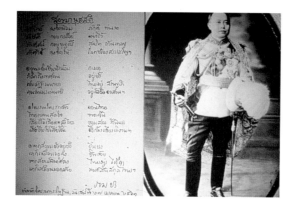

Vajiravudh College.

fervour in his subjects. Like his father, he was determined to modernize Siam while still upholding traditional Thai values and royal authority.

King Vajiravudh chose to work on issues and problems which appealed to his personal interests, largely in the literary, educational, and ideological fields. The King was also keenly interested in military affairs and formed his own paramilitary organization, the "Wild Tiger Corps," to inculcate nationalism and promote national unity. When the First World War broke out, he was determined to join the Allies in their struggle against Germany. His decision in 1917 to send Thai troops to fight in Europe was a felicitous piece of timing: although the Thai expeditionary force did not see much action. Siam's participation in the war on the Allied side earned the country and its king much praise and recognition from the international community.

The major achievements of King Vajiravudh, however, lay in the area of education and related legislation. In 1913, he compelled his subjects by law to use surnames and thus be no different from the Western nations. As a measure of his personal commitment to this idea, he himself coined hundreds of family names.

In 1921, the King issued a law on compulsory primary education which was the first step in Siam's path towards universal primary education. Two of present-day Thailand's most prestigious educational establishments were founded by King Vajiravudh: Chulalongkorn University, Siam's first Western-style university, named in honour of King Chulalongkorn, and Vajiravudh College, a boarding school for boys modelled upon the English public school.

The death of King Vajiravudh in 1925 meant that Prince Prajadhipok, his younger brother, succeeded to the throne since King Vajiravudh had no male heir. The new king (also known as Rama VII) began his reign at an unenviable juncture of both Thai and world history. The global economic depression of the late 1920's and early 1930's forced the Thai government to make economies, measures which led to some discontentment. As for Siam's internal development, the dilemma about when or whether to institute wide-ranging political reforms became more acute during this reign.

The absolute monarchy was brought to an end and gave way to a constitutional one in the reign of King Rama VII.

King Prajadhipok was a liberal and a conscientious man. A soldier by training, he nevertheless worked hard in addressing himself to Siam's problems, and his comments on various matters of government and administration in the state papers of this reign reveal him to be an admirable ruler in many ways. He was well aware of the desirability of establishing Siam in the international political community as a country with a "modern" and "liberal" constitutional system of government. The King, however, was still in the process of trying to convince the more conservative of his relatives in the Supreme State Council about the need to promulgate a constitution when matters were taken out of his hands by the bloodless "revolution", or coup d'etat, of 24 June 1932.

The promulgation of constitution by King Rama VII.

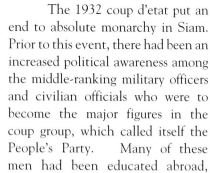

King Ananda Mahidol (Rama VIII).

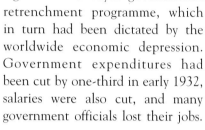

The 1932 coup d'etat put an end to absolute monarchy in Siam. Prior to this event, there had been an increased political awareness among the middle-ranking military officers and civilian officials who were to become the major figures in the coup group, which called itself the People's Party. Many of these men had been educated abroad, principally in France and Britain. There had also been a degree of discontent within the military and civilian bureaucracy resulting from the royal government's retrenchment programme, which in turn had been dictated by the worldwide economic depression. Government expenditures had been cut by one-third in early 1932, salaries were also cut, and many government officials lost their jobs.

All these factors were instrumental in motivating the coup group of 1932 to initiate a new system of government. A formal constitution was promulgated and a National Assembly set up. Siam thus became a constitutional monarchy without any bloodshed or wholesale changes in its society and economy.

After 1932: The Ascendancy of the Military

After June 1932, the country's governments alternated between democratically-elected and differing degrees of military rule. It was a period of transition, of trying to balance new political ideals and expectations with the pragmatism of power politics.

King Prajadhipok abdicated in March 1935, feeling that he could no longer cooperate with the People's Party in a constructive way. He went into exile in England, where he died in 1941. The new king was Ananda Mahidol, the ten-year-old son of Prince Mahidol of Songkla, one of King Chulalongkorn's sons. The extreme youth of the new king, and his absence from the country while pursuing his studies in Switzerland, left the People's Party with a relatively free hand in shaping the destiny of the kingdom.

During the 1940's leading figures of the People's Party dominated Thai politics. Two men in particular stood out: the civilian leader Dr. Pridi Banomyong and the young officer Luang Pibulsongkram (later Field Marshal P. Pibulsongkram). While the country experimented with various forms and degrees of democracy and several constitutions were promulgated, the two groups which held power were, alternately, the military and the civilian bureaucratic elite.

Dr. Pridi Banomyong tried to lay down the foundations of a socialistic society with his economic plan of 1933. This plan was considered to be too radical. It proposed to nationalize all land and labour resources and to have most people working for the state as government employees. These ideas were unacceptable to the more conservative elements both within the People's Party and also in the elite as a whole, which did not desire any sweeping structural changes in Thai society. Dr. Pridi was forced into temporary exile, and the National Assembly prorogued.

After 1933, Siam entered a long period of military ascendancy. The army that had been so carefully and systematically built up during the reign of King Chulalongkorn became a formidable institution. During King Vajiravudh's reign, in 1912, some officers had tried unsuccessfully to stage a coup d'etat, wanting to see Siam progress into modernity in terms of politics and government. In 1932 some senior and middle-ranking military officers had formed part of the People's Party.

Dr. Pridi Banomyong.

King Ananda Mahidol
(RamaVIII) returned from
Switzerland.

The most dynamic of these military officers was undoubtedly Luang Pibulsongkram, who came into prominence after he had played a crucial role in the defeat of a royalist counter-revolution in 1933. The Thai army was to be Field Marshal P. Pibulsongkram's power base during the next 25 years. The military had one vital advantage over other groups: an organizational strength born of being a strict and tightly-knit hierarchy. Once the military decided to involve itself in politics, it was inevitable that it would prove to be a dominant force.

The first governments of the post-1932 era tried to keep a balance between civilian and military elements so as not to alienate any important group. For instance, in 1934 the exiled Dr. Pridi Banomyong was brought back into the administration as Interior Minister largely because the Prime Minister, General Phraya Phahol Pholphayuhasena, was eager to preserve civilian support for his government. Phraya Phahol also used Luang Pibulsongkram as a minister. During the period 1934-1938 both Dr. Pridi and Luang Pibulsongkram strove hard to consolidate their political power, the former through the Thai intelligentsia and the latter through influence over the army. When Phraya Phahol resigned in 1938 Luang Pibulsongkram succeeded him as Prime Minister, signifying that the military had gained a decisive advantage in the struggle for dominance in Thai politics.

General Phraya Phahol
Pholphayuhasena.

In conformity with his view that a strongly enforced discipline backed by military strength was vital for Thailand's development he aimed at focusing nationalism to maximum intensity. He continued this policy until, in 1941, he was forced into collaboration with the occupying Japanese. Dr. Pridi, during the same period, was sympathetic to the Allies and worked with Thailand's underground resistance movement.

Field Marshal
P. Pibulsongkram.

Towards the end of World War II, Field Marshal Pibul and his collaborative government resigned and Khuang Apaivongse became the Prime Minister in 1944.

In the following year King Ananda Mahidol (Rama VIII) returned from Switzerland, and Dr. Pridi became Prime Minister in 1946. But the unexpected death of the young King generated popular dissatisfaction and once again the tide turned. Dr. Pridi was forced into exile and Field Marshal Pibul again assumed power.

This time his period of leadership was to be a long one. It would witness the establishment of parliamentary democracy in Thailand and see the emergence of the country's students as a powerful political force whose protests contributed to Field Marshal Pibul's eventual overthrow.

Major Khuang Apivongse.

In 1946, Thailand joined the United Nations, recognizing the future importance of the U.N.'s role in securing world peace. In 1950, shortly after the outbreak of war in Korea. Thailand announced its support of United Nations intervention and promptly sent a 2,000-man fighting force, smaller naval and air force contingents, and several tons of rice.

Economically, the establishment of the People's Republic of China discouraged Thailand's Chinese from sending monthly remittances and encouraged local assimilation, which in turn stimulated local growth and profits. As world demand for food products rose, the countryside began diversifying away from the rice monoculture. And in response to local demand, enterprising producers founded light manufacturing industries on city and town outskirts.

Field Marshal Sarit Thanarat.

In 1957, the premiership changed from Field Marshal Pibul to Field Marshal Sarit Thanarat. Under his vigorous personal leadership, the government apparently satisfied the requirements of the ever-burgeoning population by emphasizing economic development and national security. As a consequence of these decisive actions and policies. Field Marshal Sarit provided the nation with a sound infrastructure which successive governments could easily continue and adapt.

Following the sudden death of Field Marshal Sarit in 1963, Field Marshal Thanom Kittikachorn was appointed Prime Minister. The government led by Field

Field Marshal Thanom Kittikachorn.

Professor Sanya Dharmasakti.

M.R. Seni Pramoj.

M.R. Kukrit Pramoj.

Dr. Tanin Kraivixian.

Marshal Thanom not only concentrated on internal social and economic development but also promoted the stability of the region as a whole. Indeed, it was primarily through the initiative of Thailand that the Association of Southeast Asian Nations (ASEAN) was established in 1967 in accordance with the Bangkok Declaration. However, in response to unprecedented political confusion caused by a student uprising in October 1973 Field Marshal Thanom relinquished the premiership in favour of Professor Sanya Dharmasakti.

During the period 1973-1976, the Thai political area witnessed successive governments headed by Professor Sanya Dharmasakti, M.R. Seni Pramoj, M.R. Kukrit Pramoj, again M.R. Seni Pramoj, and finally Dr. Tanin Kraivixian, each of whom strove to develop the country in its own way.

In 1977, General Kriengsak Chamanand became the Prime Minister. His government maintained political stability, which successfully encouraged foreigners to invest in Thailand.

General Prem Tinsulanonda became premier in 1979 and headed four governments between that time and 1988, when he declined another term. During these years, insurgency-caused conflicts were greatly reduced and many groups of insurgents emerged from their jungle hideouts to peacefully surrender to government officials. Moreover, national stability and successful foreign policies brought about a great many socio-political and economic developments.

In 1982 Thailand celebrated the 2nd centennarial anniversary of Bangkok.

An elected Prime Minister, Major General Chatichai Choonhavan, took office in August of 1988. During his first year he continued the successful economic policies that have brought Thailand to the status of a newly industrialized country and was also active in foreign affairs, particularly those of neighbouring Indochina.

In 1992 the military coup d'etat led by General Sunthorn Kongsompong ousted the democratically elected Chatichai cabinet. Mr. Anand Panyarachun, a diplomat

General Kriengsak Chamanand.

General Prem Tinsulanonda.

Major General Chatichai Choonhavan.

and well-known businessman was appointed as the next Prime Minister. He led his cabinet as an interim government until his term ended in accordance with the constitution. A general election took place which resulted in an appointment of General Suchinda Kraprayoon as the Prime Minister. The cabinet led by General Suchinda Kraprayoon was ended by a political mass demonstration for democracy. After resignation of General Suchinda Kraprayoon, Mr. Anand Panyarachun was for the second time appointed as the Prime Minister. In his second period, Mr. Anand Panyarachun came with several liberalization programmes for the enhancement of economic growth and the general advancements of the country. He has also introduced a nationwide reform and revised the outmoded laws of the country resulting in greater facilitation and greater assurance to the business community.

Mr. Anand Panyarachun.

Mr. Anand Panyarachun whose rich and long experiences in diplomat career together with his outstanding performances while he was serving as the President of the ASEAN Chambers of Commerce and Industry (ASEAN-CCI) before his premiership, initiated what is later known as the ASEAN Free Trade Area or AFTA scheme whereby the trade among them will be cut to a uniform level of 0-5% within the year 2008. The new scheme was agreed upon in Singapore in January 1992 in the Fourth ASEAN Summit.

Mr. Chuan Leekpai.

The Anand II interim cabinet came to an end when Mr. Chuan Leekpai won the election in 1992 and was Prime Minister from 1992 to 1995. In mid 1995, Mr. Banharn Silpa-Archa won the election and has become Prime Minister since then.

Mr. Banharn Silpa-Archa.

THE MODERN MONARCHY

The institution of monarchy in Thailand is in many ways unique, often difficult for outsiders to fully comprehend. Not only does it have a history going back more than seven hundred years, but it also continues to function with extraordinary relevance and vitality in the contemporary world. Indeed, although the Revolution of 1932 brought an end to monarchy in its absolute form, the institution today can be said to be more powerful than ever in the sense of providing a unifying element for the country, a focal point that brings together people from all backgrounds and shades of political thought and gives them an intense awareness of being Thai. This was clearly shown by the unprecedented outpouring of public pride and personal affection that greeted the occasion in 1988 of His Majesty King Bhumibol Adulyadej's becoming the longest-reigning monarch in Thai history and is also apparent in countless other ways, large and small.

The intensity of respect felt by Thai people for their King stems in large part from the distinctive form the modern monarchy has taken under his own leadership, one that involves a remarkable degree of personal contact. At the same time, it is rooted in attitudes that can be traced to the earliest days of Thailand as a nation and in some of the past rulers who continued to serve as models of kingship.

Background to a Modern Kingship

Thai concepts of monarchy have their origins in Sukhothai, founded in the early part of the 13th century and generally regarded as the first truly independent Thai capital. Here, particularly under the reign of King Ramkhamhaeng the Great (1275-1317), was born the

King Rama I

King Rama II

King Rama III

King Rama IV

King Rama V

King Rama VI

King Rama VII

King Rama VIII

King Rama IX

The Royal House of Chakri

ideal of a *paternalistic ruler* alert to the needs of his people and aware of the fact that his duty was to guide them, a view markedly different from the divine kingship practiced by the Khmers.

This *paternalistic ideal was at times lost during the long Ayutthaya period*, when Khmer influence regarding kingship reappeared and the monarch became a lofty, inaccessible figure, rarely seen by most citizens. Nevertheless, the four-century era witnessed the reigns of some remarkable rulers, whose achievements were far-reaching.

With the founding of the Royal House of Chakri, in 1782, and the establishment of Bangkok as the capital, kingship was based primarily on adherence to the Buddhist concept of virtue. The Bangkok period produced a succession of unusually able rulers, capable of meeting a variety of challenges both to the country and to the monarchy itself.

Though it had lasted longer than most others in the world, largely due to wise rule by Chakri kings, the country's absolute monarchy finally came to an end on June 24, 1932, when a small group of civil servants and military officers staged a bloodless coup and demanded a constitution. King Prajadhipok (Rama VII), who in any case was already thinking along such lines himself and had already drafted a constitution which had been debated in the Supreme Council of State, agreed and thus became the first constitutional monarch. Three years later, unhappy with some of the results, he decided to abdicate; his nephew Prince Ananda Mahidol, then a 10-year-old student in Switzerland, was chosen to follow him as eighth in the Chakri line.

Early Years

The man who has reigned longer than any previous Thai monarch and has earned such remarkable devotion from his subjects seemed far from the throne at the time of his birth in 1927 in Cambridge, Massachusetts. King Prajadhipok still ruled at the time,

and any children he might have would be first in
succession. There was also his father, Prince Mahidol of
Songkla, then studying medicine at Harvard University,
as well as his older brother Prince Ananda Mahidol. The
future King Bhumibol Adulyadej appeared likely to spend
a more or less ordinary life, no doubt influenced by his
father's strong determination to use his education and
social position to improve public welfare, but doing so in
relative obscurity.

Fate, however, determined otherwise. Prince
Mahidol died in 1929, and the abdication of King
Prajadhipok followed in 1935. For the first 11 years of
his rule, the young King Ananda Mahidol remained
mostly in Switzerland with his mother, sister, and younger

brother, pursuing his studies while effectively cut off from his homeland by the World War. In 1946 he died in the Grand Palace while on a visit, and Prince Bhumibol Adulyadej, then 19 years old, suddenly found himself the ninth Chakri King. He subsequently returned to Luzern to complete his education, changing from science to political science and law in recognition of his new role.

Two years later, while on a visit to Fontainebleau, he met the beautiful young Mom Rajawongse Sirikit Kitiyakara, daughter of the Thai ambassador to France, HRH Prince Nakkhatrmongkol Kitiyakara, Krommamun Chandapuri Suranath, and in 1948 their engagement was announced by the Government.

They were married in Bangkok on April 28, 1950, and seven days later His Majesty was crowned in ancient ceremonies held at the splendid Grand Palace from which his ancestors had ruled the kingdom. He himself, characteristically, has chosen to take as his official

Bangkok residence the more modest Chitralada Villa, while steadfastly adhering to the momentous Oath of Succession to the Throne pledged during the coronation: "We will reign with righteousness for the benefit and happiness of the Siamese people."

As a man, King Bhumibol Adulyadej has displayed a remarkable range of talents. He is a gifted musician and composer, particularly in the field of jazz; one of his songs was featured in a Broadway musical in the early 1950's and his skills have been acknowledged by such masters as Benny Goodman and Lionel Hampton. He was an enthusiastic sailor in the early years of his rule and won the Southeast Asia Peninsula Games gold medal in 1967. In addition, he can point to impressive achievements in the fields of painting, photography, and engineering. Thanks to his international education and upbringing, he is fluent in three European languages and at ease in a variety of cultures. Undoubtedly, though, posterity will remember him most for his accomplishments as leader of the Thai nation during a critical period in its history.

The Forging of a Modern Monarchy

Despite the panoply of time-honoured ritual that attended his coronation and the reverence felt by all Thais for the monarchy as an institution–scarcely dimmed even after the 1932 Revolution–King Bhumibol Adulyadej was actually confronted by an unprecedented challenge at the time he began his rule: how to fashion a concept of kingship that met the needs of a rapidly changing society, at once traditional and creatively modern. It was a challenge as urgent as any faced by Chakri kings of the past, and the manner in which he has met it has truly defined his greatness as a ruler.

Perhaps the most important step taken by His Majesty in the process was his decision to bring the monarchy into direct contact with the provincial population. Despite the efforts of previous rulers, this had not been really feasible in the past, largely due to difficulties of travel outside the central region. It was not until 1927, after opening of the northern railway line, that the people of Chiang Mai saw their monarch for the first time, and only a few towns along the southern coast had been honoured with a royal visit. Following the abdication of King Prajadhipok, there was a period of nearly 20 years when the King was a remote personage to the vast majority of Thais, a face in a photograph or a name on an official proclamation. Many of them went about their daily lives in almost total isolation, little affected by events in far-off Bangkok and, as a result, often feeling ignored by those in power.

Generally regarded as a milestone in altering this situation is the trip made by King Bhumibol Adulyadej in 1955, when he became the first ruler to visit the northeastern provinces, traditionally the poorest and most neglected in the country, with poor roads and hamlets that became all but inaccessible in the rainy season. Together with Queen Sirikit, he spent 22 arduous days touring the region, observing at first hand the problems of the people and talking with the enthusiastic crowds who walked for miles from obscure villages just to catch a glimpse of their king. The warmth of their greeting was unmistakable; so, too, was the extent of their needs as revealed in the conversations His Majesty had with those he met.

This method of personal encounter, particularly in rural areas, has become one of the major hallmarks of King Bhumibol Adulyadej's reign. Today he and members of his family spend almost seven months of the year in one or another of the royal residences which have been built outside of Bangkok: at Chiang Mai in the North, Sakon Nakhon in the Northeast, Hua Hin on the Gulf of Thailand, and Narathiwat in the South. From these, defying discomforts and inconveniences, His Majesty has managed to visit every one of Thailand's 76 provinces, going to even the most remote villages by helicoptor, jeep, train, boat, or, on occasion, by foot, to ascertain for himself local conditions. In the process he has become not only the most travelled monarch in Thai history but also the best informed about a wide range of rural difficulties, some of them peculiar to a certain locality and others common to an entire region. Moreover, he has become a father-like figure to millions of his subjects, who are no longer amazed to find him suddenly in their village squares, available for consultation about matters both trivial and serious.

Typically, before such a visit the consults maps, aerial photographs and remote sensing to acquaint himself as thoroughly as possible with the topographical and social features of the general area. Once there he talks with resident monks and farmers, as well as government officials, soliciting first-hand information on community needs and aspirations. By comparison with the ceremonial atmosphere that surrounds royal appearances in Bangkok, these are remarkably informal sessions, with much of the initial are felt by villagers soon diminishing in actual contact with a ruler who clearly both listens and cares about their problems.

Often assisted by other members of the Royal Family, the King takes careful notes and later initiates steps to provide assistance, always working through the appropriate government agencies but sometimes using his own funds in the early stages to help a project get off the ground. He later established the Chai Pattana Foundation to help provide initial or emergency financial support for subsequent development projects. He never simply issues a directive: the impetus comes from the local population, who must agree with the proposal and cooperate to see that it is successfully implemented.

Over 1,000 small-scale "royally-suggested" projects have been started in this way, covering the whole spectrum of rural problems in Thailand, from the introduction of new crops to water conservation, from swamp drainage to the preservation of national forests. In all, the aim has been sustainable development, serving not only immediate needs but also those of future generations by conserving the present environment and seeking to restore areas that have already suffered from misuse. Some of these projects, notably those involving crop substitution, have proved so successful that the United Nations hopes to emulate them in other countries facing similar problems.

One of the earliest and most innovative was His Majesty's Hilltribe Development Project in the North, now known as the Royal Project and encompassing lowland areas as well. The migratory tribal people who live in the mountainous region that forms Thailand's borders with Laos and Myanmar had been an increasing problem to the government, partly due to their slash-and-burn technique of clearing land, thus leading to widespread destruction of the native forest, and partly to their traditional cultivation of opium poppy, base material for heroin production. The Royal Project sought to address these problems and also to improve the lives of the tribal groups, who actually derived a bare subsistence income from their role in the international drug trade.

The programme has introduced a wide variety of crops—among them such temperate-zone plants as coffee, peaches, apricots, strawberries, lychees, apples, and chrysanthemums—which bring larger profits than opium and provided assistance in both methods of growing and marketing; in addition, it has brought educational and medical facilities to permanent settlements. The results can be seen clearly not only in tribal communities who have joined the project but also in the supermarkets of Bangkok and in the numerous new export products.

International recognition of the Royal Project's effectiveness has come in many forms, including financial grants and expert assistance by several foreign governments. In 1988, it was awarded the Ramon Magsaysay Award, the Asian equivalent of the Nobel Prize, in the area of international understanding.

In the Northeast, where drought is a perennial problem, reservoirs and other water-storage facilities were built and alternative crops tested to increase the income of farmers. Swamp drainage has been a concern of royal initiated projects in southern Thailand, together with land reclamation and preservation of mangrove forests. In a number of experimental centres set up at His Majesty's initiative near the Gulf of Thailand, various agencies are demonstrating ways that surrounding villagers can improve crop yields in the sandy soil; important new sources of income like the breeding of fresh-water prawns in ponds have also been introduced with notable results.

In recent decades an alarming proportion of Thailand's native forest cover has been lost, through both indiscriminate logging operations and the need for more agricultural land by an expanding population. Among the harmful results are increased erosion and a decrease of watershed resources, as well as destruction of the natural habitat of many wildlife species. Several of His Majesty's projects are seeking to relieve this situation through reafforestation, improvement of existing

farmlands, the planting of commercial fruit orchards, and programmes aimed at educating the public on the importance of preserving those forests that remain. Their Majesties have also spearheaded efforts to raise certain endangered species of wildlife in captivity and then release them in protected areas in the hope of saving them from extinction.

A much-publicized undertaking to help Thai farmers, one made possible through His Majesty's support in its early stages, has been the Royal Rain-Making Project. Through years of experimentation, 14 different chemical formulae have been devised for varying conditions of weather, location, and topography; specially-equipped planes use these to seed clouds in areas suffering from lack of rain, with results so successful that several neighbouring countries have called on Thai experts to help them with similar problems.

Such projects have not only brought enormous benefits to Thailand's rural population but have also given the monarchy a new image, linking it more intimately with the lives of ordinary Thais than ever before. The King is not merely a symbolic figure, reigning from a distant capital; he is a trusted ally working closely with them in the ancient struggle for a better life. The pictures of him and other members of the Royal Family that are displayed in homes and business establishments all over the country are thus signs of deep affection as well as reverence for an institution.

King Bhumibol Adulyadej's agricultural interests are evident even at his residence in Bangkok. On the grounds of Chitralada Villa—within plain view of passers-by—are fields of experimental rice, a herd of dairy cattle, and a plant to manufacture powdered milk. As long ago as 1952, His Majesty had large fish ponds dug in the compound, which he stocked with a fast-breeding variety

known as *tilapia nilotica* obtained from Japan. When these proved adaptable to Thai conditions, specimens were presented to villagers throughout the kingdom, thus providing a significant new addition to the provincial diet. In 1965, Japanese Crown Prince Akihito gave His Majesty 50 fish of a different type and these, too, were bred in Chitralada ponds. Given the Thai name *pla nil* by the King, they were distributed through the Department of Fisheries and have proved extremely popular with farmers. Today, some 16 countrywide fishery stations rear over 10 million *pla nil* annually.

Also in Bangkok, King Bhumibol Adulyadej has provided the impetus for clearing and improving the Makkasan Swamp, a large body of water formerly clogged with water hyacinth in the centre of the capital. At the King's suggestion the swamp is being dredged, provided with exit channels, and transformed into a useful part of the city's flood control system.

Other Aspects of Modern Monarchy

In creating his unique version of a modern monarchy, His Majesty has been a significant force in other areas besides that of rural development. His moral leadership, personal as well as symbolic, has proven immensely important, sometimes decisive, in a number of national crises since he came to the throne, always on the side of peace and stability and remaining within the limits of his constitutional authority.

In 1973, for example, the country moved perilously close to political disorder and confusion during a confrontation between students and government forces. Both sides turned to the King for advice at the moment of greatest danger and it was largely through his intervention that serious bloodshed was averted. Firmly committed to the development of democratic principles, he has also restrained impulsive military leaders and discouraged coups as a means of resolving power struggles between various groups. The political stability which has played such an essential part in Thailand's remarkable economic growth over the past decade has been largely

due to the fact that leaders of all factions share a deep respect for his views on such matters.

King Bhumibol Adulyadej provided equally wise counsel during Thailand's struggle against a communist insurgency. Drawing on his wide experience in rural areas, he suggested solutions aimed at relieving rural poverty and inspiring confidence in the government's sincerity. Today most of the former insurgents have peacefully reassimilated into Thai life; a royal residence has been built at Khao Kho in Phetchabun Province, in the heart of what was one of the country's most insecure areas. (In this respect, it is also worth noting that even at the height of the communist problem, members of the insurgency were willing to come forward to meet the Royal Family and air their grievances.)

The King is upholder of all religions in Thailand and has actively promoted understanding between the majority of Thais and minority groups like the Muslims of the southern provinces. On his regular stays at his royal residence in Narathiwat Province, His Majesty spends much time visiting mosques throughout the region and establishing close contacts with religious leaders as well as ordinary people.

In the late 1970's, when Indochinese refugees flooded into Thailand by the hundreds of thousands, the King's compassion was one of the factors contributing to the government's decision to allow them sanctuary in a

series of camps set up along the borders. He was also very supportive in the establishment of such international organizations as ASA and ASEAN to promote socioeconomic and political cooperation within the Southeast Asian region.

For over two decades, His Majesty has devoted himself almost entirely to his numerous developmental projects and the performance of his ritual duties for the benefit of the Thai people. In earlier years, however, he travelled extensively to more than 30 countries and met nearly all the outstanding leaders of the contemporary world. Other members of the Royal Family now represent him on such trips, though he keeps in close touch with international events through his wide-ranging personal contacts.

Three recent events attest to the strength of the remarkable relationship King Bhumibol Adulyadej has established with his people. In 1982, the Royal House of Chakri celebrated its Bicentennial, an occasion of nationwide festivities that clearly showed the depth of feeling for the monarchy as an institution and for His Majesty as an individual ruler. This was even more vividly apparent in 1987 when he reached his 60th birthday, a significant milestone in any Thai life; elaborate ceremonies were held throughout Thailand for several days in December and one of the largest crowds in Thai history assembled at Sanam Luang,

across from the Grand Palace to pay homage to the man they regarded as the embodiment of national unity. Finally, in June of 1988, His Majesty was honoured as the longest-ruling Thai monarch, surpassing in that month the 42-year reign of his ancestor King Chulalongkorn. Once again the crowds assembled in record-breaking numbers and the words of the royal anthem resounded, not uttered automatically but accurately mirroring the sentiments of those who sang it:

> We, Your Majesty's loyal subjects,
> Pay homage with deep heartfelt veneration,
> To the supreme Protector of the Realm,
> The mightiest of monarchs complete with transcendent virtues,
> Under whose benevolent rule, we Your subjects,
> Receive protection and happiness,
> Prosperity and peace;
> And we wish that whatsoever Your Majesty may desire,
> The same may be fulfilled.

Traditional Royal Duties

King Bhumibol Adulyadej also presides over a large number of ritual functions, many of them deeply rooted in Thai tradition. He bestows decorations on worthy people who have performed distinguished services for the nation, sprinkles lustral water on honoured dignitaries during birthday and wedding celebrations, attends important cremation ceremonies, and casts new Buddha images at various monasteries throughout the country.

Keenly aware of the importance of education and of the value of youth to the future of Thailand, he began attending graduation ceremonies early in his reign, personally handing out degrees to the graduates of every Thai university as well as to those of military academies. The recent growth in the number of such institutions has made it necessary to delegate this responsibility to other members of the Royal Family in some cases but

His Majesty still presides over the ceremonies at older ones like Chulalongkorn and Thammasat Universities, even though they now extend over several days.

The Royal Ploughing Ceremony, a ritual marking the official start of the rice planting season that originated in Ayutthaya, was revived at His Majesty's suggestion in 1960 and is now held annually at Sanam Luang across from the Grand Palace. Prediction of the forthcoming rice, which is of considerable symbolic importance to the nation's farmers.

All new ambassadors present their credentials to His Majesty and he grants audiences to foreign heads of state, diplomats, and officials of the Thai Government, including the Prime Minister. In addition, as Head of State he convenes Parliament at the beginning of each new session and every draft law is submitted to him for his signature before promulgation. As Head of the Armed Forces, he presides each December over the Trooping of the Colours, an impressive ceremony during which the elite Royal Guards pledge their allegiance to him.

A devout Buddhist, King Bhumibol Adulyadej entered the monkhood for two weeks in 1956, as most

Thai men are expected to do at some point in their lives. Throughout the year he participates in numerous merit-making ceremonies at various temples and personally visits many of Thailand's most venerated monks.

To coordinate his active schedule, His Majesty relies on a royal bureaucracy staffed by a special category of civil servants classified as belonging to the Court and based at both the Grand Palace and Chitralada Villa, Divided into the Office of His Majesty's Principal Private Secretary and the Bureau of the Royal Household, this bureaucracy compiles the royal appointments calendar, arranges ceremonial functions, manages royal finances, supervises royal housekeeping, and performs a wide range of administrative duties; many members of the staff travel regularly with the Royal Family on provincial tours.

The King personally appoints his Privy Council, a body composed of distinguished advisers noted for their exceptional experience and knowledge of state affairs. The Privy Council reviews all draft laws and makes germane recommendations to His Majesty. In addition, it meets twice weekly to consider unusual or complex issues, such as an appeal for royal clemency or a request without precedent, before forwarding recommendations for His Majesty's attention.

Her Majesty Queen Sirikit

The dedication to public service exemplified by King Bhumibol Adulyadej's life is also found in other members of the Royal Family, who consist of Her Majesty Queen Sirikit, the Royal Children, Her Royal Highness the Princess Mother, and the King's sister Princess Galyani Vadhana. Like His Majesty, all these work untiringly for the benefit of the country, sometimes participating in projects initiated by the King and sometimes in others of their own; in doing so all have contributed significantly to the creation of Thailand's modern monarchy.

Queen Sirikit spends as much time travelling as her husband, equally indifferent to discomforts and long hours, and her interest in the welfare of rural people closely parallels his. An area in which she has taken a particularly deep interest is that of finding sources of supplementary income in the off-season or when crops are destroyed by droughts or floods. It was to combat such problems that the Foundation for the Promotion of Supplementary Occupations and Techniques (known as SUPPORT) was established in 1976 under Her Majesty's patronage, partly through funds supplied by Her Majesty and partly with public donations.

SUPPORT's primary objective is to set up women's groups and provide rural Thai women with equipment, materials, and training in cottage industries. The latter include some 18 traditional crafts which Her Majesty felt were worthy of being promoted on both local and world markets, among them embroidery and weaving in the north, a kind of ikat silk called *mudmee* in the Northeast, doll and rattanware making in the central region, and *yan lipao*, basketry woven of a strong indigenous vine, in the South. These are marketed through a chain of Chitralada Shops in Thailand and through department stores abroad. Most of the crafts are indigenous to the areas where the projects have been set up and use readily available raw materials, thus making it easier for families to acquire a second source of income for basic necessities when emergencies arise.

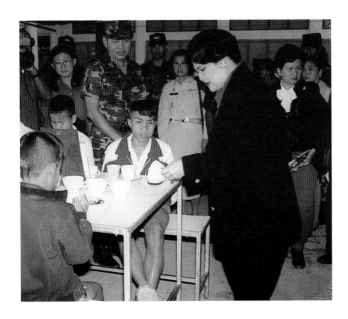

Besides individual projects in various parts of the country, SUPPORT has established two multi-craft training centres. One is in the compound of Chitralada Villa, where around 200 students attend classes taught by masters of particular crafts; the other, founded in 1980, is the Bangsai Arts and Crafts Centre, located on the Chao Phraya River near the old capital of Ayutthaya, which has an enrollment of around 300. At both students are given a daily allowance, travelling expenses, and extra pay for the crafts they produce; after training they return to their villages to pass on the skills to others.

The Queen has personally undertaken the promotion of these crafts through trips abroad to meet potential buyers and also by using them prominently in her own wardrobe; *mudmee*, for example, which was once hardly known outside the region where it was made, is now regarded as one of the most fashionable dress materials in Thailand and it was also featured in a collection by the French designer Pièrre Balmain. The Queen's interest in handicraft development led to the celebration of the Thailand Arts and Crafts Year, held from August 12, 1988 to December 31, 1989, which featured a wide variety of exhibitions, demonstrations, and other events under the auspices of the Tourism Authority of Thailand.

For her work among rural women, Queen Sirikit was awarded the prestigious Ceres Medal by the Food and Agriculture Organization of the United Nations, bringing international recognition to an achievement already well-known to countless Thais who have benefitted from it. In 1988, she was awarded an Honorary Fellowship in Great Britain's 470-year-old Royal College of Physicians, the highest honour the college confer, for her "deep concern for the health and welfare of the people of Thailand."

The Queen's efforts on behalf of the less fortunate members of society have also extended to the refugees from Indochina who have come to Thailand in such large numbers since the late 1970's. Similar handicraft training projects have been set up in the Kao Larn Red Cross Camp for women with young children, enabling them to produce goods and earn money while awaiting resettlement. Members of the northern hill tribes have benefitted as well and many are attending SUPPORT centres, where they are given new ideas to use in such traditional skills as embroidery and jewellery-making.

Sharing the King's concern over the destruction of the natural environment, Queen Sirikit is an active member of the World Wildlife Fund (Thailand) and has worked for years on behalf of conservation of forest areas as a part of watershed development and as means of helping preserve wild animals, especially those in danger of extinction. To this end, she has actively lent her support to an afforestation project in the Northeast, Thailand's most arid region, and has worked closely with concerned people to protect wildlife habitats.

Despite her deep involvement in these projects, as well as other responsibilities which include numerous royal ceremonies and serving as Colonel-in-Chief of the 21st Royal Guards Infantry Regiment, Her Majesty has also found the time to be an attentive mother, passing on to her children the same dedication to public service that has characterized the reign.

The Royal Family

Their Majesties' only son, His Royal Highness Crown Prince Maha Vajiralongkorn, was born in Bangkok in 1952. After completing his primary education in Thailand, His Royal Highness attended secondary school in England and then went to Australia's famous Royal Military College, Duntroon. Upon finishing, he returned to Thailand to take up his duties which, besides serving in the Royal Thai Army, include frequent provincial tours and representing His Majesty King Bhumibol Adulyadej at a wide variety of official functions and ceremonies. Of particular interest to His Royal Highness are the hospitals which were set up in the provinces with funds donated by the public. On several occasions, His Royal Highness has made state visits to foreign countries as His Majesty's representative.

Prince Vajiralongkorn was invested as Crown Prince by His Majesty in 1972. He married in 1977 and the following year his royal consort, Her Royal Highness Princess Somsawali, gave birth to Their Majesties' first grandchild, Her Royal Highness Princess Bajarakitiyabha. Princess Somsawali is involved in many charitable organizations and activities, particularly those dealing with public welfare, often bringing her daughter along.

His Royal Highness Crown Prince Maha Vajiralongkorn's younger sisters, Their Royal Highnesses Princess Maha Chakri Sirindhorn and Princess Chulabhorn, were born in Bangkok in 1955 and 1957 respectively. Both Princesses received their education in Thailand, from primary school through university.

His Royal Highness Crown Prince Maha Vajiralongkorn, by Royal Command, represented His Majesty the King in presiding over the Opening Ceremony of the Maulidin Nabi Celebration of Thailand, Hegira 1415, at the New Building, Ambara Gardens.

Her Royal Highness Princess Maha Chakri Sirindhorn, the first of the Royal Children to attend a local institution of higher learning, received her B.A. degree from the Faculty of Arts of Chulalongkorn University, where she majored in the Thai language. She also holds a M.A. degree in Oriental Epigraphy from Silpakorn University and a doctorate in Development Education from Srinakharinwirot University. A gifted performer on traditional Thai musical instruments, she regularly accompanies her father on his visits to his provincial projects and assists him in collecting information relevant to their operation.

Her Royal Highness Princess Chulabhorn graduated with a B.Sc. degree from Kasetsart University. A gifted scientist who was awarded the coveted Einstein Gold Medal in 1986, she also has a doctorate in Organic Chemistry from Mahidol University. On December 1, 1987, she set up the Chulabhorn Research Institute to promote scientific research in Thailand, and she has lectured on a number of occasions before academic groups abroad. In 1982 she was married to Flight Lieutenant Virayuth Didyasarin, a fighter pilot, and they now have two daughters, Their Royal Highnesses Princess Siribhachudhabhorn and Princess Adityadorn-kitikhun.

A function was held by the government on Saturday, December 27, 1986 in honour of HRH Princess Chulabhorn on her winning the Einstein Gold Medal (Best Scientist). She was the third of the world to receive the award.

Both Her Royal Highness Princess Maha Chakri Sirindhorn and Her Royal Highness Princess Chulabhorn have travelled abroad frequently to represent their country at a variety of ceremonies.

The Royal Children have always carried out their duties with great efficiency and dedication, lending valuable support to His Majesty in his many tasks of national development. In 1978 Her Royal Highness Princess Sirindhorn was bestowed with the new style of title of "*Somdech Phra Debaratanarajasuda Chao Fa Maha Chakri Sirindhorn Rathasimagunakornpiyajat Sayamborom-rajakumari*" in recognition of her services to the throne and to the nation. Throughout Thai history, succession to the throne has always been through the male line; recent constitutional amendments, however, now stipulate that if there is no male heir, the Parliament may approve succession of a royal daughter to become the ruling monarch, thus breaking a tradition of 700 years standing and providing further proof of the monarchy's modern views.

Their Royal Highnesses
Princess Maha Chakri
Sirindhorn and Princess
Chulabhorn during a State
Visit to France in 1980.

The Princess Mother

Despite her advanced age, King Bhumibol Adulyadej's mother, Her Royal Highness the Princess Mother, remains an energetic worker in the cause of national development, particularly in the field of rural health. Following a schedule that would daunt many far younger people, she regularly brings medical supplies and other necessities to remote areas of the country. One of the organizations she established to further this work is the Princess Mother's Medical Volunteer Foundation, through which several thousand volunteer doctors, dentists, nurses, and other workers devote their weekends to treating patients in some 48 of Thailand's provinces. The Princess Mother often accompanies the medical teams on their missions, appearing so regularly in the wild mountains of the North that she acquired the affectionate sobriquet of Mae Fa Luang, "The Royal Mother From Heaven." King Bhumibol Adulyadej's elder sister, Her Royal Highness Princess Galyani Vadhana, assists her mother in this work and is also active in several other

areas; she is Chairman of the Kidney Foundation, author of books on travel and culture, and former head of the French Language and Literature Department of Thammasat University.

Her Royal Highness the Princess Mother also actively supports the Border Patrol Police, an elite body of men who form Thailand's first line of defense against infiltration or incursion. Accompanied by Princess Galyani Vadhana, she makes periodic morale-boosting visits to their often isolated camps and provides them with food and other items not readily available in the border region.

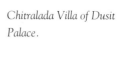
Chitralada Villa of Dusit Palace.

Royal Residences

There are two building complexes today associated with the monarchy: the Grand Palace, over 200 years old, and Chitralada Villa of Dusit Palace, the much smaller and less ornate estate which King Bhumibol Adulyadej has chosen as his family's Bangkok residence.

The resplendent Grand Palace, a 60-acre enclosure on the Chao Phraya River, is one of Thailand's best-known landmarks; today it houses the offices of His Majesty's Principal Private Secretary, the Bureau of the Royal Household, the Royal Institute, the Thai Junior Encyclopedia Project under Royal Patronage, and some offices of the Treasury Department. The earliest buildings in the palace compound, regarded as masterpieces of classic Thai architecture, were constructed in the reign of King Rama I, founder of the Royal House of Chakri, and extensive additions in both Thai and Western styles were made by subsequent rulers. Though the King no longer makes his home in the Grand Palace, its historic buildings are nonetheless still used for most of the important ceremonies associated with the Thai monarchy.

Royal coronations, for example, take place in the Phra Thinang Paisan Thaksin, one of a group of early structures of royal residences and throne halls known as the Phra Maha Monthien. This magnificently decorated

hall contains among other things the Octagonal Throne, from which the King formally receives the invitation from representatives of the people to rule over the kingdom, and the Phatthrabit Throne, from which he receives the Royal Regalia, the Royal Utensils, and the Royal Weapons of Sovereignty. The adjoining Phra Thinang Amarin Winitchai originally served as the principal Audience Hall and is still used for the Grand Audience on His Majesty's Royal Birthday Anniversary and for Royal Religious Ceremonies throughout the year.

The Phra Thinang Dusit Maha Prasat Throne Hall, also built by King Rama I, provides the setting for the annual Buddhist and Brahmin Coronation Day Anniversary Rites. It is also a custom to place the remains of kings, queens, and senior members of the Royal Family in this hall prior to their cremation, a ritual performed as in the case of Her Majesty Queen Rambhai Barni of the seventh reign who was given an elaborate traditional funeral in 1985.

The Phra Thinang Chakri Maha Prasat, a largely Western-style throne hall built by His Majesty's grandfather, King Chulalongkorn, between 1876 and 1882, is used for royal dinners and receptions and is also the place where King Bhumibol Adulyadej receives the credentials of newly arrived foreign ambassadors to Thailand.

Wat Phra Kaeo or the Temple of the Emerald Buddha which occupies one section of the palace compound, serves as the royal chapel and houses Thailand's most revered Buddha image. His Majesty performs a number of important religious ceremonies here during the year, among them the ritual changing of the image's jewel-encrusted regalia at the beginning of the hot, cool, and rainy seasons.

Chitralada Villa in Bangkok serves not merely as a Royal Residence but also performs a number of other functions; within the same compound are a hospital which serves the royal staff and needy people, a school, and assorted experimental agricultural facilities. In addition, six other royal palaces are maintained at Bang Pa-in north of Bangkok, Hua Hin on the east coast of the Gulf of Thailand, the northern city of Chiang Mai, Sakon Nakhon in the Northeast, Narathiwat in the South, and Khao Kho in Phetchabun Province. The latter, most recent of the provincial palaces to be built, is in an area formerly regarded as one of the worst centres of the communist insurgency.

Royal Regalia

One of King Bhumibol Adulyadej's most spectacular legacies from his ancestors is his fleet of ornately carved *royal barges*. Predominantly gold and scarlet, these were mostly constructed during the reigns of early Chakri kings and resemble the barges that were used by Ayutthaya kings for transport. Powered by brilliantly-costumed, chanting oarsmen, they have been used to carry His Majesty to the riverside Wat Arun (the Temple of Dawn) to present monks with robes after the annual Rains Retreat.

His Majesty the King accepts a ceremonially caparisoned albino elephant.

Another royal perogative ensures that all albino or "white" elephants found in Thailand (known as "significantly auspicious elephants") become the King's exclusive property. The discovery of a white elephant is considered an auspicious omen, the animals being presented to the monarch so that his reign may prosper. Regarded as an honorary human being, each "significantly auspicious elephant" is awarded a lordly title and thereafter leads a correspondingly lordly life. King Bhumibol Adulyadej has had seventeen white elephants (eleven still living), the most any Thai king has ever owned, which is regarded as an extremely auspicious sign for the success of his reign.

The Garuda, a mythical half-bird, half-human figure which in Hindu legend served as the mount for the god Vishnu, adorns King Bhumibol Adulyadej's septer and royal standard, as in former times the King was considered an incarnation of Vishnu; thus it is used on Government stationary, as badges on caps for civil service officials, as technically government endeavours are in the service of the King. Moreover, the Garuda signifies the concept of "By Royal Appointment" and the symbol is awarded, at His Majesty's personal discretion, as a sign of royal approval to business companies that have rendered outstanding economic and charitable services to Thailand. Such an award is rarely bestowed and is considered a great honour by recipients.

As do other monarchs, King Bhumibol Adulyadej enjoys the perogative of bestowing awards and honours on government employees and ordinary citizens who have served the country with civic, administrative, or diplomatic distinction, and to individuals who have rendered great services to the Crown. One distinctive, probably unique feature of Thai royalty is that royal titles are not inherited in perpetuity but lapse gradually over five generations. Thai titles descend through Chao Fa, Phra Ong Chao, Mom Chao, Mom Rajawongse, and Mom Luang. The Children of anyone rank inherit the next lowest rank on the father's side, so that a male Mom Chao's male or female child is a Mom Rajawongse, while a male Mom Luang's child is a plain Mister or Miss. Once titles have lapsed, families of royal descent can add "Na Ayutthaya", or "of Ayutthaya," to their surnames to indicate royal ancestry.

A Monarchy for the Times

Adhering to the traditional close relationship between King and people, yet daring to be innovative, Thailand's modern monarchy meets needs that are at once old and new. This makes it the central element in the traditional Thai triad of nation, king, and religion, binding the diverse elments of the country in a literal as well as a symbolic way. Much of its extraordinary success is due to the dedication and personal example of the ninth Chakri ruler, who in 1987 was popularly acclaimed as a "Maharaj", or King Bhumibol Adulyadej "the Great," by his loyal and loving subjects.

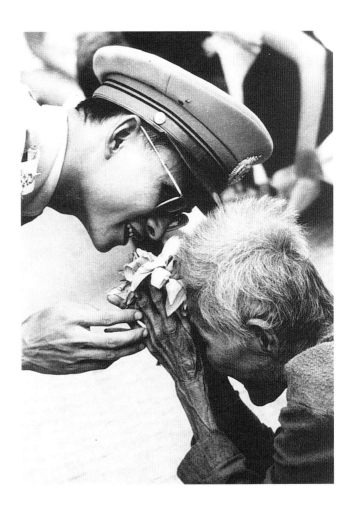

THE CORONATION GOLDEN JUBILEE
THE CELEBRATION TO MARK THE 50TH ANNIVERSARY OF THE ACCESSION TO THE THRONE OF HIS MAJESTY KING BHUMIBOL ADULYADEJ
B.E. 2539 (1996 A.D.)

His Majesty King Bhumibol Adulyadej, Rama IX of the Royal House of Chakri acceded to the Throne on 9th June, 1946. On the accession day, he proclaimed:

"We shall rule in righteousness for the benefit of the people of Siam".

Since then, His Majesty in his utmost preseverance, industriousness and devotion has gone to all corners in his kingdom to fight the ills and bestow happiness to his people. Thailand has enjoyed progress and prosperity in the areas of economy, administration, international relations, agriculture, science and technology, culture and the preservation of the national identity . His mercy and merit which shower upon his people and those who need his protection and assistance have made their lives happy, secure and peaceful. Catastrophes, miseries and threats have been dispelled by his supreme omnipotence. People's lives and their livelihood under his righteous rule have been well maintained, which have contributed greatly to the stable growth and prosperity of the nation.

On June 9, 1971, His Majesty celebrated the 25th Anniversary, or the Silver Jubilee of His Accession to the Throne, which brought enjoy and delights to all of his subjects.

Later, on July 2, 1988, a special state ceremony was organised to commemorate the auspicious occasion of outpacing the length of other Thai monarchs in the history. Up to that time, His Majesty's reign had broken the longest reigning record of 42 years and 23 days.

The upcoming *June 9, 1996*, will be another auspicious occasion in the history of the Thai people when they will all join in the jubilant and festive mood for the grandest celebration of the 50th Anniversary of His Majesty's Accession to the Throne, or the 50th year of his reign.

The Royal Ceremonial Emblem commemorating The Fiftieth Anniversary (Golden Jubilee) Celebrations of His Majesty's Accession to the Throne

The emblem's symbolic meaning :

The seal shown in the centre of the emblem is the official seal of His Majesty King Bhumibol Adulyadej (Rama IX), resting on the tusks of two white elephants, above a two-tiered tray. The upper part comprises the seal of the Royal House of Chakri and the Royal Crown.

The white elephants carry a seven-tiered *chatra*(the royal umbrella of state), a royal regalia. Under the two-tiered tray is the Thai numeral for fifty. The inscription on the blue ribbon says, "The Fiftieth Anniversary Celebrations of His Majesty's Accession to the Throne".

The elephants – traditional conveyance in the past–stand ready to serve the King in the same way that his loyal subjects are ready to tend to his needs, while at the same time, benefiting from the shade of the protective royal umbrella of state.

According to ancient Brahmin belief, white elephants are evocative of might and intelligence, and thus represent His Majesty's righteousness and wisdom.

The elephant also symbolizes longevity, and was once portrayed on the country's national flag. This represents Thailand's long history dating back thousands of years.

The emblem therefore embodies the honour and dignity of His Majesty the King and the Royal House of Chakri, the country's national identity, the love and high esteem which the people of Thailand have for their great King, and the long and proud history of the Kingdom of Thailand.

THE LAND AND ITS PEOPLE

Approximately the size of France, covering an area of some 513,115 square kilometres, Thailand displays considerable geographical and climatic variety in its four major regions. The far north, where the nation's borders meet those of Myanmar and Laos, is mountainous with valleys watered by a number of rivers and streams; during the winter months temperatures are cool enough to permit the cultivation of such temperate-zone crops as coffee, lychees, and strawberries. The rolling North-eastern Plateau, by contrast, suffers from frequent droughts, although these are being alleviated by an increasing number of reservoirs and other man-made water

Bird's eye view of Bangkok, the capital.

facilities. The Central Plain region, through which flows the Chao Phraya River, is one of the most fertile rice-growing areas in the world and has been the scene of Thailand's greatest historical development. The narrow Southern Peninsula, stretching to Malaysia, has coastlines with spectacular beaches along both the Gulf of Thailand and the Indian Ocean and lofty jungled mountains in many areas.

Hilltribes are among the minority population of Thailand.

The country is blessed with an equal variety of natural resources. Though logging is now restricted in the teak forests of the north, the region contains rich deposits of flourite, wolfram, and tungsten and its riverine valleys support a large number of orchards and farms. Potash is plentiful in the northeast, and mulberry plantations have traditionally sustained the cultivation of silkworms. Both flourite and gems are mined in the west, while some of the finest sapphires in the world come from the mountains of the southeast. The Chao Phraya valley is a vast network of irrigation canals which supply water not only to countless rice fields but also to vegetable farms and fruit orchards. Natural gas deposits in the Gulf of Thailand are supplying energy for many development projects, particularly along the Eastern Seaboard. In addition to a plentiful supply of seafood, the south has extensive deposits of tin and huge plantations of coconuts, cashews, and other fruits.

Though the great majority of Thailand's 50 million people are ethnically Thai and Buddhist, the country has a substantial number of minority groups who have historically lived together in harmony. Of these the Chinese are perhaps the most numerous, particularly in urban areas, though they have become so thoroughly assimilated it would be difficult to isolate them as a distinct group. Similarly, while there are Laos and Khmer groups in the northeast and west, nearly all regard themselves as Thai, culturally as well as by nationality. More clearly defined are the Muslims, who are mainly concentrated in the southern provinces, and assorted hilltribes who live in the far north; there are also sizeable communities of Hindus and Sikhs in large cities like Bangkok.

Oil has been the country's largest import item for quite some time. The situation may soon change when rich deposits of natural gas in the Gulf of Thailand are fully exploited.

Whatever the layout of a village may be, home for villagers is usually a simpler wooden house on stilts with a steeply sloping roof.

The Family

Perhaps the best way to comprehend Thai social values is to focus on its basic unit, the family, and in particular the rural family in its typical village setting. Generally this will be an extended family, with several generations living under one roof, or at least under several roofs within the same compound; and it is here that the Thai child learns codes of behaviour that will guide him throughout much of his later life, whether it is spent in the village or beyond.

In a village, home is usually a simple wooden house raised on posts; domestic animals like buffalos, pigs, and chickens are kept below, and the family lives above, often in a single room. There is little privacy, though this is not as highly regarded as in Western countries, and the communal life style instills a strong sense of social harmony in which tact, compromise, and tolerance are

A Thai family always extends beyond the nucleus of parents and their offspring. Here, in a rural household, mother, aunt and daughters enjoy themselves.

essential. The father is regarded as the leader, but the mother also plays a significant role, particularly in the family finances.

When small, children are treated permissively by various members of the family, which as likely as not will include grandparents and sometimes more distant relatives as well. Respect for elders is taught very early, however, and by the time a child walks he is aware of his position in the family hierarchy, a distinction that applies not only to the relationship between parents and children but also to that between siblings of different ages. This same delineation of roles also applies to the wider world outside the family and will remain deeply ingrained throughout life, thus explaining the reluctance of younger Thais to oppose or otherwise confront a senior during their subsequent careers in business or government.

Buffaloes are usually taken care of by young village boys to help their hard-working parents. While their animals are grazing, they enjoy various games.

A sense of responsibility is also inculcated in early childhood. Each child is assigned certain duties according to age and ability—feeding livestock, leading the family buffalo to graze in nearby pastures, taking care of younger brothers and sisters while parents are at work in the fields. As they grow older, responsibilities increase and they are allowed to participate in family discussions, with their opinions taken into account when important decisions are made.

One of the prime responsibilities placed on children is that of taking care of parents in their old age, a prominent feature of the Thai concept of family. There

Thai children usually accompany their grandparents to the wat to take care of them and to listen to the monks' teaching.

is no feeling of being inconvenienced by this duty of caring for aged parents; on the contrary, their acquired wisdom gives them an honoured place in the household, and their counsel is actively sought in teaching their grandchildren and great-grandchildren to be responsible adults with the same traditional values.

Village Organization and Leadership

Beyond the family, the next larger unit of social organization is the village. Although there are regional variations in house styles and crop cultivations, and the setting may vary, in essence Thai villages are remarkably similar, revolving around well-defined climatic, religious, and farming seasons.

The typical village contains around 100 to 150 households, or an average of 500 to 700 inhabitants. The houses are nearly all simple wooden structures, elevated on stilts as protection against flooding and unwelcome animal intruders and also to improve air circulation. A small wooden granary, also on stilts, is often found beside the house, together with large earthenware jars in which rainwater is stored for drinking. Most villages now have electricity but water for washing and cooking comes from canals, rivers, or ponds, or, in the arid northeast, from communal wells.

On the village outskirts are the local school and the *wat*, or Buddhist monastery, sometimes adjacent to one another, sometimes at opposite ends of the village. The school is generally a simple wooden building, perhaps a single room where several classes are held simultaneously; an essential feature is the flag-pole upon which the Thai flag is ceremoniously raised each school morning and lowered in the evening. The monastery, constructed and maintained largely through local donations and thus reflecting the village's wealth, is often separated from the community by an open field to give the resident monks maximum privacy and seclusion for their religious activities. This grassy expanse also serves as the village common, a place where children assemble to play kickball and where local fetes are held.

The village is self-governing, led by an elected headman, or *phu-yai-ban,* who until recent years was always a man; since 1983, however, women have also been elected to the position. A candidate is not affiliated with any political party but must be a literate Thai householder who has resided in the village at least six months and be at least 25 years old. If he retains the villagers' esteem, the *phu-yai-ban* can remain in the post until retirement at 60 through repeated reelections; by the same token, he can be removed if he forfeits their respect.

The village headman regularly delivers the government's policy to his villagers, and leads the discussion to find a solution to local problems.

The *phu-yai-ban* preserves the social harmony valued so highly by all Thais by skilfully settling minor disputes, taking care to ensure that neither party feels cheated or loses face. In addition, he keeps the village birth and death records and acts as a spokesman for the community in negotiations with the government bureaucracy.

Administratively, neighbouring villagers are organized into groups known as *tambon* which depending on topography and population density, consist of two to 28 villages. The *phu-yai-ban* within each *tambon* elect one of themselves to be *kamnan,* or commune head-person. Thailand has nearly 5,000 *tambons* at present. The *kamnan* is chairman of a committee which often includes a government school headmaster, as agricultural extension worker, and sometimes a Health Department doctor or paramedic in charge of a local clinic. It also contains at least two men selected by the *nai amphoe* (or district officer, who is the *kamnan's* immediate superior) or appointed by the provincial governor.

This committee is responsible for deciding which villages should have new roads, irrigation budgets and health services, while the *kamnan's* main individual responsibilities are to see that justice prevails within the commune, to maintain records and statistics, to help preserve peace, to assist in collecting taxes, and to act as the intermediary between the district officer and all village headpersons in his *tambon.*

Most young Thai men enter the monkhood for spiritual training and to gain merit for themselves and their parents. A man who has not been ordained is not considered a mature adult. Accompanied by music, a nak leads the procession from home to the wat. His relatives and friends dance to the music in a festive mood.

The *wat* is the focal point of the village, symbolizing the Buddhist religion and also acting as the major unifying element, particularly during festivals and merit-making ceremonies when it also becomes a social centre for young and old alike. Abbots and senior monks frequently enjoy more prestige and moral persuasion than the village head, and in times of personal crisis they are often the first whose advice is sought. Within the *wat* the abbot has absolute administrative, clerical, custodial, disciplinary, and spiritual responsibilities, and they determine the monastery's relationship with the village. If an abbot is scholarly, meditative, and retiring, the monastery is unlikely to concern itself much with mundane village affairs. On the other hand, if one is a dynamic personality he may make the *wat* a community centre with a subtle but powerful influence on social action. Every young man in the village, before he starts his own family, will spend a period of study and reflection in the *wat*, thus increasing the influence of Buddhism.

A nak is ordained in the ordination hall, attended by all monks in the wat. The nak changes his white gown for a saffron robe.

Social Values

Buddhist teachings are at the root of the typical Thai villager's sincere consideration for others, embodied in the virtue known as *namchai*, "water of the heart," a concept encompassing spontaneous warmth and compassion that allows families to make anonymous sacrifices for friends and to extend hospitality to strangers. For example, a stranger visiting a village will rarely be seen as an intruder and a subject for suspicion and distrust. Much more likely, the villagers will have the *namchai* to take him in, feed him, offer him a bed in one of their homes, and generally treat him as a friend. Buddhism also lies behind such common expressions as *mai pen rai* (or "never mind, it doesn't matter") when something unfortunate happens, reflecting the feeling that one must gracefully submit to external forces beyond one's control, such as the effects of past karma.

Although highly individualistic and resisting regimentation, Thais nevertheless realize that inner freedom is best preserved in an emotionally and physically stable environment. Therefore, they believe that social harmony is best maintained by avoiding any unnecessary friction in their contracts with others. From this has grown the strong Thai feeling of *krengchai*,

Larger social groups within the village are formed spontaneously to help one another in various activities which a single family could not manage unassisted.

which means an extreme reluctance to impose on anyone or disturb his personal equilibrium by direct criticism, challenge, or confrontation. In general, people will do their utmost to avoid personal conflict.

Outward expressions of anger are also regarded as dangerous to social harmony and as being obvious signs of ignorance, crudity, and immaturity. Indeed, during normal social intercourse, strong public.

Within such a behavioural framework, Thais share very definite views on what constitutes friendship and enjoyment. Sincere friendship among Thais is extremely intense; the language is rich in expressions which reflect the degree of involvement and willing self-sacrifice. Such relationships are found particularly among men. A *"phuan tai"*-literally, "death friend"-is a companion for whom it would be an honour to die. Should a friend become involved in difficulties, his friend feels an obligation to help him, regardless of the danger to himself, because *"tong chuai phuan"*-"One must help one's friends." This requirement is a sensitive point of honour and explains many circumstance that often baffle outsiders. Displays of dismay, despair, displeasure, disapproval, or enthusiasm are frowned upon.

Accordingly, the person who is, or appears to be serenely indifferent *(choei choei)* is respected for having what is considered an important virtue.

On the level of acquaintanceship, politeness predominates. When greeting people, Thais will usually show their concern for others' health by remarking how "thin" or "fat" he or she has become. The remark is intended as a gesture of friendship.

Individual Life Cycles

A Thai baby officially becomes "someone" after its name is chosen-frequently by the village abbot–and entered in the village head's records. Soon after birth the child will be given a nickname, nearly always of one syllable. Intimates will continue to call him or her by this nickname for the rest of his life and may indeed have to think for a while to remember the proper name.

Childhood is a carefree, cossetted time. By the age of four, children regularly meet to play beyond the family compound, with boys and girls generally segregating and roaming freely throughout the village. Boys play

Girls at play.

Village children attend government schools where a standard curriculum is used nationwide.

make-believe games, fly kites, plow imaginary fields, and hunt insects and harmless reptiles. Girls nurse make-shift dolls, "sell" mud-pies in make-believe markets, play games emulating their mothers, and look after younger brothers and sisters.

Gradually the children are drawn into work patterns. Around eight years of age, girls give increasing help with household chores and boys assume greater responsibilities such as feeding domestic animals and guarding the family buffalo as it grazes or wallows.

Children attend the government village school to be taught from a standard nationwide curriculum. They acquire varying degrees of literacy and study Buddhist ethics and Thai history. All receive a comprehensive education and by coming into contact with neighbouring villages' children and visiting the provincial capital on school trips they enjoy a broadening of social experience.

Having assumed ever-increasing workloads and responsibilities, youths of 15 and 16 are already regarded as fully mature adult labourers. Between graduation from school and marriage at around 20, most village males go into the monastery, usually for the duration of one rainy season, in order to make merit for themselves and their parents; in some areas a man who has never been a monk is avoided by marriageable girls, who regard him as a *khon dip*, literally an "unripe person."

The village girl's entrance into adolescence is a gentle one. Courtship is confined initially to communal work groups during planting and harvesting and at monastery-centred festivals and activities. There may be extensive banter between boys and girls but, individually, young people tend to be shy and "whirlwind courtships" are exceedingly rare. Emotional relationships mature slowly and customarily involve chaperoned meetings at the girl's house.

Most young people select their own marriage partners. Rarely is parental disapproval voiced since marriages often take place between families within the same village, further strengthening and widening communal ties. A marriage is sometimes presented as a *fait accompli* by children who work in towns or cities and are thus beyond parental control. In many parts of the country it is the custom for the groom to move in with the bride's family, thus providing extra labour for the family fields and also avoiding friction between mother and daughter-in-law.

Early in the morning, in accordance with traditional Thai belief that married life should begin with merit-making, the bride and groom feed village monks and present them with small gifts. In return, the monks bless the couple and the house or room where they will live.

An elder pours sacred onto the bride and groom's hands to bless the couple in a local wedding ceremony.

The village marriage ceremony bestows no official validity on their union but is merely a public proclamation that the two people will live together as man and wife. The young couple's wrists are ceremoniously bound together in the presence of village elders and they are led to the marriage chamber as guests feast, drink, sing, and dance. Later, their marriage is officially registered at the district office and becomes a fact of law. Daily tasks are generally divided equally between husband and wife. Women normally do the household chores, but they work in the fields during planting and harvesting. Men perform heavy tasks and fieldwork, fetch water, and occasionally clean their own clothes. Thai village men are often very good cooks and sometimes help prepare the food for festivals.

After marriage, every couple eagerly awaits the birth of its first child, which usually comes during the first year. Children have a high position in rural and cultural values, since there is strength in numbers, a vital sense of continuity is ensured, and many hands make farming activities easier. Often there exists an unspoken preference for boys since they alone may be ordained as priests to gain merit for themselves and their parents, but no love is witheld if the child proves to be a girl.

Everyday village dress is simple. Men generally wear shorts, a simple shirt, and their versatile *phakhaoma* —a checkered rectangle of cloth loosely worn around the waist which, at a moment's notice, can serve as a turban

Buddhists at a merit-making ceremony.

In a widespread, complex pattern of communal cooperation, farmers join to transplant rice seedlings into each family's prepared fields.

for protection against the sun, a loincloth to preserve modesty during public bathing, a sweat-aborbing towel, or a hammock.

Women wear the *phasin* (the Thai version of the sarong) and a simple blouse or bodice. Children wear similar clothing as their parents except when they are dressed in their school uniforms.

The Seasonal Cycle

The rice planting season usually begins in April or May. Rice is by far the most important of all Thai crops and the principal food for people throughout the country. Whether boiled and eaten plain, distilled into

Monks lead the candle-light procession, participated in by laymen who walk behind.

a liquor known as *lao khao,* or transformed into sweets and noodles, rice and its cultivation comprise a central pillar of Thai life. *Kin khao,* the Thai expression for "to eat," literally means "to eat rice." The grain provides major government revenues and for centuries has been Thailand's leading agricultural export.

Visakha Puja, the year's greatest religious holiday which commemorates the Buddha's birth, enlightenment, and death, comes during seeding and ploughing. Village elders attend temple celebrations and sermons during the day, while those who have been working all day in the fields return at dusk to join the solemn candle or torchlit procession that

Streams of candle-light surround the Marble Temple of Wat Benchamabophit and the occasion of a candle-light procession.

circumambulates the monastery chapel three times. Each person carries flowers, three glowing incense sticks, and a lighted candle in silent homage to the Buddha, his teaching, and his disciples.

Shortly after transplanting is completed, usually towards the end of May, the first of the annual monsoon rains arrive to inundate farmland. Daily rainfall replenishes the fields and while the rice is growing much of the family's time is taken up with Rains Retreat observances.

During this annual three-month period (*Phansa* in Thai), Buddhist monks are required to remain in their monasteries overnight, a tradition which predates Buddhism. In ancient India, all holy men, mendicants and sage spent three months of the rainy season in permanent dwellings, thus avoiding unnecessary travel during the period when crops were still new for fear they might accidentally tread on young plants. In deference to popular opinion, the Buddha decreed that his followers should also abide by this tradition. This initiated a move away from an itinerant life to a more or less settled existence since the advantages of communal living became apparent.

Phansa represents a time of renewed spiritual vigour. The monk meditates more, studies more, and teaches more. Laymen, too, traditionally endeavour to be more conscientious, perhaps abstaining from liquor

The "nak" is carried in a procession around the "Bot" or the ordination hall three times before entering it for the ordination ceremony.

and cigarettes and giving extra financial and physical support to local monasteries. *Phansa* is also ordinarily the season for temporary ordinations. Young men enter the monkhood for spiritual training, to gain merit for themselves and their parents, and to conform to the widespread feeling that a man who has not been a monk cannot be considered a mature adult.

The Buddhist ordination is a mixture of religious solemnity, merit-making, and boisterous celebration reflecting the Thai belief that the three most important events in a man's life are his birth, his ordination, and his marriage. The ordination ritual itself originated over 2,500 years ago as the Sangha (the Buddhist monastic order) took shape and has changed little to this day. Socially, it is something in which the entire village

Sometimes the "nak" rides a white "horse" in the procession to imitate the Lord Buddha who left his worldly palace on the back of a white horse.

participates. Local monks comprise the presiding chapter and preceptors, while villagers gain merit by accompanying the tonsured, white-robed candidate for monkhood (known as the *nak*) in a colourful procession to the monastery, often marked by joyous dancing and the infectious throb of long drums.

Symbolism permeates every aspect of the ordination ceremony. The *nak's* white robe connotes purity and the royal umbrella held over his head reminds participants of the royal heritage Prince Siddhartha Gautama renounced during his spiritual quest to become the Buddha. The *nak* leads the villagers in a triple circumabulation of the monastery chapel to evoke the Buddhist Triple Gem—the Buddha, the Dhamma, and the Sangha (the Teacher, the Teaching, and the Taught).

Once the rains have ended, the daily rhythm of fieldwork is increasingly concerned with keeping birds away from the ripening rice. During this time fish are abundant in rain-swollen streams and fields. Methods and equipment for freshwater fishing vary from region to region and depending on where the fish are being sought—canals, rivers, ponds, or rice fields.

In early November, one of the most beautiful of Thai festivals, Loy Krathong, takes place. *Loy* means "to float," and a *krathong* is a lotus-shaped vessel traditionally made of banana leaves. The *krathong* usually contains a candle, three incense sticks, some flowers, and coins. By

On the full moon night of the twelfth lunar month, krathongs are floated to pay respect to Mae Khong Kha, the Goddess of the water.

Harvesting is a laborious task which requires cooperative hands.

Out of the harvest season, the farmers and people throughout the country celebrate the traditional Thai New Year, also known as the Songkran festival.

the light of the full moon, people light the candles and incense, make a wish, and launch their *krathongs* on the nearest body of water. The Goddess of the water who plays such an important role in rural life is thus honoured, and it is also commonly believed that the *krathongs* carry away the past year's sins as well as the hopes of the launcher for the future. Moonlit waterways throughout Thailand are covered with tiny, flickering lights representing millions of silent aspirations.

By late November or early December, rice in the north and the central plains is ready to be harvested. Wherever possible, water is drained to allow fields to dry. Harvesting schedules are determined by common consent within each village. Early each morning, cooperative work groups go into the fields with sickles to harvest each farmer's crop. Around noon, the host family sends food to the fieldworkers, and after lunch work resumes until dark when the host family provides another meal.

The cut rice is spread in the fields to dry for several days before being bundled in sheaves and taken to the family compound, where it is threshed and winnowed. Except in the South, where later monsoons arrive late in the year, harvesting usually ends in January to February. Then the farm family turns its energies to activities neglected during the rice harvest. Buildings, tools, and fences are repaired and secondary crops are either planted or harvested.

The hot dry season after the rice harvest is marked by the important Songkran festival, which celebrates the traditional Thai New Year. At this time people from rural areas who are working in the city usually return home to celebrate. Songkran is observed with special elan in the North where, because it occurs during a time of relative leisure, it becomes a three to five day festival of entertaining and socializing.

People sprinkle scented water on the Buddha image.

A thorough house cleaning, sprinkling of Buddha images with lustral water, memorial ceremonies, merit-making presentation of gifts to monks, elders, and spirits, the release of caged birds and fish, pilgrimages to holy shrines, parades, dancing, and uninhibited, good-natured water throwing are all features of the Songkran celebration.

Around this time, showers signal the dry season's approaching end, and villagers once more prepare for rice planting as one annual cycle ends and another begins.

Leisure Activities

A penchant for *khwam sanuk* combines with a natural gregariousness to ensure that both spontaneous and formal leisure activities are vital parts of the Thai village's social fabric.

Rice cultivation demands consistent hard work, but the communal gatherings that result set the stage for all types of group activities from feasting to courting.

Villagers enjoy a folk entertainment.

Some evenings after a hard day's work, many villagers, instead of going to bed, gather around bonfires to talk. Young people sing and court. Older people chat, smoke, and drink homemade rice liquor, a mild or potent brew depending on the brewer's skill and the ingredients at hand.

There may be a rhyming song contest and a lot of friendly banter between old and young as individuals try to outdo each other in composing choruses with familiar themes. Local musicians may play reed instruments, bamboo flutes, hand cymbals, and drums to accompany singers, providing both inspiration and humour.

As people usually settled near water, a courting song is sometime sung as the "boat song"

The tomtom drum dance owes its liveliness to the encouraging rhythm of the drums.

Ordinations, particularly when a number of families pool resources for a group ceremony, are often celebrated with similar festivity. Enormous feasts are prepared. Electric generators may be rented, a band organized, and a folk dance drama troupe engaged to keep revellers spellbound until the early hours with satiric comic opera performances featuring outrageous puns and double entendres, sly ribaldry, and popular folk songs.

Throughout the year, villagers share a common interest in gambling, travelling *(pai thieo)*, and sports. With many, gambling is a passion. The national lottery excites imaginations in every province, as do cockfights and such exotic competitions as fish and beetle fighting. Card games are a pastime favoured by both sexes and almost everyone can play Thai chess.

Pai thieo by foot, boat, bus, motorbike, or rail is a favourite way to relax when time allows. Travelling makes the villager less insular and personal relations with family and friends are treasured as much for the opportunities they afford for travel as for the affection upon which they are based.

Besides national celebrations, there are regional festivals like the northeast *Ngan Hae Bang Fai*, or skyrocket festival, in May or June of each year. Traditionally a time of letting off steam, the festival's high point comes when, amid much merry-making, villagers

fire homemade rockets, some of them 20 metres tall, to ensure a plentiful rainfall for the forthcoming rice season.

Takro and kite flying are popular traditional sports. *Takro* is played by a loosely formed circle of men who use their feet, knees, thighs, chests, and shoulders to acrobatically pass a woven rattan ball to one another, endeavouring to keep it in the air as long as possible and eventually kick it into a basket hanging high above their heads. (There is also a professional version of *takro*, known as sepak takro, which is played by teams from various ASEAN countries.)

Kites are flown mostly during the breezy hot season. Popular in Thailand since at least the founding of Sukhothai, kites have been used effectively in warfare:

Colourful kites can be seen everywhere at Sanam Luang in Bangkok during the flying season.

an Ayutthaya governor quelled a northeast city-state's rebellion in 1690 by flying huge kites, called *chulas*, over the beseiged city and bombing it into submission with jars of explosives.

In addition to being an individual pleasure, kite flying can be a competitive sport. Opposing teams fly male *(chula)* and female *(pakpao)* kites in a surrogate battle of the sexes. The small agile *pakpaos* try to bring down the more cumbersome *chula*, while the male kite seeks to snare the female kites and bring them back into male territory.

During temple fairs, another popular sport is the unique martial art of Thai boxing. A form of self-defense developed during the Ayutthaya period, Thai boxing

Some of the herbs and spices used in cooking Thai food.

forbids biting, spitting, or wrestling. On the other hand, the contestants may punch, kick, and shove, and unrestrainedly use their bare feet, legs, knees, elbows, shoulders, and fists to savage each other. A vicious kick in the throat, an elbow smash to the eyes, a knee in the stomach, or a whiplash kick in the chest can immediately floor the sturdiest of opponents. Nowadays boxers wear conventional boxing gloves, a somewhat humane development considering that less than 50 years ago they customarily bound their fists with hemp which contained liberal quantities of ground glass.

The major portion of Thai cuisine is highly spiced and chilli hot, thanks to the addition of a variety of chillies, large and small, some more potent than others. The burning sensation of Thai chillies has caused much fanning of mouths by stunned foreigners on their first sampling but increased experience often brings enthusiastic approval, as attested by the popularity of Thai restaurants today throughout the world.

The ideal traditional Thai meal aims at being a harmonious blend of spicy, subtle, sweet, and sour and is meant to be appealing to eye, nose, and palate. A large central bowl of rice may be accompanied by a clear soup (perhaps bitter melons stuffed with minced pork), a steamed dish (mussels in curry sauce), a fried dish (fish with ginger), a hot salad (sliced beef on a bed of greens with chillies, onions, mint, lemon juice, and more chillies), and a variety of sauces and condiments, of which the most essential is *nam pla* (fermented fish sauce), into which food can be dipped. This is normally followed by a sweet dessert (bananas coated with sugared coconut and deep fried, for example) and, finally, fresh fruit (such as mangoes, durian, papaya, jackfruit, watermelon, and many more) of which Thailand boasts a year-round supply.

Food varies from region to region, with modifications of standard dishes and also local specialities. In Chiang Mai, for example, the food is generally milder than that of the central region; *naem*, a spicy pork sausage, is a northern delicacy.

Northeastern food tends to be very spicy, with explosive salads and special broiled, minced meat dishes mined with miniature, high-voltage green chillies. Glutinous rice is more popular in this region than steamed rice and exotic dishes like fried ants and grasshoppers and frog curry are not uncommon.

Southern cuisine makes delicious use of the creatures which team in the nearby seas. Lobsters, crabs, scallops, fish, and squid are common ingredients and unusual delicacies like jellyfish salad can also be found. In the southernmost provinces, where there is a large Muslim community, sweet, mild, and spicy curries abound.

Thai food is not only spicy but also colourful, often beautifully decorated with delicate vegetable carvings.

Some Thai sweets.

Foreign foods have also found a place in the Thai diet. Some of these go far back into history, like the egg-based Portuguese sweets which were introduced in the Ayutthaya period, while others like bread and cake are more recent acquisitions.

To please the eye, Thai cooks pursue the ancient art of fruit and vegetable carving to transform tables into visual feasts. Originally an aristocratic art practiced at the royal court, vegetable carving flourished throughout the Ayutthaya period, when a deft hand could fashion a white radish rose in a matter of minutes. It reached its zenith during the Bangkok reign of King Rama II when court ladies created flowers, fish, vases, bowls, and other decorative objects from watermelons, cucumbers, tomatoes, onions, and other unlikely garden produce. On a somewhat broader scale the art is still practiced today: there are few more charming surprises than discovering tomato roses and cucumber primroses with a local fast lunch.

The art of fruit and vegetable carving is purposed solely to add pleasure to the eye.

Urban Life

In terms of present-day Thailand, to speak of urban life essentially means to speak of Bangkok, for though many provincial capitals have grown rapidly in recent years the national capital is still the ultimate city to every Thailand. One out of ten Thais lives in Bangkok, which is 45 times

bigger than Chiang Mai, the second most populous city. The metropolitan area now covers some 1,537 square kilometres on both sides of the Chao Phraya River.

Almost all major domestic and foreign companies are located in the capital, as are all government ministries and most of the country's leading educational, sporting, and cultural facilities. The greater part of Thailand's imports and exports pass through Bangkok (though this may change when the Eastern Seaboard Project gets underway) and 90 percent of the motor vehicles in the nation are registered there. It is the focal point of Thailand's aviation, railroad, and communications

King Rama IX bridge over the Chao Phraya River.

network, as well as the chief destination for the majority of tourists who come annually to occupy its more than 20,000 hotel rooms.

Given such facts, it is not surprising that Bangkok acts as a magnet for people from all parts of the country. They come to be educated at its schools, colleges, and universities, to find employment in its numerous factories and commercial firms, or simply to see its famous buildings and monuments and enjoy its highly varied pleasures. Both metaphorically and literally, all Thai roads converge on the capital.

The highrising of modern Bangkok.

By contrast, provincial cities tend to reflect regional characteristics. For example, Hat Yai, the south's major city, is growing rapidly but it is still very much a projection of the tin and rubber industries which dominate the region. Chiang Mai in the North is both a coordination point for the agriculture of the area and also famous as a centre of northern culture and traditions. Similarly, such northeastern cities as Nakhon Ratchasima and Khon Kaen, while prospering on local development, are essentially provincial in all senses of the world.

Only Bangkok, with its huge, diverse population, its shopping centres and highrise office buildings, and its cosmopolitan sophistication presents itself as a city in the international sense of the term. Thus to understand modern urban culture in Thailand, it is necessary to examine the capital in some detail.

Bangkok's in the 1990's

Numerous districts in Bangkok are centres in themselves, each unified by common features rooted either in ethnic character of a specific function or business. Thus Ratchadamnoen Avenue and its environs remain the centre for government ministries and inter-national agencies, while there is a major concentration of commerce in Chinatown. Silom Road has become the primary banking and financial district and the Sukhumvit Road area is predominantly a middle-class residential section. Those seeking entertainment are attracted by the neon glare of Patpong and New Phetchaburi Roads, where there are hundreds of bars and restaurants.

Outlying residential districts, meanwhile, continue to expand rapidly as more housing estates and shopping complexes are built to accommodate both the flow of migrants converging on the capital from up-country and the new generation of young married couples who are increasingly leaving their parents' homes for places of their own. Heavy industry, too, is concentrating on the outer fringes of the city, with industrial parks springing up along major highways leading out into the country. To facilitate communication between the suburbs and downtown areas, an elevated expressway has been built. A ring road project, the major portions of which have been completed, will also relieve congestion by permitting through traffic to bypass the city centre.

Modern department stores are well patronized by children and teenagers.

Older Bangkok residents live in separate, private houses, located either in high-density neighbourhoods or, increasingly rare, in relatively spacious compounds in long-established residential areas like Dusit and Bangkapi. Rising land values, however, are producing new housing concepts, especially in the more congested inner city. Though Western-style apartment buildings are inhabited mainly by foreigners, more and more Thais are moving into "town houses," projects in which they own the actual land and building but share a common wall with their neighbours; hundreds of these projects have been constructed in the city, some consisting of several dozen units in an area that once contained a single dwelling.

As the 1990's got underway the biggest residential boom was in condominium construction. This era dawned with the passage of the Condominium Act by Parliament in 1979. According to a survey conducted in 1982, there were 48 condo projects being implemented in the country, most of them in Bangkok; another survey at the end of the decade found more than 220 such

projects, with those in the capital being concentrated on Sukhumvit and Rachadapisek Roads and along the Chao Phraya River. An important factor in the sale of condominium units has been a desire to escape the traffic jams which add hours to suburban commuting times.

Throughout Bangkok, lining main roads and side streets, are innumerable two-three-and four-storey shophouses which contain specialty shops, restaurants, or small factories that are generally family concerns. Workers and family are commonly housed on upper floors. Such dwellings rarely have recreational space or gardens, though imaginative roof-top plantings can be glimpsed on some. Automobiles are generally parked inside on the ground floor and children play on the sidewalks outside.

Poorer people often live in single-storey houses made of scrap lumber, concentrated around the port area and in certain suburbs. Government public housing usually takes the form of lowrise blocks of simple flats located throughout the city.

As building expansion is becoming impossible horizontally in the inner city, Bangkok today is growing vertically to accommodate both office and residential construction.

The rapid growth of Bangkok has severely strained its facilities and led to a number of serious problems. The city now has over a million registered motor vehicles and because of the limited road surface traffic congestion is heavy in downtown areas. Moreover, some parts of the city are sinking due to the pumping of water from artesian wells to supply suburban projects and drainage is inadequate in others; both have resulted in periodic flooding during the rainy season. Experts are presently working on elaborate plans to relieve these problems, among them an elevated system of rapid public transportation and extensive flood-control projects.

Bangkok's population is predominately young. Over half the residents are under 30. Numerous new schools, both public and private, have emerged to meet the needs of this high concentration of young people, as well as two "open" universities for those who cannot be accommodated by the older institutions of higher learning. The young have also influenced the life of the city in other ways—most of the capital's shopping centres are youth-oriented, are its entertainment facilities.

The city's cultural life is greatly enriched by its minority communities. Chinese and Indians account for nearly 10 percent of the capital's population and contribute to its variety of cuisines and festivals. Japanese and Asians from neighbouring countries also figure prominently in the city's cosmopolitan atmosphere.

Western influence has been instrumental in creating a taste for new fashions and new life-styles, reflected in such things as golf and tennis, delicatessens and boutiques, music and drama, libraries and popular games, architecture and interior decoration. Fast foods from the West, too, like hamburgers and pizzas, have become popular with young and old alike.

Leisure in the city

The stress of city life make leisure activities vital, and weekends find Bangkokians dedicated to having a good time. Sometimes there are local temple fairs

featuring food and traditional forms of entertainment like the ever-popular *li-ke*. Sporting events draw large crowds, whether they be of purely local interest or involve foreign footballers, boxers, or gymnasts. Several museums, a planetarium, art galleries, and a cultural centre can be visited for instruction as well as relaxation. There are dozens of modern air-conditioned cinemas throughout Bangkok, most of them showing Thai and Western movies. The most popular local productions are melo-dramas with equal measures of comedy, romance, and epic adventure.

Several amusement parks are located on Bangkok's outskirts, with carousels, Ferris wheels, roller coasters, shooting galleries, and ice cream stalls to keep young visitors cheerfully occupied for hours. Lumpini Park, in the heart of the city, is crowded on weekends with footballers and strollers, as well as joggers and others in search of physical fitness. Chatuchak Park on the outskirts is the site of the famous Weekend Market featuring several acres of stalls selling a remarkable assortment of goods: household pets, every conceivable

kind of fruit, fresh vegetables and spices, clothing, Buddha amulets, various handicrafts, potted plants and trees, secondhand books and records, and probably, if one is persistent, the proverbial kitchen sink. The new Rama IX Park, presented to the city on the occasion of His Majesty King Bhumibol Adulyadej's 60th birthday, is another popular place to escape the city's clamour; Thailand's only true botanical garden, it also features an imposing pavilion with displays of the king's life and interest.

Bangkok boasts some of the most varied nightlife in the Orient. Visiting ballet, operatic, and folk dance troupes from Europe, the U.S., and various Asian countries frequently appear, and film festivals are held by foreign cultural organizations like the Alliance Française, the Goethe Institute, and the British Council. Patrons of nightclubs and supperclubs, many of them in the city's leading hotels, are entertained by international as well as local performers. Discotheques with the latest gadgetry flash and throb to the insistent beat of music played at top volume.

Hotels on the Chao Phraya River, Bangkok.

Nightlife in Bangkok.

Siam Square and Siam Centre, commercial areas, show strong Western.

Bangkok's cosmopolitan quality is particularly evident in the incredible variety of foods offered by its countless restaurants. Diners in the city have a choice of French, Danish, Italain, German, Japanese, Middle Eastern, Swiss, English, Mexican, Korean, Indian, Vietnamese, Burmese, and American fastfood outlets, as well as of course, superb Chinese and Thai cuisine.

Although Bangkok abounds in markets, shops, and department stores selling every possible kind of merchandise, those who prefer to spend the day at home in the city's residential lanes can buy what they need from itinerant vendours who bring necessities right to the door-step, selling charcoal (for cooking), fruit, ice cream, noodle dishes, grilled chicken, handmade brooms, pots and pans, and countless other items.

Urban Values

Buddhism is at the centre of the Thai view of life and forms the foundation of most attitudes, in the city as well as in the village. But just as even the toughest material will change its shape under pressure, Buddhism has undergone certain alterations caused by the stress of Bangkok's fast-paced urban life style.

In the village, the *wat* is the heart of social as well as religious life. Bangkok's monasteries today inevitably play less of a social role and are normally visited only for religious observances or for one of the festivals scattered throughout the Buddhist year. Accessibility is the main

problem: in rural areas the *wat* is generally just a short walk away, while in the city a visit often entails a long, hot drive in heavy traffic. Therefore, many Bangkok homes have a room set aside for family Buddha images and a small altar. This little private sanctuary serves as a place for prayer and meditation in the morning and evening–daily rituals that in a village setting would be more often performed at the *wat*.

Urban surroundings also rob many monasteries of the tranquil atmosphere which characterizes their upcountry counterparts. Nevertheless, monks continue to practice their meditation in them, apparently undisturbed, by the bustling life outside, just as they go out each morning to collect food offerings from city dwellers as anxious to make merit as villagers. Many Bangkok residents also go there to study meditation during their off-duty hours from work.

Formerly everday life was highly structured and circumscribed by Brahmanic ritualistic taboos, and some of these still linger in modern society. Wednesday, for example, was deemed an inappropriate day on which to cut hair and accordingly, some Bangkok barber shops close each Wednesday.

Astrology also retains its ancient influence and is used by many people to determine auspicious dates for major undertakings. Today it enjoys a kind of reassurance-consultancy role, as certain types of psychological counselling do in the West. Buddhist monks, Brahmans, and professional astrologers cast horoscopes according to which the day and hour to embark on a trip are decided. Purchasing land, starting a new business, or opening a shop are also often subject to an astrologer's calculations, and few couples would agree to be married without first determining the suitability of their union and the most auspicious day and minute for the ceremony.

Traditional Thai life-styles, which survive virtually intact in upcountry villages, have undergone extensive reshaping under the pressures of urban demands. Family ties in the city, for example, are not as pervasive as in the village, and young married couples often set up housekeeping on their own.

Modernization has greatly extended the range of employment opportunities open to people migrating to the city. A decade or so ago, virtually the only acceptable course available to a newly-arrived girl was to take a position as a domestic. Nowadays, she may prefer a job

in one of the light industries-sorting transistors, assembling pocket calculators, or working in one of Bangkok's huge textile plants. An incidental effect of this development has been the introduction of an increasing number of labour-saving electrical appliances into middle-and upper-class homes. Considered a wasteful extravagance only a few years ago, washing machines, vacuum cleaners, and microwave ovens are now popular household items available at all department stores.

Despite all the apparent changes, however, traditional Thai values are still strong beneath the surface of urban life, a reflection, no doubt, of the fact that the over-whelming majority of city dwellers have come from village backgrounds and also of the potent strength of Thai cultural heritage, which over the centuries has so often demonstrated its ability to bend without breaking.

Social Welfare

Origin of Organized Social Welfare

As elsewhere in the world, the history of social welfare in Thailand can be traced back for centuries in the form of charity or the humanitarian concern of people, deeply rooted in Buddhist philosophy. This is evidenced by the fact that the Thai people never fall to help each other in the time of distress.

Buddhist monasteries have marked their place in the development of social welfare in Thailand. They perform their secondary function that has greatly contributed to the social welfare of the people in a variety of areas, particularly, in education, training, employment and rehabilitation, long before social welfare was officially established in Thailand.

Some of the children are cared for at Wat Sa Kaeo, Ang Thong Province.

Family institution plays an important role in establishing an individual framework of social welfare. While babies and young children are generally cared for by grand-parents or other elder members of the family, it is customary for Thai people to take good

care of the elderly in their families. The concept of gratitude is well ingrained in the mind of the people since their early childhood. Generosity-at-heart is also an underlying national characteristic that results in the willingness to help those in need. This can be witnessed in Thailand's tremendous efforts to shoulder the inevitable burden of refugees in Thailand after the fightings in Indochina in the past two decades.

However, it was not until 1883 that the first social welfare organization, The Red Cross Society, was founded by the royal initiation, to help wounded soldiers. During the preceding year, the first orphanage had also been set up. And in 1910 one of the leading private welfare agencies, the Poh Teck Tung Foundation was established. The establishment of the Department of Public Welfare in 1940 demonstrated the prime concern of the government for the welfare of the Thai people.

Since then, private social welfare agencies, taking the form of associations, foundations, groups and organizations, have flourished in response to increasing welfare problems, and the needs of people. As a result, the National Culture Act enacted in 1942 to control and supervise such agencies. New social legislation came into force and intensive social programmes were put into operation. The significance of social welfare is increasingly recognized and constitutes an integral part of national development policy.

Gemstone cutting is one of the vocational courses open to disabled military and police personnel run by the Veterans Welfare Association.

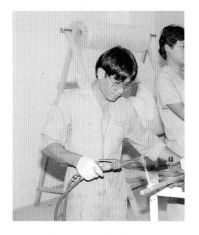

Disabled veterans in the Veterans Hospital produce artificial limbs for their colleagues.

The Veterans Welfare Association promotes sport among disabled veterans and supports them to attend the international sporting events for the disabled.

Typing is one of the vocational courses taught to veterans to allow them to earn their living.

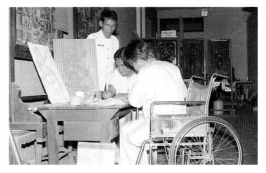

Those veterans who have an artistic flair are taught production skills and carving.

The wide array of social welfare activities in Thailand fall under the jurisdiction of government departments, state enterprises and local self government bodies. Apart from these, the non-governmental sector not only participates actively in the provision of social welfare services to the people but also takes the initiative in developing new services. These concerted efforts have been developed and expanded ceaselessly to satisfy humanitarian concern and to fulfil the basic human rights of the people.

However, the Department of Public Welfare is the principal government agency, extending its services to needy and distressed people throughout the country. The nature of its welfare programme is remedial, preventive, curative and developmental in order to enable people being helped to become productive citizens. Its services are extended to specific target groups of children, women, the elderly, the disabled, the destitute and discharged mental patients, the disaster victims, needy families, poor and homeless persons and the hilltribes. On the other hand, non-governmental social welfare organizations (NGOs) play a supportive role to the government organizations. It is estimated that there are over 3,200 NGOs in the country, with operations ranging from rural and slum development, to primary health care, women's and child development. Major coordinating bodies of NGOs are the National Council on Social Welfare under the Royal Patronage of His Majesty the King, and the National

Council of Women of Thailand under the Royal Patronage of Her Majesty the Queen. Both government and non-government social welfare organizations follow the same precept, that is to "help people to stand on their feet."

The Role of Thai Women in Society

The household management is not only the responsibility weighing substantially on Thai women. From time inmemorial, they have participated professionally and noteworthily in the Thai social fabric whether they be in the paddy fields, in the forests, in fishermen's village, in factories, in traditional or modern offices of the government or business enterprises or in private homes all over the country, etc.

The above statement is confirmed from the survey made by the National Statistical Office in 1992 that out of 32.9 millions Thai aged above 13 years old in the labour force, 15.2 millions (46.1%) were working parallelly with their male counterparts. Out of this force, 19.71 millions or 59.9% are in agricultural sector while 3.6 millions or 10.9% were in manufacturing area. The number has been increasing rapidly in the last 20 years due to the national policy for open investment and investment incentives, the result of which has brought about extensively export promotion. Statistically, for the main export manufacturing products that are the sources of a gigantic sum of national income of 634,385 millions baht in 1992 (i.e. gems and jewellery, textiles and garments electrical and electronic products, agro-industrial foods etc.), it is reported that female workers have 4 times outnumbered those of male one. In the fields that require expertise in rendering services such as in tourist industry which also generates a big share of national income, the role of Thai women involving in the industry has to be principally taken into consideration. Therefore, it is presently fair to say that Thai female labour force plays a vital role in the social and economic life of the country.

According to the constitution, women have rights in all aspects accorded to Thai citizens. Most

importantly perhaps is the right which constitutes to their participation in the professional labour force : their right to acquiring modern education, the results of which open venues for their professional participation in governmental, non-governmental and political sectors of the country. In 1985, for example, out of 716,181 government officials, 54.4% females occupied the posts of varied profession of school teachers, university professors, scientists, doctors, architects, engineers, judges, public

prostutor, military and police officers, airline pilots, bank presidents, ambassadors, etc. In fact, we had the first woman member of parliament in 1949 as well as several women ministers in the cabinet in the past 20 years and most recently in 1993 the first woman governor of a province marked history of female participation in the high-ranking national administration.

Although considerable problems still confront Thai female labour force. To quote only a few vital ones : inequality in job opportunity compared with that of men, security in industrial work, social blases towards female workers, etc. As years pass by, women role in the economic and social life of the country cannot be ignored. On the contrary, the issue is become increasing tremendously.

RELIGION

Religion plays a very important role in Thai life. Considered an essential pillar of society, it is not only the major moral force of the Thai family and community but has also contributed to the moulding of this freedom-loving, individualistic, and tolerant people for many centuries. That there is complete freedom of worship in Thailand, without ethnic or racial discrimination, should therefore come as no surprise to any serious student of Thai society.

Out of the estimated 55 million people in Thailand, about 95 percent are Buddhists, while about 4 percent are Muslims, 0.5 percent Christians, and the remainder Brahmins, Hindus, Sikhs, Confucians and others. Despite the fact that Buddhism is the state religion and that the king must be of the Buddhist faith, both the king and the government uphold and support all religions accepted by the people, according to the constitution and in reality. Thus amidst a rich diversity of beliefs, the people of Thailand have always lived together in peace and harmony.

Buddhism

Buddhism, the great eastern religion founded by the Indian Prince Siddhartha Gautama 600 years before the birth of Christ, first appeared in Thailand during the 3rd century B.C. in the area of the present day provincial capital Nakhon Pathom. Once established, it proved such a durable and pervasive force that some ethnic groups who migrated into that area during the Dvaravati period readily adopted it as their state religion.

At its inception, Buddhism had been a reaction against Brahmanism, eschewing Brahmanism's emphasis on caste and dogma regarding sacrifice and ritual. At the

"Phra Phuttha Chinnarat" in Phitsanulok Province is one of Thailand's most revered image.

The Lord Buddha preached to royal family after his enlightenment.

same time, it modified Brahmanic concepts of karma and rebirth.

Briefly, Buddhism teaches that one's life does not begin with birth and end with death but is a link in a chain of lives, each conditioned by volitional acts (karma) committed in previous existences. The concept of karma, the law of cause and effect, suggests that selfishness and craving result in suffering. Conversely, compassion and love bring happiness and well-being. Therefore, only by eliminating desire can one find peace of mind. The ideal Buddhist aspiration is to attain perfection through Nirvana (Nibbhana), an indescribable, immutable state unconditioned by desire, suffering, or further rebirth, in which a person simply is, yet is completely at one with his surroundings.

After its introduction into Thailand, Buddhism gained wide acceptance because its emphasis on tolerance and individual initiative complemented the Thais' cherished sense of inner freedom. Fundamentally, Buddhism is an empirical way of life. Free of dogma, it is a flexible moral, ethical, and philosophical framework within which people find room to fashion their own salvation.

*His Majesty the King, accompanied by
Her Majesty the Queen, performed religious
ceremonies and presented offerings to members
of the Buddhist clergy at Wat Phra Si
Rattanasatsadaram and the Amarin Winitchai
Throne Hall.*

His Majesty the King in his monkhood.

Sukhothai's King Ramkhamhaeng (1275-1317 A.D.) established Theravada Buddhism as Thailand's dominant religion. It reached its height under the reign of King Ramkhamhaeng's grandson, King Li Thai (1347-1368 A.D.), when about 30 volumes of the Buddhist scriptures were studied and rewritten by the king into one volume, the Tribhumikatha, a treatise on Buddhist cosmology and the three planes of existence–Sensuous, Corporeal, and Incorporeal. Not only was this the first Buddhist treatise by a Thai, but it was also the first known Thai Buddhist and didactic literary work. The Tribhumikatha's impact on religious arts such as mural paintings can be seen today in many monasteries in various provinces.

Through the centuries Buddhism has been the main driving force in Thai cultural development. Much of classical Thai art, particularly architecture, sculpture, painting, and early literature, is really Buddhist art. Then, as now, Buddhism coloured everyday Thai life.

Although Buddhism became the primary and state religion, Thais always subscribed to the ideal of religious freedom. Thai constitutions have stipulated that Thai kings must be Buddhists, but monarchs are invariably entitled "Upholder of All Religions". Consequently, the government, through the Religious Affairs Department; annually allocates funds to finance religious education and to construct, maintain, and restore monasteries, mosques, and churches.

At present Thailand is the location of the headquarters of the World Fellowship of Buddhists (WFB), an international Buddhist organization consisting of 98 regional centres in 37 countries which promotes coordination and cooperation to enhance Buddhism throughout the world.

H.E. Professor Sanya Dhamasakti, former Prime Minister and present President of the Privy Council of H.M. the King, has been unanimously elected President of the WFB twice consecutively.

His Majesty the King at a Mahayana Buddhist ceremony.

Mahayana Buddhists

Mahayana Buddhists are found primarily among Thailand's ethnic Chinese and Vietnamese. There are some 21 major Chinese monasteries and 25 meeting halls. Mahayana monks are easily distinguished from Theravada monks by their orange jackets and trousers.

A Chinese monastery in Bangkok's China Town.

Strict vegetarians, they eat only food prepared by their monasteries and are not required to be celibate. Their daily routine is concerned with elaborate rituals and with preparation for the funerals and burials over which they preside.

Vietnamese monks are found in 13 major monasteries. Though dressed like the Chinese monks, they are not subject to special dietary regulations and make daily morning food collections.

Muslims

Muslims comprise Thailand's largest religious minority and are concentrated mainly in the southernmost provinces of Narathiwat, Pattani, Yala, and Satun. Islam is said to have been introduced to the Malay Peninsula by Arab traders and adventurers during the 13th century. Most Thai Muslims are of Malay descent, reflecting the common cultural heritage Thailand's southernmost provinces share with Malaysia.

His Majesty the King and Her Majesty the Queen granting an audience to the Thai Muslims while visiting their village in southern Thailand.

The Central Mosque in Pattani Province.

Ninety-nine percent Sunni and one percent Shi'ite, Thai Muslims enjoy inspirational and financial support from His Majesty the King, who provided money for translating the Koran into Thai. Each year the King or his representative also presides during celebrations commemorating the Prophet Muhammad's birthday. Moreover, His Majesty appoints a respected Muslim religious leader as Chularajamontri, or State Counsellor for all Islamic affairs. The government also provides funds for building and renovating mosques.

In some southern provinces where the Muslim population is substantial, government-employed Muslims are allowed to leave for important Muslim festivals and allowed to work half-days on Friday, the Muslim holy day. In such provinces family and inheritance cases are judged according to Koranic law with a Muslim religious judge, or *kadi*, sitting on the bench. In addition, one four months' leave with full salary is also granted to allow an employee to make the Haj, the pilgrimage to Mecca.

There are approximately 2,000 mosques in Thailand, about 100 of which are in Bangkok. Some 200 Muslim schools offer secular as well as religious instruction. All in all, Thailand's Muslims enjoy full state support and are free to teach and practice their religion according to their own tenets.

Christians

Christianity was introduced to Thailand by European missionaries in the 16th and 17th centuries. These early Catholic missionaries were later joined by Protestants of the Presbyterian, Baptist, and Seventh-Day Adventist sects. Their converts mainly came from ethnic minorities such as the immigrant Chinese. Despite the small number of Thai converts, Christians have made several major contributions in the fields of health and education.

Thailand's first printing press was introduced by Christians, and King Mongkut (Rama IV) learned English and Latin from Christian missionaries.

His Majesty the King gave a warm welcome to His Holiness Pope John Paul II during his State Visit to Thailand between 10-11 May 1984.

Though King Mongkut reportedly told one of his missionary friends "What you teach us to do is admirable, but what you teach us to believe is foolish," during his monkhood before ascending the throne, he nonetheless allowed Christian missionaries to give lectures, even in his own monastery. Christians introduced Westery surgery, made the first smallpox vaccinations, trained the first doctors in Western medicine, and wrote the first Thai-English dictionaries.

Thailand's Christian population is estimated at 0.5% of the total.

Hindus and Sikhs

The approximately 20,000 Indians residing in Thailand are almost equally divided between Hindus and Sikhs. The Hindu community is mostly concentrated in Bangkok, where it worships at four main Hindu temples. There are also several Brahman shrines at which Hindus and Buddhists alike worship. The Hindus operate their own school where the curriculum is based on the Thai education system, though in addition to Thai it teaches Hindi, Sanskrit, and English.

The Sikhs, too, are concentrated mainly in Bangkok. Divided into two sects, they worship at two different temples. Collectively, the Sikhs operate a free school for poor children, regardless of caste, creed, or religion, and through several charitable association they support the aged and the sick.

His Majesty the King granting an audience to representatives of the Sikh community in Thailand, who presented His Majesty with Buddha images at Wat Bovornnives.

*In the past, Buddhist monks
played an important role in
the country's education.*

EDUCATION

In the early days of Thai history, education primarily revolved around two institutions, one religious and the other royal. Buddhist monks gave basic education to boys in classes set up within the compounds of monasteries, while children of the royal household and from families of the nobility were educated in order to serve in the court and govern in the provinces. The mass of society was made up of farmers, who saw little need for literacy. Village history, lore, and local philosophy were transmitted orally.

During the reign of King Rama V (1863-1910A.D.) there was increased recognition of the need for educated people to staff the growing bureaucracy. As a result, the Thai education system was modernized and made more accessible to the general public. This began with the 1898 Education Proclamation, which was strongly influenced by the British system and in which two educational paths were stipulated: the academic and the vocational.

Wat Mahan School has been established within the Buddhist monastery compound in order to educate children.

Administrative Structure

There are three major government agencies responsible for the provision and development of education in Thailand: the National Education Commission, the Ministry of Education and the Ministry of University Affairs. The National Education Commission is mainly responsible for the educational policies, planning and research at the national level. The Ministry of Education is responsible for the provision of basic education nationwide. Its areas of responsibility include the provision of pre-school education, primary education, secondary education, teacher education, vocational and technical education, curriculum development and non-formal education, while the Ministry of University Affairs is responsible for the management of state universities. A small number of specialized schools are operated by the Ministry of Interior, the Ministry of Public Health, the Ministry of Defence and the Ministry of Transport and Communications.

Formal Education

The first formal comprehensive education plan was introduced in 1932. This plan highlighted four years of elementary education and eight years of secondary schooling. This system was further refined in 1936, when five levels of education were featured; preprimary or kindergarten, primary, secondary, pre-university, and higher education. The educational plan of 1951 was noteworthy in that it facilitated special and adult education.

As part of the emphasis on national development since 1960, a major goal of the educational system has been to harmonize and comply with economic and political plans. The government faced the challenge of widespread illiteracy, as well as the massive task of training young men and women for the dynamic development process in the shortest time possible. Recently, it has had to modify instruction to include the specialized skills required by industries such as computer

H.R.H. Princess Maha Chakri Sirindhorn has always paid special attention to education for young people.

Girl-guides and crippled boyscouts stand hand in hand during their gathering.

Outdoor activity.

Classroom atmosphere.

UNESCO also provided assistance to the Department of General Education in its production of AIDS educational materials and its training of teachers.

The Science School; Mahidol Witthayanuson, is a secondary school that promotes mathematics and science teaching learning at the upper secondary level. It is located in the groups of Mahidol University on Salaya Campus in Nakhon Pathom Province.

science and environmental engineering, together with new branches of medicine. The most recent changes were brought about by the educational plan of 1977, which called for six years of compulsory primary schooling, three years of lower secondary education for those who plan to enter special occupations and three years of upper secondary education for those who wish or enter higher education or a university. This system was launched in May 1978, beginning with the first grade at both the primary and secondary levels, and continued until the cycle of six grades at both levels was fully implemented in 1983.

The current system of formal education consists of four levels of education: one or two years of pre-school education; six years of compulsory primary education; six years of secondary education: three years at the lower secondary level and three years at the upper secondary level and higher education.

Efforts to raise the overall educational standards of the nation to meet the development needs in technology and advanced agricultural methods result in the expansion of basic education from six to nine years, covering six years of primary education and three years of lower-secondary education, in rural areas to form a broader basis for future training and employment.

Science lesson.

Apprenticeship.

Non-formal Education

Non-formal education, including adult education, introduced in Thailand in 1940 in an attempt to provide education for those who miss schooling opportunities, is an indispensible component of the present educational system that complements the formal system of education. Educational programmes offered emphasize basic education, news and information literacy (level 1-4) and vocational skills training which are available throughout the country.

There are over 500 public libraries throughout the country, most of which offer mobile services to people in rural areas. Practical reading materials are also available at over 30,000 village reading centres formed by village committees.

Embroidery course.

There are at least 38 national museums for public reference and interest.

The Non-formal Education Department established *Thaicom* Distance Education Centre in October 1993 to plan and manage the satellite distance education project. The experimental

Hair dressing course.

period of this project is from 1994-1998. The centre coordinates with agencies concerned from both the public and private sectors in the management of televised distance education through satellite broadcast and the development of such multi-media, as texts or self-learning manuals, learning kits, television/radio programmes, video/cassette tapes.

Special training services are also provided for disadvantaged groups in urban and rural areas, new labour market entrants, the unemployed, and certain categories of people such as ex-convicts, homeless, and sexually-exploited persons who require skills to earn their living and make them active contributors to society.

(Below left) Sewing course.

Little hilltribe children in attention to their teacher.

These children have been developed in terms of physical, intellectual, emotional and social aspects so that they may become self-reliant and contribute weaningfully to society in which they live.

Special and Welfare Education

Special education refers to the provision of education for all kinds of disabled and handicapped children, including the deaf, the blind, and the mentally retarded, while welfare education caters to the culturally and socially handicapped such as hilltribe children, slum children, and children of lepers. To ensure that such children receive an equal opportunity in education, and education suitable for their abilities, special schools and welfare schools equipped with special educational programmes and facilities have been established throughout the country.

The mainstreaming or integrated programmes for the disabled in regular schools.

Kurudayada Teacher Training Programme

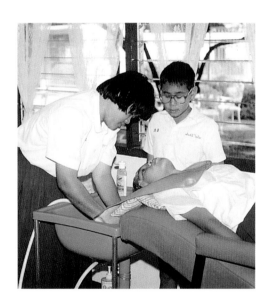

Entrepreneurial competencies.

The "School vegetables" spearhead an awareness–building on environmental problems in the community. It is by far the most practical way to allow students to earn while they learn.

Vocational Schools and Specialized Institutes

Seeing the necessity to adapt the educational system to the development and labour needs of the country, vocational education and training has been given much promotion. Various types of courses and training programmes are offered and administered by the Department of Vocational Education and the Institute of Technology and Vocational Education.

There are eight levels of studies programmed to suit the student's previous academic background, ranging from the semi-skilled level, offered to students who have completed the lower secondary level, to technical teacher training programmes (degree level), open to holders of Higher Certificates of Technical Education with high academic records and a desire to become technical teachers at colleges and vocational training centres.

Teacher education has undergone various changes since 1892, when the first teacher training school for elementary school teachers was founded. In the 1960's a large number of teacher training institutes were established to meet an urgent demand for more teachers. This expansion was precipitated by three major factors; the extension of compulsory education, population growth, and the availability of secondary education to a larger population. The attention that has been paid to expanding teacher education was evident in the dramatic increase in teachers. However, this effort was concentrated on the quantitative rather than on the qualitative. At present there is a concern for improving the quality of the teacher education programmes. The Kurudayada Teacher Training Programme is one of the innovative projects designed to upgrade the image of the teaching profession and to significantly increase the quality of the teachers. The programme emphasises a strict recruitment process for teacher candidates. Those who indicate a positive attitude towards a teaching career and wish to enroll for the programme must have attained at least 3.0 grade-point average from the secondary school level and must actively involve themselves in educational activities designed by the Office of National Primary Education Commission (ONPEC).

Higher Education

Higher education is the principal concern of the Ministry of University Affairs, which coordinates the operation of 18 state universities and 28 privately operated universities and colleges (1994). Education at this level copes with thousands of secondary school graduates wishing to continue their further studies.

Most of the privately-run colleges offer courses and programmes leaning heavily towards science and technology. It is clear that these colleges are responding both to the increasing demands of a large number of high school graduates and also to current needs for advanced technology.

Admission to state universities is through a competitive national university entrance examination, held annually in April by Ministry of University Affairs.

At present there are at least 45 universities and 36 teacher training colleges in Thailand offering Diplomas and Degrees. The first university, Chulalongkorn University was founded in 1917. In keeping with a government plan to decentralize education, many universities are located in large regional centres throughout the country. These include Chiang

Chulalongkorn University.

Thammasat University.

Mai University in the North, Khon Kaen University in the Northeast, and Prince of Songkla University in the South. These universities offer a wide variety of courses at the undergraduate, graduate, and post-graduate levels, covering such fields as Agriculture, Archaeology, Architecture, Arts, Business Administration, Education, Economics, Engineering, Humanities, Law, Medicine and Nursing, Science, and Statistics. Scholarships are provided by the government and private sector for outstanding and needy students.

The language of instruction at most state-run universities is Thai, with the exception of the economics and engineering major courses at Chulalongkorn University, Mahidol University and Thammasat

Ramkhamhaeng University.

Sukhothaithammathirat University.

University, which are conducted in English. Special courses are taught in English at the discretion of a university.

In addition to conventional universities, two open universities have been established to expand educational opportunities for working people and secondary school graduates. One of these, Ramkhamhaeng University, provides campus instruction in Science and Humanities, supplemented by television and radio programmes, while the other, Sukhothaithammathirat University, employs television and radio programmes as well as correspondance courses and cassette tapes. The latter is said to be the most modern and best equipped open university in Southeast Asia.

Not all of the institutes at the higher education level come under the responsibility of the Office of University Affairs. The Police Cadet Academy at Sampran District, for example, is under the supervision of the Police Education Bureau, whereas Chulachomklao Royal Military Academy at Khao Cha-ngok is both academically and financially the responsibility of the Institute of Army Academies of the Ministry of Defence. Such academies offer Bachelor's Degrees to their graduates who go on to serve as police or military officers.

Education beyond the Bachelor's Degree level is also available for military officers. The Armed Forces

Staff College is reserved for high-ranking officers at administrative level who wish to pursue special training in military planning and administration.

Education at a degree level is also extended to Buddhist monks. There are two Buddhist universities, Mahamakut University and Mahachulalongkorn University, established with the approval of the Ecclesiastical Elders' Council and budgetary support from the Department of Religious Affairs, Ministry of Education.

Although the large majority of students at the university level are in social science or humanities, applied science and technology is gaining in importance, King Mongkut's Institute of Technology (KMIT) is an example of such an attempt to increase graduates in these needed areas. KMIT provides direct, relevant technical training both at the Bachelor's and Master's Degree levels in the fields of engineering and architecture for the development of the nation.

Programmes of studies at the Master's Degree level are offered in at least 30 universities, whereas those at the Doctorate's Degree level are offered at over 10 universities, some of which offer evening classes.

International Programmes in Education

To encourage international cooperation in education as a means of promotion high technology in Southeast Asia, Thailand is the home of the Asian Institute of Technology (AIT), where over 1,000 students from Asia and elsewhere attend courses in 4 academic schools: Management, Civil Engineering, Advanced Technologies, Environment, Resources and Development. About 150 professors from Asia and the Western countries form teaching staff at AIT. Courses in Management, Development, and Computer Sciences are offered throughout the year. The Asian Disaster Preparation Centre at AIT is also a unique training institute in this region.

His Majesty the King's visit to the Regional Computer Centre at the Asian Institute of Technology, Bangkok in 1987.

Joint programmes at the international level are also conducted in other universities such as the SASIN Graduate Institute of Business Administration, operated jointly between Chulalongkorn University, Northwestern University and the University of Pennsylvania in the U.S.

OutLook for Thailand in The Seventh Plan

Thailand has undergone rapid changes during the last two decades. The pace is likely to continue or even accelerate during the period of the Seventh National Economic and Social Development Plan (1992 - 1996). Thailand is being transformed from an agricultural country to an agro-industrial or even an industrialized country. Thai society is changing from being a traditionally rural one to an urban society. Thai people are faced with these changes to which they must adapt themselves. Therefore, they need the kind of education that prepares them adequately for new demands and new lifestyles. The current basic education of six years must be extended to at least nine years or the lower secondary level. Self-study materials and other electronic media such as computer and television will play an increasingly significant role in an educational system that is becoming more flexible and accessible to everyone at all levels and

New technology adopted to educational aid.

at all times. The existing learning network must be expanded to attain a national coverage. There must be more decentralization of administrative power and more public or local participation in developing the curriculum to suit the local needs. These are the new dimensions of education for the future.

A group of students join hands in the school cleaning up campaign.

THE ARTS

From Classical to Popular Arts

Most classical Thai art originated in or under the patronage of the royal courts. It is an amalgam of the finest cultural traditions of Asia, blended and stamped into unique forms instantly recognizable as Thai.

Classical art encompasses Buddhist art as represented in religious architecture, decorative murals, and Buddha images. The art reflected the complex formal structure and etiquette of court culture, with its heavy Indian influences, and expressed both religious and intellectual impulses. Entertainment was considered to be of secondary value in this category of art.

Another category is popular art, which arose from age-old village realities and the rites associated with birth, death, and the seasonal cycle of crop cultivation.

When speaking of Thai art in general one is able to distinguish between these two groups. On the other hand, different as they are, they are complementary and mutually reinforce each other. Much classical or court-inspired art later evolved into simpler forms which found popular appeal. Classical drama, for example, moved into the realm of popular culture in the form of comic folk-operas.

Traditional Thai Manual Arts

During the Ayutthaya period, writers, painters, dancers, sculptors, architects, musicians, and skilled craftsmen came under the royal patronage of kings and the nobility. Thai architects and artists were responsible for building and decorating palaces, monasteries, and shrines in conventionally acceptable forms and styles. Unlike their Western counterparts, they were not expected to display revolutionary originality or inventiveness. Thus art and craftsmanship were

A Buddhist temple in Ayutthaya Province reflects the glorious past of this ancient capital.

Loha Prasat, a multitiered architecture at Wat Ratchanatda, Bangkok.

transmitted from generation to generation according to rigid discipline.

In an attempt to provide general training to Thai craftsmen, especially those who worked in the palaces, the Krom Chang Sip Mu (Organization of the Ten Crafts) was established. According to Prince Pradit Worakarn, who was given charge of the Chang Sip Mu Department during the reign of King Rama V, the original organization in fact covered at least 13 different craftsmen: drawers, paper-makers, engravers, figure-makers, modellers, plasterers, lacquerers, metal beaters, turners, moulders, wood-carvers, sculptors, and carpenters.

In the Bangkok period, these were grouped into 10 divisions: drawing (which included draughtsmen, painters, muralists, and manuscript illustrators), engraving (woodcarvers, engravers on metal, precious metal inlay), turning (lathe-workers, carpenters and

joiners, glass mosaic workers), sculpting (paper sculptors, decorative fruit and vegetable carvers), modelling (beeswax moulders and bronze casters, mask and puppet makers), figure making (dummy and prototype makers), moulding (craftsmen in bronze and metal casting), plastering (bricklayers, lime plasterers, stucco workers and sculptors), lacquering (masters of lacquerware and mother-of-pearl inlay), and beating (metal beaters and finishers of metal articles).

The reflections of the finest craftsmanship of Thai craftsmen.

Contemporary Thai arts and crafts, though modernized to some extent through improved technology, are still very much inspired by tradition. Ranging from delicately wrought silverware to numerous utilitarian items of everyday life, they are part of the kingdom's rich cultural heritage.

Painting

Classical Thai painting was confined to temple and palace interiors and book illustrations. Mural painting was developed to a high degree in the belief that walls should enhance the beauty of the religious and royal objects they surrounded.

A mural painting depicting an episode from the Buddha's life.

Traditional Thai painting was typically Asian in that conventional perspective was ignored and figures were large or small depending on their importance. Shadows were unknown and space was neutral rather than atmospheric. Figures were two dimensional and landscapes were merely sketchily-treated backdrops for detailed action. A technique of pictorial composition called "apportioning areas" was employed, comparable to the "bird's eye view" of Western painting. By this method, the positions of the key scenes were assigned first and then closed off with "space transformers" that effectively isolated them from considerations of perspective by doing away with any surrounding intermediate or middle ground.

The traditional Thai painter had five primary pigments, the close equivalents of scarlet lake, yellow ochre, ultramarine blue, pipe-clay white, and pot-black. With these he was able to produce as many other colours.

All were tempera colours, finely ground powders that were stirred into bowls containing a glue binder, using sticks to work it to the desired strength and consistency. With these colours the traditional artists created uniquely beautiful compositions in the form of temple murals, cloth banners, and manuscript illustrations.

The earliest surviving murals are characterized by earth colours made from natural pigments. They depicted excerpts from the Jataka stories, episodes from the Buddha's life, scenes of Buddhist heaven and hells, rows of gods, and scenes of contemporary Thai life. The murals in Bangkok's Wat Suthat and Thon Buri's Wat Suwannaram are particularly fine examples.

The traditional painting technique continued into the Bangkok period, when colours became richer thanks to pigments imported from China. Around the middle of the 19th century, artists began using chemical pigments and Western perspective. Spatial values were eschewed for atmospheric effects, and opulent gold leaf and bold primary colours radically altered the delicate harmony of the old subdued earth colours.

Thai painters with distinguished works generally reach scholarly professional level of artistic skill. Some of them have been recognized and awarded with the status of the "National Artist" including for example, Fua Hariphitak, Chalerm Nakeeraksa, Sanit Dispandha and Tawee Nanthakwang.

Besides, Thai painters, though trained in the traditional style, have been currently influenced by Western style and technique. However, some have been able to integrate the various styles and thus create their own expression of art. Chakrapan Posayakrit, for example, while best known for his portraits is also a painter of scenes and characters based on literature which manage to convey a flavour that is at once modern and traditional. Another internationally contemporary artist is Tawan Dachanee, who has experimented extensively with his medium.

Heroine from a Thai literature through the imagination of a renowned painter, Chakrapan Posayakrit.

Sculpture

Thai sculptors of the past concentrated almost exclusively on Buddha images, producing works that rank among the world's greatest expressions of Buddhist art. These have ranged in size from Sukhothai's gigantic seated Buddha at Wat Si Chum, which measures 11 metres from knee to knee, to tiny, fingernail-sized Buddhas worn as amulets. Their greatest achievements were during the Sukhothai period, when the smoothness and sheen of cast metals perfectly matched the graceful elongated simplicity of the basic form. To emphazise the spiritual qualities of Buddhism, Thai sculptors eschewed anatomical details such as muscles and bone structure, realizing that these would only distract from the enigmatic serenity that was their goal.

Phra Atchana, the seated Buddha at Wat Si Chum, is one of the finest examples of Sukhothai sculpture.

Thai sculpture received a boost in 1933 when an Italian sculptor, Corado Feroci founded the Fine Arts School which in 1943 became Silpakorn University. Having first arrived in Thailand in 1924 to work with the Royal Fine Arts Department on the creation of monumental sculptures, Feroci is today remembered as the father of modern art in Thailand. He became a Thai citizen in 1944, changing his name to Silpa Bhirasri, and served as Dean of the Painting and Sculpture Faculty until his death in 1962.

Many of his students have been awarded with the "National Artist" status. These include, for example, Paitoon Muangsoomboon, Chit Rianpracha and Pimarn Moolpramook whose works have appeared in various places such as at the Benjasiri Gardens in Bangkok. Another artist who is well-known among the Thais and abroad is Misiem Yip-in-tsoi. She took up painting first, and then sculpture. She achieved great success in the latter field. Examples of her works,

much of which depict children, can be seen in many private collections as well as in a sculpture garden she established in Nakhon Pathom near Bangkok.

Many modern Thai sculptors have experimented with the artistic possibilities of new methods borrowed

The statue of King Rama I by Corado Feroci, better known as Silpa Bhirasri, the founder of Silpakorn University.

A modern sculpture by Misiem Yip-in-tsoi at Rai Mae Fa Luang, Chiang Rai Province.

from industrial technology to create works both simple and incredibly complex in meaning and effect. Others have taken objects out of their ordinary environment and turned them into arresting works of art. In one exhibition at the art gallery of the National Museum, buffalo horns and hides, rice sacks, dried rice stalks, sickles and other implements were used to create the essence of being on a farm.

Lacquerware and Mother-of-Pearl Inlay

The art of making lacquer originally came to Thailand from China, probably by way of Burma–now Myanmar, but over the centuries distinctively Thai designs and techniques were evolved. It became a notable handicraft in the northern province of Chiang Mai and is still made there in a number of households.

Lacquerware is a local hand-crafted product of Chiang Mai.

Lacquerware begins with finely-woven bamboo basketry or well-seasoned wood which has been carved or shaped on a lathe into the desired shape. To this is

first applied a basic coating material called *samuk*, consisting of the ashes of burnt rice-paddy husks or ground clay mixed with *rak*, or black lacquer, obtained from a tree which grows in the northern hills. When dry, this is polished with soap-stone and then another coating is applied. This process is repeated again and again for up to fifteen times, building up a rigid base of durable lacquer. At the end, a final polishing is given with a sandpaper-like leaf called *bai-nod*.

The object is then ready for several coats of pure black lacquer, from three to six coatings. The final layer is polished with water and powdered fired clay, giving it a glistening shine.

A design is then applied by either the method called *lai kud* or the one called *lai rot nam*. If the object is to be in colour, *lai kud* is used, while *lai rot nam* is for objects with gold designs. At the end of the process the colour or gold stands out against a background of glossy black.

The use of mother of pearl to adorn objects has a long history in Thailand. Stucco pieces embedded with bits of shell have been found at monuments dating back to the Dvaravati period (6th to 11th centuries A.D.), and same form of the art may have existed even before along the coastal region.

Temple door panels intricately inlaid with mother-of-pearl.

But these early efforts were crude compared with the magnificent works achieved by techniques perfected in the late Ayutthaya and early Bangkok periods, when temple doors and windows, manuscript boxes, alms bowls, and numerous other items were splendidly decorated by the painstaking process the Thais call *khruang muk*. The craft continues to thrive today in the production of exquisitely detailed furniture, mirror frames, boxes, and trays that are the pride of many owners both in Thailand and abroad.

The Thai mother-of-pearl inlay technique involves the patient cutting of the luminescent *muk fai,* or flame snail, indigenous to the Gulf of Thailand. The outer surface of this shell is removed with a special knife and the pearly inner shell is cut into fairly flat pieces, each about two and a half centimetres long. Sanded flat, they are glued to wooden surfaces to form patterns or scenes and the area in between filled with lacquer.

Pottery

Handsome pots dating back more than 5,000 years have been found at Ban Chiang in northeastern Thailand, and the art of shaping and firing clay has continued to the present day. Simple earthenware vessels are still used for cooking and storage, while more sophisticated glazed pottery is also being produced by methods introduced from China 700 years ago.

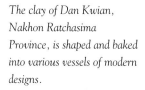

The clay of Dan Kwian, Nakhon Ratchasima Province, is shaped and baked into various vessels of modern designs.

Almost every region of the country has its own traditional pottery. The North, for example, makes fine low-fired pots and water jugs, lightly glazed with terra cotta and oil to make them capable of holding liquids;

by northern custom, one of these pots is placed outside most temples and private homes so that thirsty strangers can stop and refresh themselves. Dark brown pottery in a wide variety of shapes, from flower pots to fanciful animals, is produced at kilns near the north-eastern city of Nakhon Ratchasima and Ratchaburi, west of Bangkok, is noted for its beautifully decorated water storage jars, yellowish-green in colour and adorned with dragons and swirling floral motifs.

According to tradition, the art of making delicate, blue-green celadon began at the end of the 13th century, when King Ramkhamhaeng of Sukhothai brought 300 Chinese potters to his kingdom. Within a short time, the high-fired stoneware was being traded throughout Southeast Asia, all the way to the Philippines and Indonesia.

Glazed ware celadon is made in the North using the same technique as in Sukhothai period.

The celadon industry declined with Sukhothai but has been revived in recent years in the northern city of Chiang Mai. The technique is still the same as in ancient times, using a clear glaze made from feldspar, limestone, ash, and a small amount of red clay. The wood used for firing the kilns comes from a small jungle tree that grows north of Chiang Mai, the ash of which is supposed to help impart the typical celadon colour. Several companies are now making the stoneware, which is becoming a noted Thai export once again.

Weaving: From Thai Silk to Home-spun Hilltribe Cloths

The gorgeously irridescent, nubby Thai silk may have originated in northeastern Thailand, where cloth

Hand-woven silk is one of the famous exported products of Thailand.

weaving is a traditional folk craft. Rearing their own silkworms and spinning and dyeing the yarn, northeast village women use primitive hand looms to produce shimmering bolts of cloth for sale in faraway markets.

Though it prospered in early Bangkok, the silk industry went into a long decline starting in the latter part of the 19th century when cheaper, factory-produced fabrics from China and Japan began to flood the market. An attempt to improve production was made during the reign of King Chulalongkorn, when Japanese experts were brought in and a Department of Sericulture was established, but the effort enjoyed limited success. A few years after World War II, an American named Jim Thompson revived the industry and made the silk known to international markets. There are a number of silk companies today, many of them in or around Bangkok, but the Northeast is still the main centre of production; near the northeastern town of Pak Thong Chai, the company Jim Thompson founded has built the largest hand-weaving facility in the world.

Besides plain and printed silks of various weights, a number of special weaves have become celebrated. One of these is called *mudmee*, a kind of ikat which is a specialty of the Northeast. Thanks to the encouragement of Her Majesty Queen Sirikit, *mudmee* is now in wide use. Another sought-after silk is richly brocaded with gold and silver thread in traditional Thai patterns. This requires the most time and skill to make and is therefore the most expensive, used mainly on such ceremonial occasions as weddings.

The diversified designs of mudmee silk are based on the tie-dye technique.

Thai silk is today the best known of all the country's handicrafts, found not only in countless local shops but also throughout the world. It is exported worldwide in plain lengths, plaids, brocades, stripes, prints, and checks and is supported by a massive manufacturing and sales infrastructure, a far cry from its humble origins.

Supple handwoven Thai cotton is also popular. Made in a variety of weights for both clothing and home furnishings, it is being exported in increasing quantities.

A hilltribe girl in her tribal costume.

Fine embroidery is one of the traditional crafts of the northern hilltribes, with the Hmong and Yao people being particularly skilled at creating splendid, boldly-coloured geometric designs. In long strips, these are used to edge a skirt or jacket, in squares to enhance a vest or shoulder bag, in larger pieces to make a handsome quilt. Her Majesty Queen Sirikit has long been an admirer of tribal embroidery and has helped to promote the craft, particularly on homespun cloths such as cotton and local hemp that produces a fabric resembling linen, among fashionable ladies in Bangkok and in other countries as well.

Nielloware

The art of *khruang thom*, as the Thais call nielloware, is believed to have come to the country during the Ayutthaya period. The precise origin is uncertain; some scholars say it came from China, while others give Persia as the source. In any case, it became a major craft in southern Thailand, particularly in Nakhon Si Thammarat, and is still practiced there.

Fine nielloware is usually made of pure silver, sometimes later plated with gold. The metal is bought by the craftsmen in thin sheets, from which the desired shaped is cut and welded into a crude, three-dimensional form. After the design has been engraved—usually traditional, such as Thai flame or an intricate floral motif—an oxidizing solution is applied to the parts in high relief, turning them a permanent blue-black. The piece is then filed to remove all the rough edges and given a final polishing.

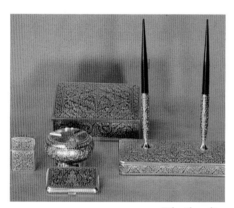

Nielloware can be made into different shapes for different purposes.

Nielloware objects have been made in almost every conceivable shape, from elaborate coffee and tea sets to fittings for handbags and buttons. It is one of Thailand's most distinctive and beautiful crafts.

Silverware

Though silverware is made in several parts of Thailand, the most famous centre is Chiang Mai, where it has been a prominent local handicraft for at least a thousand years. In ancient times, it was concentrated in a village called Wua Lai, just outside the city wall; the village has long been absorbed by the modern city but the area where it stood is still noted for its silver.

Northern silversmiths have applied their skills to a great variety of objects, from goblets to swords, but their most common products have been ceremonial bowls and boxes of assorted sizes. These are usually adorned with elaborate decorations, either figures or traditional Thai motifs.

SUPPORT

Handicrafts like silverware, nielloware, lacquerware, and mother-of-pearl inlay were once produced only in artisans' homes. Today these traditional skills, some of which were in danger of disappearing, are being gradually expanded to non-artisans, especially in rural areas. A leading factor in this has been the Foundation for the Promotion of Supplementary Occupations and Related Techniques, popularly known as SUPPORT, founded by Her Majesty Queen Sirikit to provide Thai farmers with sufficient training to enable them to turn out high-quality crafts and thus earn extra income between crops or in times of difficulty. SUPPORT has set up numerous projects throughout the country as well as retail outlets, and the Queen has personally undertaken several trips abroad to promote the handicrafts on the world market. Another stimulus came in 1988-89, which was designated as Thai Arts and Crafts Year, when 104 projects were set up to promote and market handicrafts by the Tourism Authority of Thailand. In this way, many of Thailand's most treasured traditional crafts have been revived and are now finding new admirers outside the country.

In the year 1992 to mark the auspicious occasion on the 60th anniversary of Her Majesty the Queen the

Silverware is listed among the numerous items of Thai handicrafts.

Products of the SUPPORT Foundation.

SUPPORT Museum was inaugurated at the Aphisek Dusit Pavilion in Dusit Palace, Bangkok. The main collections in this museum contain masterpieces of art from the SUPPORT Foundation. It opens daily for the public.

Music

Since ancient times, the Thai people have known how to make musical instruments or to copy the patterns of others and adapt them to their own uses. In fact, there are several kinds of musical instruments which the Thais apparently devised before they came in contact with the culture of India, which was widespread in Southeast Asia before they migrated there.

Later, when the Thai people were establishing their kingdoms and had come into contact with Indian culture, particularly with Indian instruments which the Mon and Khmer cultures had absorbed first, they assimilated this musical culture into their own.

From this contact, the Thais created several new kinds of musical instruments such as the *phin, sang, pi chanai, krachap pi, chakhe,* and *thon,* which are mentioned in the Tribhumikatha, one of the first books written in Thai, and on a stone inscription from the time of King Ramkhamhaeng of the Sukhothai period. Some songs of the Sukhothai period are still sung at present, such as *Phleng Thep Thong.*

During the Ayutthaya period the instrumental ensemble was composed of four to eight musicians. Songs became much longer and singing technique was improved. Many Ayutthaya songs were composed in a form of musical suite called *Phleng Rua,* which was a series of songs. Poets contributed lyrics in the form of short stories, mostly from the Ramakian. Many Ayutthaya songs are still employed in Thai plays today.

In the beginning of the Bangkok period, after a long period of war, there was a remarkable revival of Thai arts, especially music and drama. The size of the instrumental ensemble was enlarged to 12 musicians and several masterpieces of Thai literature were produced as theatrical performances accompanied by music. Beautiful lyrics written by contemporary poets were fitted into melodies of the Ayutthaya period.

All Thai musicians in the past received their training from their teachers, through constant playing and singing in their presence. With nothing else to rely upon except their own memory, it was only through much hard work that they gained their technical experience and practical knowledge in playing and singing.

Later when Thailand began to have contact with Western European nations and the United States, the Thais adopted such Western instruments as the bass drum, the violin, and the organ.

To save the national music from extinction, modern Thai musicians are trying to devise a system in

The Bangkok Symphony Orchestra.

which this traditional music can be rendered into Western notation and later edited. According to a book written by Sir Hubert Perry, entitled "Evolution of the Art of Music":

"The Thai scale system is…extraordinary. It is not now pentatonic, though supposed to be derived originally from the Javanese system. The scale consists of seven notes which should by right be exactly equidistant from one another; that is, each step is a little less than a semitone and three-quarters. So that they have neither a perfect fourth nor a true fifth in their system, and both their thirds and sixths are between major and minor; and not a single note between a starting note and its octave agrees with any of the notes of the European scale…Their sense of the right relations of the notes of the scale are so highly developed that their musicians can tell by ear directly a note which is not true to their singular theory. Moreover, with this scale, they have developed a kind of musical art in the highest degree complicated and extensive."

In all, there are about 50 types of Thai musical instruments, including many local versions of flutes, stringed instruments, and gongs used for all kinds of

A Thai musical ensemble.

occasions: festivals, folk theater, marriages, funerals, and social evenings after harvesting.

Princess Maha Chakri Sirindhorn is a distinctive patroness of Thai music.

The best known Thai musician for both the revival and conservation of the Thai music are Montree Tramote and Khunying Phaitoon Kittivan. Both of them were also awarded the status of "National Artists" in Thai music.

Her Royal Highness Princess Maha Chakri Sirindhorn is an accomplished performer of several Thai classical musical instruments. She has become an active leader for the movement to revive interest in the rich cultural value of Thai music among the younger generations.

The Western classical music tradition was introduced to Thailand before the turn of the century. Its development was nurtured by Phra Chen Duriyang, who had studied the stringed instruments and piano with his German father. Phra Chen established Thailand's first orchestra in the Royal Entertainment Department and taught many young Thai musicians. By the late 1920's, other small orchestras had been established as

His Majesty the King (1st from left) joining a jazz band.

part of the branches of the Thai armed services, and in 1934 Phra Chen's orchestra was transferred to and became the nucleus of the Fine Arts Department. Thai musicians have shown marked improvement in style and technique over the years and they have taught a new generation of musicians. Following a drive spearheaded by the musicians, the Bangkok Symphony Orchestra was established in July 1982 and gave its first public concert in November of that year.

Popular Western music, introduced in the 1950's, was also widely accepted by the Thai people and today there are a large number of modern groups, some producing music that combines elements of both pop and traditional Thai.

The Bangkok Symphony Orchestra in concert.

Music plays an important part in the life of the Thai royal family. His Majesty King Bhumibol Adulyadej is an internationally-recognized jazz musician with numerous original compositions to his credit, one of which was featured in a Broadway show in the 1950's.

The crowning success for His Majesty's music came in 1964 when NQ Tonkunstler Orchestra played a selection of his compositions at the Vienna Concert Hall. These were also broadcast throughout Austria where they enjoyed resounding success. Two days later, the world's renowned Institute of Music and Arts of the City of Vienna conferred its Honorary Membership upon His Majesty the King in recognition of his outstanding musical achievements. He became the 23rd Honorary Member of the Institute since its establishment in 1817, and **the first Asian composer to receive this honour.**

Up to now, the music world has recognized His Majesty the King as one of the great living composers. His works will surely keep his place among those of the great masters of music and will not only delight the present day audience but it will also do so for generations to come.

The Music Association of Thailand whose objectives are to promote Thai music and safeguard the welfare of musicians, is under the royal patronage.

Drama

In the purely classical form, Thai drama and dance are indivisible.

The *khon* masked drama is derived from Indian temple rituals and dancing and draws its story line from the Ramakian, the Thai version of the Indian epic Ramayana. During the Ayutthaya period, the *khon* was acted by accomplished male court retainers playing both

"The Battle", a spectacular war scene from the Ramakian, in a Khon masked drama.

Khon masks are works of art that require master craftsmanship.

male and female roles because until the 19th century the movements were thought too strenuous for women to perform. By the mid 1800's both men and women were appearing on stage together.

Khon performances are characterized by vigorous, highly-formalized action. Acting and dancing are inseparable, each step having a definite meaning which is emphasized by precisely defined music to suggest walking, marching, laughing, etc. Because some actors and actresses are masked and cannot speak, narrative verses are usually recited and sung by a chorus that sits with the accompanying woodwind, gong, and drum ensemble. The leading male and female performers do not wear masks and on some occasions they may speak.

The ornate papier mache masks, decorated with gold, lacquer, and paste jewels, are works of art and perfectly portray the protagonists' personalities. Costumes are made of rich brocades adorned with sparkling costume jewellery and closely resemble the apparel of royalty and celestial beings in classical Thai mural paintings. Major characters are readily identifiable by the predominant colours of their costumes. *Phra Ram*, the hero, wears deep green, while his brother, *Phra Lak*, wears gold and the monkey-god *Hanuman* wears white.

Khon productions were originally so long—more than 20 hours—that performances were staged on two consecutive days. Indeed, a performance of the entire Ramakian (with 311 characters) would take more than one month (720 hours plus) of continuous performance. King Rama II's shorter version of the epic is used for dramatic purposes and contemporary adaptations of certain episodes are as short as three hours.

Lakhon dance drama is less formal and actors, with the exceptions of monkeys, ogres, and other non-human, non-celestial beings, do not wear masks. *Lakhon* plots are drawn mainly from the Ramakian, the Jatakas, and folk stories, *Khon* and *Lakhon* costumes are identical, but *Lakhon* dance movements are more graceful, sensual, and fluid, the upper torso and hands being particularly expressive with conventionalized movements portraying specific emotions.

Lakhon is subdivided into numerous variations, the major three being *Lakhon Chatri*, *Lakhon Nok*, and *Lakhon Nai*. Simplest of all in form and presentation, *Lakhon Chatri* is often seen at popular shrines, such as Bangkok's *Lak Muang* (City Pillar) where dancers are hired by supplicants whose wishes have been granted to perform for the shrine deity.

An expressive movement of the classical Thai dance.

Lakhon Nai drama was originally presented only by court ladies in the palace. It was graceful, romantic, and highly stylized. *Lakhon Nok* plays, on the other hand, were performed outside the palace and acted only by men. Filled with lively music, off-colour humour, and rapid, animated movements, *Lakhon Nok* was the ancestor of the enormously popular *Li-ke* folk theater which is still a feature of many provincial festivals.

Li-ke, a burlesque of *Lakhon* containing elements of pantomime, comic folk opera, and social satire, is generally performed against a simply painted backdrop during temple fairs. Its court-derived stories are embellished with local references and anecdotes, and spontaneous dialogue is freighted with outrageous puns and double entendres.

Two neglected dramatic forms are *Nang Yai* shadow play and *hun* marionettes, both regular forms of entertainment in Ayutthaya. In *Nang Yai*, intricately fashioned cowhide figures, some two metres tall, are held against a brilliant backlit white screen. Bearers of the figures dance their parts, the movements of which were later to provide the pattern for *Khon* and *Lakhon*.

The *Nang Talung*, a more popular shadow play found mainly in the south of Thailand, closely resembles the Indonesian *Wayang*. Beautifully fashioned *Nang Talung* figures are smaller than their *Nang Yai* counterparts and are often constructed to have one moveable part—an arm, a leg, or a chin. Concealed from audiences, the manipulators are skilled singers and comedians whose repartee keeps the action bubbling.

Hun marionettes, seldom seen today, are superbly crafted figures which differ from European marionettes in that they are manipulated from concealed threads pulled from below rather than above. A more popular version is *Hun Krabok* (literally "cylindrical model") which are similar to Punch and Judy style hand puppets.

Architecture

Admitting Indian, Khmer, and other external influences, Thai Buddhist architects developed their own distinctive styles of soaring multitiered rooftops and towering spires straining toward the sky. Harmoniously combining two apparently paradoxical elements, flamboyancy and serenity, the style perfectly mirrors the Thai soul. Although most early Thai buildings were made of wood and have long since disappeared, taking with them the architectural principals according to

which they were built, a developmental history of Thai architecture can still be traced through surviving stone temples.

Early Sukhothai monuments were strongly Khmer-influenced. In the Khmer manner, sandstone was used to form door parts, lintels, and rectangular windows. Around the 12th century, brick replaced sandstone as the favoured building material. Bricks were carefully laid without mortar, bound with vegetable glue, and then sheathed in carved stone. Later, architects used stucco, a sand, lime, and glue mixture strengthened by a terra cotta armature, to cover the brick walls. In the heavily forested north, wood was employed in temple construction and craftsmen attained great skill in carving decorative elements.

Chinese influence can also be seen in ornamental decoration, particularly the use of porcelain fragments in various colours and adornments that afford the finest Thai architecture its harmonious, polychromatic effect. This art reached its highest expression during the first half of the 19th century.

Spires of Thai Buddhist architecture soaring side by side within the compound of Wat Phra Kaeo.

Materials such as glass mosaic pieces highlighted gables and pillars, as well as wooden and stucco figures, and other decorative techniques utilized lacquer, gilt, mother-of-pearl inlay, gold leaf, and porcelain fragments to obtain the desired effect of gleaming elegance.

The most spectacular Buddhist architecture is to be seen at Bangkok's *Wat Phra Kaeo* (Temple of the Emerald Buddha) which contains more exquisite carving and decoration per square centimetre than any comparable site in the world. Within the temple compound, almost every surface is covered with inspired decoration. Incorporating so many colours and materials, the complex is a near psychedelic yet unified mixture of multitiered ochre, blue, orange, and green tiled roofs, towering fanged dragons staring at a golden Ayutthaya-style chedi, marble prangs, priceless mother-of-pearl inlaid doors, bronze lions, gilt Garudas, Chinese statuary, and tiny tinkling bronze wind bells suspended from scarlet and gold lacquered eaves and is, above all, the Thai ideal of a skillfully-arranged complex imparting reverence and serenity.

Bangkok's *Wat Benchamabophit* (the Marble Temple) is renowned as the most impressive example of modern Thai Buddhist architecture. Built in 1899 by King Chulalongkorn, the temple is constructed of white Italian marble and surmounted by multitiered orange tiled roofs.

In addition to religious structures, a distinctive Thai style of domestic architecture also evolved, employing prefabricated panels hung on a framework of stout pillars and using wooden pegs instead of nails for joining. Various forms developed in different regions of the country, perhaps the best known being the central

The Marble Temple, Bangkok.

Skyscrapers are rapidly becoming a familiar sight in major cities of Thailand, especially Bangkok.

plains style with its steep roofs, decoratively carved bargeboards, and slightly inward-leaning walls that give it a memorable sense of elegant grace.

Traditional Thai architecture declined around 1900 when buildings were increasingly in European styles. Old-style craftsmen and builders who worked on temples, palaces, and traditional homes found that prevailing tastes required them to master Western techniques and construction of classic buildings almost ceased, especially in the capital. From the late 1940's European influence grew rapidly and local architects enthusiastically embraced the concepts of such Western pioneers as Frank Lloyd Wright and Mies Van der Rohe.

Like other forms of art in the early 1990's, Thai architecture has been revolutionized by new industrial materials and by the example of the pure functionalism of machines. Modern Thai architects seem to be guided by Western principles of structure, plan, and functionalism, so that their works resemble those to be seen in any large city of the world, reflecting not only individual taste but also such matters as zoning regulations, ecology, and energy consumption.

Literature

Early Thai literature was primarily concerned with religion and until the mid-19th century was in verse form. Thai verse was written exclusively by the aristocracy or royalty, the only educated classes able to do so. The tradition of authorship by kings can be seen in all periods of the country's history, from Sukhothai up to Bangkok. Two Chakri monarchs, King Rama II (1809-1824) and King Rama VI (1910-1925), were distinguished poets and stalwart patrons of Thai arts.

One of the most important Thai literary works is the *Ramakian*, a uniquely Thai version of the Indian epic, the Ramayana. Early Thai versions of the *Ramakian* were lost in the destruction of Ayutthaya. The longest of the three present versions was written in 1798 by the first Chakri King, Rama I, and a group of intimates, who incorporated Thai and Buddhist elements into it to preserve oral knowledge of Ayutthaya state rites and traditions. Indeed, King Rama I's *Ramakian* is the major historical source of medieval Thai courtly traditions.

King Rama II, a great poet of Rattanakosin period.

King Rama II composed two episodes of the *Ramakian* for classical drama purposes and wrote several other epic poems, including the *Inao*, a romance with a Javanese background. The *Inao* is a treasure trove of historical information on early 19th century Thai customs, habits, and manners and figures prominently in the repertoire of classical drama.

Another major Thai literary figure was Sunthon Phu (1786-1855), a poetic genius and well-beloved commoner. Sunthon Phu's enduring achievement (apart from his legendary personal adventures) was to write superbly well in common language about common feelings and the common folk. Easily understood by all classes, his work became widely accepted. His major works were *Phra Aphai Mani*, a romantic adventure, and nine *Nirats* mostly written during a pilgrimage, associating romantic memories with the places he visited in central and eastern Thailand.

Both King Rama V and Rama VI were also distinguished writers whose creativity contained the rich intellectual heritage in several prose and verse forms. Among outstanding literary works of King Rama V were

Ngo Pa and the well-known collection of *Klai Ban* or Far Away from Home, on his journey to Europe in 1906-7. Those well-known works of King Rama VI were *Matthana Phatha, Phra non Kham Luang*, and several patriotic articles entitled, *Muang Thai Chong Tun Thoet* or Wake up–all Thais, etc.

An outstanding writer and scholar was Phya Anuman Rajadhon, who was born in 1888 and died in 1969. Interested in all aspects of Thai culture, from language to folklore, Phya Anuman wrote dozens of books on such subjects and served as an inspiration to numerous younger Thais who are now prominent in academic fields.

Moving into the modern age about 1900 onward, most of the Thai readers are well acquainted with the work of Dokmaisod whose real name is M.L. Boobpha Nimmanhaemindha. She was a novelist in the pioneering age. Her best known works were for example, *Phu Di, Nung Nai Roi, Nit, Chaichana Khong Luang Naruban*, etc. Many of her works have been assigned as books for external reading for students at the secondary and tertiary levels of education today.

Malai Choopinij, in his pen name Mae Anong and Noi Intanon, was an expert in his own right in both full length and short stories. *Thung Maharat*, a novel based on rural life, and *Long Phrai*, which is about the adventure in the forest, are some of his best-known literary works.

Mai Muang Doem the pen name of Kan Phungbun Na Ayudhya, whose novel *Khun Suk*, won much admiration during his time and was on several occasions adapted for television drama.

Yakhop, a pen name of Chot Praephan, whose most popular work is *Phu Chana Sip Thit*, a legend of Burmese royal court, which has been adapted by many script writers for television drama as well as stage drama enjoyed by nationwide audiences.

Sri Burapha, a popular novelist, whose real name was Kularb Sai Pradit. His most famous work is a love

Former Prime Minister
M.R. Kukrit Pramoj.

story entitled *Khang Lang Phap*, or literally Behind the Portrait.

Another leading literary figure is former Prime Minister M.R. Kukrit Pramoj, whose works have been prolific. They appeared in various forms including short stories, articles, columns and critiques. He is generally regarded as the best Thai short story author. His collection of short stories, the so-called *Lai Chiwit*, is considered an exemplary work embodying the finest Thai prose, an appreciation of which is essential for the appraisal of Thai contemporary literature. His most outstanding novel, *Si Phandin*, or Four Reigns, revolves around the court life from the reign of King Rama V to Rama VIII offering a vivid portrait of Thai society in those long years of the four interesting reigns.

Krisna Asokesin, or Sukanya Cholasuk, is another very successful and famous novelist. She has written a collection of over one hundred novels on love and complexities of family life. She has won both domestic and international awards. Her well-known novels, *Rua Manut* and *Tawan Tok Din*, won the SEATO Literary Awards. She was also awarded the National Artist status.

National Artist
Seni Saowaphong.

Seni Saowaphong or Sakdichai Bamrungphong is the doyen of modern writers. His novels and short stories deal with class conflicts, exploitation, and urban society. *Pisat*, Evil Spirits, his most popular novel, is about the conflict between new and old generations. He also won the National Artist status.

The late Suwanee Sukhontha, a former painter, was a highly successful woman writer. Her best novel, *Khao Chu Kan*, His Name is Kan, won a SEATO Literary Award. It is about a young doctor who sacrifices a brilliant career in one of the nation's leading hospitals to work in a rural area where peasants have no access to modern medicines.

Suwat Woradilok, a novelist under the pen name Rapeeporn, whose work under the title of *Phandin Mai* is well-known among novel readers. Kamsing Srinok, who is also known under the pen name of Lao Kam Hom, is a low-profiled but powerful writer, whose short stories recreate northeastern village life. His most acclaimed short story, *Fa Bo Kan* is about the hardship the Northeasterners must face during a cruel drought. Both Suwat Woradilok and Kamsing Srinok won the National Artist status.

Kampoon Boonthavi, who wrote *Luk Isan*; Chart Korbjitti, whose works are *Kham Phiphaksa*, The Judgement, and *Wela*; Vanich Charungkichanand, with his collection of short stories entitled *Soi Dieo Kan*, are all awardees of the Southeast Asian Writers Award (SEAWRITE).

National Artists Suwat Woradilok.

Other well-known contemporary female novelists whose names are worth mentioning here are : the late Supa Devakul, who was not only a popular known novelist but also a stage and television playwright; Wimol Siripaibul, with her well-known pen names Thomayanti and Rose-la-rain, Penkae Wong Sa-Nga or her real name Penkae Vajanasuntorn, Nopakun Jittayasotorn, under her pen name Man Supiti, and Winita Dithiyon, under her pen name Wor Winichaikul.

Kamsing Srinok.

Angkarn Kalayanapong is a leading Thai contemporary poet whose language is most eloquent and impressive. One of his distinguished works, *Lamnam Phu Kradung* draws great admiration as its literary work paints the beauty and vitality of nature and campaigns against environmental degradations. He has won both the SEAWRITE Award and the National Artist status.

Another popular Thai contemporary poet, Naowarat Phongpaiboon, writes in a traditional style although his topics are current. His odes to such emotions as love, despair, and hope are laced with beautiful

lyrics. He has won both the SEAWRITE Award and the National Artist status. His most famous work, entitled *Khian Phaendin*, is the fruit of his journey to all corners of Thailand from where he recorded the beauty and admiration of local landscapes in words and wins utmost popularity among the Thais.

The transformation of the world by science and technology is one of the things that separates present day literary works from those of the past. Writers depend not only upon a general public perception of reality, as in the past, but also upon their own instincts and insights which they express as a kind to personal vision, sometimes to make their readers see and think in a new way.

It was inevitable that Thai artists in the age of technology would find new subjects and forms of expression in addition to more foreign influences, the arts have begun to move in different directions which modern Thais can relate to. Yet the beauty of the old has not lost its ability to inspire, and despite the inroads made by modern culture, it continues to hold its own and even to show signs of revival in many areas.

Publishing

Christian missionaries introduced Thailand's first printing press in 1835. Nineteenth-century interest in publishing was confined mostly to the royal court and foreign groups of missionaries and businessmen. No fewer than seven English-language newspapers began and ceased publication between 1844 and 1877.

One royal publication, the *Royal Gazette*, founded in 1858 by King Mongkut (Rama IV), exists to the present day as the official medium for acts, decrees, ministerial proclamations, and public announcements of newly-promulgated laws.

Daily newspapers came into their own during King Vajiravudh (Rama VI)'s reign when 20 dailies, including one Chinese and two English-language publications, were being printed. The King, himself a skilled writer, used several pen names to write newspaper articles commenting on issues of the day.

Thai publishing at present is a lively business. A glance at any ordinary news-stand reveals hundreds of different local newspapers, magazines, and paperback books on every conceivable subject. Many foreign best-sellers are translated into Thai soon after their appearance abroad.

Thai newspapers.

Publications often change constantly through time. Magazines and newspapers will adhere to certain current topics of popular interest to the public. By that nature, they may continue or cease operation as they deem fit. Among the well established Thai language newspapers, *Thai Rath* has the largest circulation and, like most other newspapers elsewhere, is inclined towards sensational news. Its chief competitors, *Daily News* and *Matichon* have also won a fair degree of popularity among the Thai readers who often demonstrate the distinctive taste for both entertainment and information.

Sin Sian Yit Pao is the leading Chinese-language newspaper, while the *Nation Review* and the *Bangkok Post* are the major English-language papers.

Satrisarn editor Khun Nillawan Pinthong, receiving "the best magazine" award from Princess Maha Chakri Sirindhorn.

Magazines in both English and Thai will cater to a wide spectrum of tastes. Some are targetting principally at woman readers through such attractions as the serialized romantic stories and house-keeping tips, while the others will focus on interior design, fashion, sports, and business. Standards of production have dramatically improved during recent years and high quality colour printing has been quite common. In this diverse range of the Thai magazine market, *Satrisarn* is considered the oldest, and *Sakulthai Weekly* the most popular among the well educated readers. Both have been awarded *"the best magazine"* for youth readers by the National Youth Office of Thailand. In 1994 *Sakulthai* received the Phra Kieo Thongkham Award for outstanding use of the Thai language from Chulalongkorn University.

Radio and Television

Thailand has 480 radio stations. Many fall under the aegis of the governmental Public Relations Department which is responsible for Radio Thailand, the official government broadcasting station, which transmits the local and international news mandatorily broadcast by all Thai stations. Radio Thailand is also the official channel for government information.

Along with the Thai Television Company, Ltd., the Post and Telegraph Department, the Royal Thai Army, Navy, and Air Force, the Police Department, Kasetsart and Chulalongkorn Universities, and the Ministry of Education all operate radio stations. Except for the Education Ministry and Radio Thailand broadcasts, all other stations are commercial and rely heavily on advertising revenue to cover operating costs. Programming tends to resemble the commercial format popular in other countries, with music and talk shows the dominant fare.

In 1955 Thailand was the first country in Southeast Asia to begin the regular television services. Today their are 5 channels including Channel 9 and 11 which are run by the government, Channel 5 and 7 run by the Army leaving Channel 3 as the only Channel run by private enterprise. All stations except channel 11 are commercial.

The programmes therefore must meet with the acceptance and appeal of the audience at large, hence the selection and design of which must be properly done. Variety and talk shows are among the most popular and largely imported from the U.S. television series, the Chinese dramas and the Japanese cartoons. Equally popular are the locally produced serialized drama and the quiz and game shows. Among the younger audiences the U.S. and Japanese cartoons have won a sizable market. Similarly, the local programmes specially designed and created for youth and children are also doing well. Educational programmes which are introduced as a part of the courses offered by the open-university are broadcasted to enthusiastic audiences who pursue their studies for the academic degrees through this media. Sports programmes, particularly local and overseas soccer, boxing matches, golfing and snooker from local sources and live telecast from overseas are among some of the items that seem to attract great appeal from the Thai public.

Besides the regular channels, Thailand has at last 10 privately owned cable television programmes which broadcast in both Thai and English.

Films

The great majority of Thai films are unashamedly made for entertainment purposes and consequently enjoy large audiences. Tightly budgeted, they commonly feature actors and actresses with proven box-office appeal who may be obliged to portray as many as 20 different roles in 20 different films being shot concurrently. The films they star in usually include everything; pathos, romance, hatred, love, loss, gain, joy, despair, violence, gentility, comedy and tragedy are interwoven around a major plot and several sub-plots.

Among the most popular film makers both from the past and the current ones are H.R.H. Prince Panupan Yukgla, Dokdin Kanyamal, Piak Poster, M.C. Chatri Chaloem Yukol and Cherd Songsri, etc.

There have been attempts by movie directors to produce more films with a social message, but these have not been very successful money-making ventures. One such director is veteran film maker Wichit Khunawut; among his works are *Khon Phu Khao* (Mountain People), which dealt with the northern hilltribes, and *Luk Isan* (Son of the Northeast) about the hard life in Thailand's northeast.

Thai movie-makers are also often involved in foreign films shot in Thailand. There have been an increasing number of these in recent years, among the best known being *The Man With The Golden Gun*, *The Killing Fields*, *The Deer Hunter*, and *Air America*.

Historic Thai films are treasured by the National Film Archives under the Department of Fine Arts whose collection includes the footage of King Chulalongkorn (Rama V) on one of his visits to England towards the end of the 19th century as well as the featured film specially filmed by His Majesty King Prajadhipok (Rama VII) himself and many other rare items.

THE CHARACTER AND STRUCTURE OF THE ECONOMY

Traditionally an agrarian nation, today Thailand boasts a complex, multi-faceted economy embracing industries employing the latest and most sophisticated technology.

Several important factors have contributed to the country's enviable growth. Its principal comparative advantage has been the abundance and diversity of its natural resources. Blessed with large expanses of fertile land and ideal growing conditions, Thailand not only enjoys agricultural self-sufficiency but is also the only net food exporter in Asia and one of the largest food exporters in the world.

Growth and diversification into new industrial areas have to a large extent been initiated by the dynamic private sector. Innovative private enterprise broadened the nation's agrarian base by exploiting the value-added potential of basic staple crops, and at the same time expanded into new product areas in response to world demand. With the government providing infrastructural support and exerting relatively limited control over private industry, a free enterprise system has emerged which has allowed development to take place at a rapid rate consistent with the needs and resources available.

With its agrarian base as the bedrock, the economy has experienced steady growth. The introduction of improved technology and marketing

The arduous rice-field work is year-long. In April or May, farmers start planting seedlings in their well-ploughed fields. By late November or early December, cooperative work groups use sickles to harvest the crops. Cut rice is threshed, and the paddy is then ready to be winnowed and taken to market.

expertise has made Thailand a world leader in the sales of staple commodities. It has also transformed the country into a fast-rising manufacturer of sophisticated products built to international standards which find ready acceptance in world markets.

Thailand's primary money earners in the late 1970s were the crops grown on its rich land. Today agricultural products are produced in such quantities that in many commodities the country ranks as the world's number one supplier. Thus besides being the world's foremost exporter of tapioca and rice, it is a leader in the production of frozen shrimp, canned pineapple, natural rubber and sugar. Moreover, Thailand's industrial sector produces a wide number of goods ranging from textiles including the famous Thai silk and ready-made garments to integrated circuits, plastics, jewellery, footwear, knocked-down furniture and fibre-glass yachts. In recent years in fact, manufacturing has surpassed agricultural products in Thailand's GNP, while tourism has replaced agricultural products as Thailand's largest source of foreign exchange. The country's rich reserves of minerals are eagerly sought by the world's industries. In recent years, local factories have been established to manufacture industrial goods from the ores and thereby enhance their value.

Bounty of the Land and Sea

Rice forms the core of the Thai economic system. The staple food of the nation, it was the country's largest single foreign exchange earner for well over a century. Thailand is the world's leading exporter of rice, earning 32,958 million baht in 1993. In recent years though, agriculturalists have found new uses for paddy land. At the same time, modern technology has opened up new or formerly arid land to crop cultivation. The Northeast and Southeast, previously considered two of the least fertile areas, are now producing tapioca in large quantities and in 1993, it ranked seventh after rice, earning 21,600 million baht.

The world sugar shortage of the mid-1970s triggered a boom in Thai cane sugar production. In 1993 sugar had an export earning of 14,820 million baht. In addition to raw cane and granulated white sugar, molasses, a by-product of sugar manufacturing, has been gaining importance. World markets have been requiring molasses in increasing quantities as an ingredient in animal feed. Additional amounts are refined locally to produce ethyl alcohol. However, due to diversification in the economy since 1987, sugar was not ranked in the top ten export earners.

Cassava cultivation on a major scale was not resumed until 1958, when it was taken up by farmers in the Northeast. Foreign demand for tapioca then increased so dramatically that Thailand is now the world's leading exporter. Local factories process it into flour, which is used industrially, and into the chips and pellets sold as animal feed.

Thailand is the world's largest producer of natural rubber. Production in 1993 was 1,484,000 tons earning 29,183 million baht. This substantially higher output was due largely to higher world demand and the effects of the AIDS epidemic on the demand for rubber products. Rubber plantations occupied mainly in the South.

Also in demand abroad are Thailand's numerous garden variety beans. These include mung beans, soya beans and black matpe beans–the source of the famed Far Eastern beansprouts associated throughout the world with oriental cooking. The soya bean is processed into vegetable oil by domestic factories. Other crops grown for their oils include coconuts, peanuts, castor seeds and mint.

Canned rambutan and longan have found ready markets overseas but by far the most important of the country's fruit exports is canned pineapple, of which Thailand is the world's leading exporter. In 1993 canned and processed food earned 42,605 million baht.

Flowers are also an important export item. Thailand is one of the world's biggest suppliers of orchids. There are about 2,000 commercial growers, mostly in the Bangkok area. Major markets are Japan and European countries.

In the past, beef production was a profitable farming sideline but in recent years growing demand brought about by the increase in population and urbanization and by a rising standard of living has led to specialization in livestock breeding and commercial stockfarming using scientific methods. High-quality cattle, pigs and poultry have been imported to improve local breeds through cross-breeding. It has also been shown that cattle thrive on coconut plantations if the space between the trees is planted with suitable grass.

Thailand has export markets for beef in Singapore and Hong Kong and is trying to gain entrance into the potentially large Japanese market. Increased scientific beef cattle production will also be a boon to the fast-growing leather and tanning industry.

Thailand's wide variety of hard and soft-wood forests has created a burgeoning wood industry. Tropical evergreens, hill evergreens, mangroves, deciduous dipterocarps and mixed deciduous are processed to produce firewood, stick lac, gum benzoin, rattan used in the manufacture of cane furniture, bamboo used both for furniture and paper, dyes, tanning bark and a huge variety of medicinal herbs, leaves and roots.

Thailand's waters are every bit as bountiful as its fields and forests. Thailand is the world's foremost exporter of frozen shrimp; squid and cuttlefish are also popular export items. According to the Fisheries Department, a fleet of more than 16,000 powered vessels plying the waters off the country's roughly 3,000 km. coastline approximately 2.6 million tons of marine products a year.

Freshwater fish abound. Besides the many varieties which breed naturally in rivers, lakes and streams, there are those raised by rice farmers in their flooded paddy fields and harvested together with the rice. In addition, the Fisheries Department is vigorously promoting freshwater aquaculture by farmers with large ponds. Freshwater prawns are also plentiful.

Mineral reserves in Thailand are rich and varied, with 1993 exports earning of 3,980 million baht. Tin, for centuries the biggest moneymaker among Thai minerals, remains so today, with the country ranking fourth behind Brazil, Indonesia, and Malaysia.

Gemstones, among them the legendary Siamese rubies and sapphires, have also long been mined in Thailand. Thailand's coloured gems market is one of the world's largest. Export of gems and jewellery in 1993 ranked third among exports, earning 40,921 million baht. In addition, many different minerals, ores and metals are being exported. The major minerals, exported, are fluorite, zinc, barite, gypsum, feldspar, antimony, lead ore and dolomite.

Minerals mined but not exported include limestone, marl, lignite, potash, kaolinite, ball clay, quartz and tantalum, all of which are used by local manufacturers.

In recent years, the limelight has shifted to other modern buried treasures: natural gas and oil in the Gulf of Thailand. The country's dependence on imported oil rose from 50 percent of the total energy consumption in 1962 to 75 percent in 1981. By producing and utilizing indigenous sources of energy for substitution, such as natural gas, lignite, hydro-power and non-conventional energy sources, Thailand has reduced her dependence on imported oil. Thus, dependence on foreign energy sources was down to 62 percent in 1993.

Natural gas and oil have been discovered in the North, Northeast, and in the Gulf of Thailand. The new Eastern Seaboard industrial centre comprises a gas separation plant, a petrochemical complex and other manufacturing facilities. Located in three eastern provinces—Chon Buri, Rayong and Chachoengsao—it covers 8.3 million hectares of land. After the successful laying of a 425 km. natural gas submarine transmission pipeline, from the Erawan gas field in the Gulf of Thailand to the onshore terminal and then to the Bang Pakong and south Bangkok power plants, the gas came on stream in 1981.

As a government-owned enterprise, the Petroleum Authority of Thailand (PTT) is engaged in the business of oil supply, oil refinery, gas pipeline operation, gas-processing plant operation and petroleum industry. With the cooperation of other government agencies, PTT has been responsible for the development and exploitation of fossil fuel resources in the country.

Sector Performance

Over the past two decades, the national income has increased by approximately eight percent per year. Moreover, growth has been broadly based, with all economic sectors participating in the development process.

The fabric of the Thai economy remained virtually unchanged up to the late 1950s. In the early 1960s, the industrial and service sectors began supplementing agriculture as significant income and employment generators. Today, Thailand is still predominantly an agrarian country, with about 57 percent of its working population engaged in agricultural production and earning about 12 percent of the national income. Over the years, however, the industrial and service sectors have been increasing their shares of the total GDP.

Significant structural changes in the Thai economy have taken place since the early 1960s. Agriculture's share of the national income declined steadily from about 40 percent in 1960 to 12 percent in 1993. At the same time, the manufacturing sector expanded very rapidly, increasing its portion of the national income from 13 percent in 1960 to 37 percent in 1993. Such a structural change does not, however, imply that agricultural output failed to rise during the period. On the contrary, it increased by about five percent per year. Moreover, a high degree of diversification took place, enabling Thailand to boost its export items from only three major commodities namely rice, teak and rubber in the early 1950s to more than 10 main agricultural products in 1993.

The industrialization process initiated during the 1960s was geared towards import-substitution. It was succeeded in the 1970s by a drive to produce export-oriented items. By the mid-1970s Thailand was exporting manufactured goods ranging from cement to watch parts, and including canned fruit, garments, chemical products, transport equipment and television sets. In 1993 manufactured exports accounted for about 81 percent of total export earnings.

International trade is vital to the Thai economy. Thailand's entry into foreign markets in the mid-19th century enabled its economy to expand rapidly. Today, export and import transactions together account for about half of the national income. Although there were annual deficits in the balance of trade, the balance of payments recorded continuous surpluses throughout the 1960s and early 1970s. Sharp increases in oil prices since 1970, however, affected the balance of payments position severely. Large tourist earnings and foreign capital inflow put the balance of payments back into a surplus position.

The public sector supports the growth process by providing developmental facilities through the construction of basic infrastructure and by creating a conducive environment for the private sector to operate effectively.

Despite the steady increase in population, real per capital income has doubled over the past two decades. At current prices, it increased from 4,000 baht per head in 1970 to 53,215 baht per head in 1993. The proportion of the country's population living at the subsistence level has declined from around half in the early 1960s to less than a quarter in recent years.

In short, the performance of the Thai economy over the past two decades has ranked high among developing countries. Some basic economic problems such as income disparity, the need to conserve natural resources, the uncertainty of export markets, and the need for improving administrative efficiency, remain to be solved but judging by past performance as well as from the present economic outlook, it is clear that Thailand has the potential to expand its economy and thereby improve the welfare of its citizens.

The Agriculture and Mining Sectors

The agriculture sector's contribution to the Gross Domestic Product declined from 39.4 percent in 1961 to 12.2 percent in 1993 due primarily to the rapid expansion of other sectors of the economy. However, agriculture will continue to be a dominant sector of the Thai economy for years to come.

In 1993, farm population comprised approximately 57 percent of the total labour force. If the people indirectly engaged in agri-business industries were also included in the estimate, labour force absorption by agriculture totaled 57.2 percent.

Agriculture exports were the major source of foreign exchange earning during the 1960s and 1970s. However, as Thailand's progress towards industrialization increased, manufactured exports gained importance. In 1993, exports of agricultural products amounted to only about 18.1 percent of total exports compared with the share of 40 percent in 1982.

Major Crops

Field crops, which accounted for 50 percent of agricultural output in 1993, increased at an annual average rate of 8 percent between 1961 and 1993. Agricultural production was still dominated by seven major crops: rice, tapioca, rubber, maize, sugar-cane, mung beans and tobacco leaves, most of which were grown primarily for export.

Since 1970 the increase in crop production have come from both the expansion of cultivated areas and improvements in yields. In response to high agricultural prices, the total area planted has continued to increase. Furthermore, farmers are switching from crops with relatively low returns per hectare to those with higher earnings. Performance, however, varies considerably: sugar-cane, rubber and tapioca yields have been increasing significantly, rice and maize yields growing slowly, and kenaf yield declining. The trend towards crop diversification continues in response to price incentives as the proportion of cropped area devoted to rice declines.

Although the national average rice yield has remained low, a recent trend clearly indicates certain structural changes in production. At present, rice cultivation is undertaken in intensive irrigated areas, wet-season irrigated areas, and rainfed areas. Intensive irrigated areas, which enable farmers to produce at least two crops a year, increased phenomenally from 407,488 hectares in 1977/78 to 4,240,000 hectares in 1992/93.

Furthermore, there is ample evidence that yields in both intensive and wet-season irrigated areas have risen sharply during the past five years. About four million hectares of paddy land now benefit from wet-season flood control to keep fields free of excess water which would damage crops. Nevertheless, the remaining six million hectares represent rice production in rainfed areas where limited access to modern technology and inputs results in low yields.

Livestock

Livestock production is second in importance in the agricultural sector. Between 1988 and 1993, its share of the total GDP of agriculture declined from 1.7 percent to 1.3 percent.

The Government has been trying to improve beef and dairy production through cross-breeding and artificial insemination using high-grade stock imported from United States, Switzerland, Germany, Denmark, and Australia. Likewise, indigenous breeds of swine have been improved through cross-breeding with pure-breds imported from abroad. The Livestock Department has set up swine breeding centres throughout the country and has conducted a nationwide artificial insemination programme.

Of all livestock raised for the market, poultry has improved the most. Pure-bred chickens are popular among poultry raisers and research in breeding and management with the aim of improving egg production and feed conversion rate has been conducted with great success. As a result, frozen chickens have become one of the country's important exports.

Forestry

A 1993 satellite photo survey showed that forest areas in Thailand had diminished to only 13.35 million hectares or about 26 percent of the country's total land area. Thus, during 1973-1993 deforestation had claimed about 8.8 million hectares. Most of the devasted forest areas are located in the Northeast, the North, the upper part of the Central Plains and the West; where there was extensive slash-and-burn agricultural practive by villagers and illegal log poaching.

In view of the depletion of forest resources and the government's restrictions on cutting, the growth rate of forestry output declined from an annual average of 2.61 percent during the Second Five-Year Plan (1967-1971) to 0.25 percent during the Fifth Five-Year Plan (1982-1986). The Royal Forest Department undertook various reforestation projects in various areas of 607,492 hectares in 1980, 648,512 hectares in 1987 and about 1,000,000 hectares in 1993.

Fisheries

Thailand's fishing industry is dependent on marine catches. Fish from natural fresh waters, commercial fish farms, and irrigated paddy fields account for less than 10 percent of the total catch. The remainder comes from the sea.

During the Fifth Five-Year Plan (1982-1986) fishery output increased by an annual average of 2.45 percent as compared with the 4.49 percent per year during the Fourth Plan (1977-1981), 3.4 percent per year during the Third Plan (1972-1976), and 18.6 percent per year during the Second Plan (1967-1971). Depletion of marine resources during the Sixth Five-Year Plan (1987-1991) reduced fishery output so much that the government is effectively enforcing regulated fishing to ensure sustainable yields for both present and future generations. An alternative which the government has undertaken to encourage the production of fish helps to expand freshwater fish farms to offset declining marine catches. Towards this end, about 45 freshwater fishery stations have been set up.

To overcome the effect of 200-mile economic zone, the government has promoted private joint fishing ventures with foreign countries aimed at alleviating the problem of limited fishing sources, in addition to private joint ventures in the waters of Indonesia, Malaysia, Bangladesh, Australia, India, Vietnam, Cambodia and Myanmar. Further expansion of such joint ventures holds bright prospects.

Mining

The mining industry in Thailand is dominated by tin. However, with later developments, the output of other minerals such as fluorite, gypsum and lignite has become more prominent. In addition, significant increases in the output of a number of other minerals such as iron, antimony, manganese and lead have been achieved. During the Third Five-Year Plan (1972-1976), new mineral deposits were found and output expanded to include tungsten (wolfram and scheelite), barite and zinc. The value of zinc production rose from 377.4 million baht in 1984 to 1,974 million baht in 1993. Mineral output in Thailand to a significant extent depends on foreign demand as domestic consumption remains low.

During the past decade, the mining sector expanded slowly. Its share in the total Gross Domestic Product remained fairly stable at about 2.5 percent.

The Manufacturing Sector

Thailand's industries have traditionally been closely linked with agriculture. From the post-war years up to the late 1950s, the major processing facilities were rice mills, sawmills, sugar mills, ice factories, textile and gunnybag factories, tobacco leaf curing plants and cottage or household industries, such as fabric weaving and basketry, to supply local needs. All these industries grew up as a result of free market forces and with limited government assistance.

Modern industrialization started in the early 1960s. Although the first Industrial Promotion Act was promulgated in 1954, it was only implemented in 1960 with the establishment of the Board of Investment. The Act was revised in 1962 to promote investment in specific activities, mainly through tariff protection, tax holidays and reduction of taxes on imported raw materials and machinery. A new law was introduced in 1972 in accordance with the government's shift in policy from an import-substitution to an export-oriented economy.

Growing at an average rate of approximately 10 percent per year since 1960, in 1993 manufacturing accounted for more than 24 percent of the national income; employed 10 percent of the entire labour force; and accounted for 64 percent of exports, making it the nation's largest sector.

In 1960, industrial activity was concentrated on food processing, which accounted for over one-third of total manufactured products. Other significant products were beverages, tobacco, garments and chemical compounds. From 1960 to 1969, the fastest growing was the petroleum products industry, averaging 103.1 percent per year. However, between 1980-1989 the average growth rate declined to only 5 percent per year as a result of the diversification of the industrial sector.

Intermediate products, among them machinery, electrical machinery, iron and steel, metal products, and non-metallic products also expanded rapidly. As a result of the relatively high growth rates of these industries structural change took place in this sector. Instead of concentrating on a few industries, the manufacturing sector's activities broadened to encompass several new groups of industries. Thus, in 1970 more intermediate products were manufactured, e.g. electrical machinery, transportation equipment, textiles and garments not only to substitute for imported products, but also for exported products.

Between 1986 and 1988, textiles and garments was the most important industry, accounting for 29.2 percent of principal export, while canned food accounted for 12.7 percent in 1988.

Between 1970 to 1993, the share of tobacco products in Gross Domestic Product declined from 8.5

percent to 0.85 percent, non-metallic mineral products decreased from 4 percent to 2 percent, and rubber and rubber products from 2.6 percent to 0.68 percent while general machinery and electrical machinery increased from 5 percent to 12 percent.

Viewing the past two decades of industrial development in Thailand, the following observations can be made:

- A high degree of diversification has taken place in the industrial sector. As a result, industrial activity in Thailand today has become more evenly distributed among many groups of industries and is more complex than in the 1960s.

- The growth of manufacturing output during the 1960s was characterized by import substitution. Since the 1960s, the share of consumer and manufactured goods among Thailand's total imports declined continuously, while that of intermediate and capital goods increased. By the 1970s, the Thai economy reached the stage where component parts and other intermediate capital goods could be produced locally. As a result, the imported content of many locally-made industrial products is decreasing.

- In the early 1960s, Thai exports consisted almost entirely of primary commodities. A decade later the manufacturing sector had developed to the extent that locally-made products were competing on world markets. Thereafter export-oriented industries began to gain prominence. Part of this shift resulted from a widespread concern in the early 1970s over limited demand in the domestic market. Also conducive circumstances in the world market at that time called for a shift in policies from producing for domestic markets to producing for export. The textile boom which started in 1972 came basically in response to export potential. The import quota on Japanese goods imposed by the U.S. enabled Thai textiles to capture a larger share of that market. The sugar boom which began in 1974 was in response to the sudden increase in the world price. Production of other items such as food products, animal feed, chemical products, pharmaceuticals, iron and steel products, and electrical components also grew in response to domestic and foreign demands.

One important aspect of industrial development in Thailand has been the private sector's rapid response to shifting market demands. This is reflected in the changing structure of manufactured imports and exports since the early 1960s.

In 1955, Thailand's imports of manufactured goods accounted for about 75 percent of the total value of imports. By 1993 the proportion had declined to about 28 percent but capital goods such as machinery and transport equipment, increased from 28.9 to about 45.8 percent. Import of raw materials also increased remarkably.

On the export side, Thailand's manufactured exports contributed about 2.4 percent of total export earnings in 1957. This had risen to 64.45 percent by 1993. For the period 1983-1993, the share of basic manufactured goods rose from 17.8 percent to 18.23 percent, and machinery increased from 5.7 percent to 30.0 percent while the export of miscellaneous manufactured goods increased from 10.1 percent to 20.8 percent.

In the current phase of Thailand's industrial development, dating from the realignment of the Japanese yen and other major currencies, the country is benefiting from a major regional restructuring of manufacturing. Production of a new range of intermediate manufactures is being fuelled by a wave of foreign investment and industrial relocation from Japan, Taiwan and other Asian NIEs, in addition to the U.S. and other countries.

On the whole, Thailand's manufacturing sector's performance has been impressive. With its ability to expand and adapt to world market conditions, the country can look forward to further diversification and growth and to resultant increased prosperity.

Taking into consideration the availability of resources and the potential of projects already underway, one may expect the following industries to grow in significance over the next decade.

Agro-based industries. At present Thailand has abundant supplies of farm produce. The advantage of establishing additional food processing industries is, therefore, apparent. Large-scale commercial livestock production offers unlimited growth potential. Other agro-based industries with good prospects include palm oil, vegetable oil, canned fruit, and paper pulp.

Non-ferrous construction materials. Thailand's cement industry is reputedly the largest in Southeast Asia; prior to 1975, the country was a net exporter. But during the uncertain period following the oil crises, the Thai government took measures to control inflation by freezing the prices of major commodities including cement. As a result, investment in this industry was delayed, and the country became a net importer of cement. By mid-1979, however, with government encouragement, a massive expansion of capacity was underway which turned Thailand back into a net exporter of cement by 1982. Other construction materials with strong potential are aluminium, glass and ceramics. The economic boom of 1987-89 led to another surge in the construction sector.

Light machinery and equipment. Effective January 1, 1987, the Thai government in July 1986, advised local passenger car assembly plants that they must use locally-produced components not less than 54 percent. This measure has helped to accelerate the production of automotive components. The prospect is further enhanced by the cooperation among ASEAN countries to expand intra-ASEAN trade which would enlarge the market for individual countries. Other activities include production of agricultural machinery, diesel engines, drilling and welding machines.

Chemical products. With current market demand, the chemical products industry is expected to expand rapidly over the next few years. Items in this group include herbicides, pesticides, acetylene black, glue gelatin and cellulose acetate.

Mineral processing industries. Developments in this sector point to future expansion of zinc, rock salt and gypsum processing facilities.

In summary, Thailand's prospects for industrial exports in the near future appear bright. This assessment is based on five major factors: capable producers who now have a strong and flexible agricultural base; much closer contact with world markets than before; low-cost skilled labour capable of producing advanced industrial products; the dynamism of East Asian trade and investment growth, and a relatively well-functioning economic system free from distortion by high levels of protection or rapid inflation.

Tourism

Tourism has been Thailand's highest income generator since 1982, having grown at a healthy 16 percent per annum since 1980. In 1994 visitor arrivals reached a record 6.16 million.

The Tourism Authority of Thailand has worked closely with other agencies to develop tourism resources in the most efficient way. For example, with the Board of Investment it periodically reviews policy regarding promotion of investment in tourist-related facilities, while it works with funding institutions to determine which tourism projects should receive investment.

The Organized Financial Market

Thailand has a substantial number of financial institutions, namely, commercial banks, finance companies, agricultural cooperatives, savings cooperatives, life insurance companies, pawnshops and credit fonciers. In addition, there are a number of specialized financial institutions, namely, the Government Savings Bank, the Bank of Agriculture and Agricultural Cooperatives (BAAC), the Industrial Finance Corporation of Thailand (IFCT), the Government Housing Bank, and the Export Import Bank of Thailand (EXIMBANK).

Within the organized financial markets, commercial banking is the most important institution in the Thai economy; it will likely maintain this position in the future.

With regard to the outstanding amounts of credit extended by the various institutions, commercial banks also pay the leading and most active role, accounting for 72 percent in 1992. Finance companies accounted for about 18 percent and the remaining 10 percent was shared by other institutions.

The Bank of Thailand

The Bank of Thailand was established in 1942 to act as the country's central bank. Its function is to issue notes, act as banker to the government and other banks, act as fiscal agent of the government in its dealing with international monetary organizations, manage public debt, maintain exchange controls, supervise commercial banks and manage public credit fonciers.

As banker to the government, the Bank of Thailand holds the main accounts of the Government as well as those of government enterprises. It extends loans to the Government through the purchase of treasury bills and government bonds, and advises it regarding the formulation and implementation of monetary policy. The Bank of Thailand has three branches in the provinces—a southern branch at Songkhla, a north-eastern branch at Khon Kaen, and a northern branch at Lampang.

Under the Commercial Banking Act of 1962 and its revision of 1979, the Bank of Thailand is entrusted with supervising the commercial banks and has the power to prescribe the cash reserve ratio, the maximum rates for loans and deposits, and the ratio of capital funds to risk assets. The Bank also acts as a lender of last resort for commercial banks by giving short-term loans against government securities and making available rediscount facilities. In 1979, a repurchase market was established whereby the Bank of Thailand bought and sold government bonds with an agreement to repurchase or resell. It is considered one of the best central banks in Asia.

As of 1993, there were 15 local commercial banks with 2,700 branches, including head offices: 757 in Bangkok and 1,943 in the provinces. In addition, there were 39 overseas branches of Thai banks, and 14 foreign banks (with 2 branches) registered abroad but operating in Thailand. The commercial banking network reaches practically every town in the country.

The commercial banks in Thailand had total assets of 2,756.9 billion baht of which more than 79 percent was in the form of bill, loans, and overdrafts. Commercial bank lendings are concentrated to a large extent on manufacturing (24.3 percent), wholesale and retail trade (17.9 percent) mostly in the form of working capital financing, and imports and exports (11 percent).

The commercial banks normally provide credit in the form of overdrafts which are on a short-term basis but may be rolled over on a year-to-year basis. Due to fluctuations in interest rates both in the international and domestic markets, commercial banks at present encourage customers to utilize term loans instead of overdrafts. Moreover, many commercial banks also provide guarantees for foreign and domestic loans, most of which are in the form of short and medium-term for local companies purchasing machinery and equipment from overseas manufacturers.

To further improve the role of commercial banks, the Commercial Banking Act of 1979 stipulated requirements for reducing the banks involvement in non-banking activities, encouraging lending to selected sectors and promoting a better relationship between the banks and their clients.

To promote Thailand as a regional financial centre, the Bank of Thailand implemented foreign exchange liberalization and in 1993 authorized 46 commercial banks to operate International Banking Facilities by providing loans in foreign currency to foreign and local borrowers. Of these, 20 banks were newly-established foreign banks in Thailand.

Other Sources of Finance

Finance companies cannot take deposits, but they can raise funds by issuing promissory notes or similar instruments; these, in turn, are lent to businesses and individuals. Finance companies came into existence in 1969 and have grown rapidly, reaching a total of 91 as of December 1993. Of these, 20 companies are licensed to offer only finance services, 71 to provide both finance and securities services, and 13 to offer only securities services and 17 credit fonciers companies. Finance companies are not subject to the same interest rate restrictions as commercial banks on their promissory notes, but are subject to the same restrictions on lending rates.

Many finance companies also perform the functions of investment banks by underwriting and marketing the securities of private sector companies. While some of the larger, finance companies have been moving towards term lending, the bulk of their assets are still concentrated on short-term consumer financing and cheque discounting services. With the passing of the Finance Business, Securities and Credit Fonciers Business Act of 1979 and its revision of 1983, all finance companies are to be authorized and regulated by the Ministry of Finance and the Bank of Thailand.

Agricultural cooperatives are organized by farmers for concerted efforts in agricultural activities including the provision of credit to members, while savings cooperatives are formed on an occupational basis with most of the members being salary earners. The agricultural cooperatives obtain most of their funds from the BAAC and lend them directly to member farmers. The savings cooperatives, on the other hand, obtain their loanable funds through a payroll withholding system. The loans given by the savings cooperatives are mostly for meeting current needs, or unexpected expenses or for financing the purchase of consumer goods.

There are at present 12 life insurance companies in Bangkok with branches throughout the country. Of the different types of life insurance, endownment is the most popular, accounting for about 80 percent of all policies sold. The Life Insurance Act (1958) requires each company to maintain security deposits of two million baht and capital funds of five million baht. It also specifies the various forms of investment into which life insurance companies may put their funds.

Credit fonciers finance the purchase of land or housing construction. They may not mobilize funds from the general public but must rely on their own resources or borrowings. There are at present 17 such companies, most of them operating in Bangkok.

The Government Savings Bank is the only wholly government-owned savings bank in the country. With 528 branches at the end of 1993, it has been very successful in mobilizing household savings and invests over 90 percent of its deposits in government bonds.

The Industrial Finance Corporation of Thailand (IFCT) was established in 1959. Functioning along the lines of a private development institution, it is the only industrial development bank in Thailand. Its sources of funds at present are borrowings from several institutions, namely, the Thai government, the Bank of Thailand, the World Bank, the Asian Development Bank, the Kreditanstalt fur Wiederaufban and the Japan Export-Import Bank. During the past few years, it has borrowed from the international market. Its capital, retained earnings, and debenture issues also provide loanable funds.

The IFCT makes term loans for financing fixed assets and permanent working capital. Loans are repayable up to 15 years but the average maturity is seven to eight years, including a grace period of two to three years. In addition to lending activities, it also provides specialized services to industries and has introduced securities underwriting services.

The Small Industries Finance Office (SIFO) was established in 1964 as an office in the Industrial Promotion Department of the Ministry of Industry. Its principal objective is to provide financial assistance to small industrial enterprises including cottage and handicraft industries. The SIFO's source of funds is limited to government budget appropriations. These funds are deposited with a government-owned bank, which supplements them at a ratio of three to one. Medium and long-term loans of up to one million baht are made at low interest rates. Approval of loan applications is given by SIFO, but collateral evaluation and lending operations are undertaken by the government bank. In 1993, the operations of SIFO were taken over by the Small Industry Finance Corporation (SIFC), with increased loan ceiling up to five million baht per borrower. The sources of funding are from the Thai Government and financial institutions.

The Government Housing Bank, established in 1953, is entirely owned by the government. Its basic function is to provide financing facilities to low-income families to obtain houses of their own. Its sources of funds are borrowings from the government, the Government Savings Bank, the commercial banks, its own capital and retained earnings, and limited savings deposits from the public.

The Export Import Bank of Thailand was established in 1994. Its basic function is to provide medium-term credit for agricultural export, long-term credit for capital goods export, export insurance service, investment guarantee for overseas investment of Thai investors and financing small and new exporters without access to commercial bank lending. The bank also finances import of machinery and equipment used for export production and import of goods beneficial to environment. Its source of funding is from the Bank of Thailand and financial institutions, local and overseas.

The Capital Market

The Securities Exchange of Thailand (SET) was established in 1974 under the supervision of the Ministry of Finance and the Bank of Thailand. In 1993, there were 347 companies listed on the SET. Its trading volume expanded rapidly in the early period of its establishment, and, recently it has become popular with offshore investors. Capital gain tax is not levied on profit on sale of listed securities on the SET. Dividends received from listed companies also receive favourable treatment.

To closely monitor and supervise the operations of SET, the Office of the Securities and Exchange Commission (SEC) was established in 1992. In the same year, to give new dimension to the capital market, seven mutual fund management companies were licensed to give the general public a chance to participate in the investment through Unit Trusts.

The Role of the Public Sector

Thailand is predominantly a free market economy with the private sector generating most of the economic activity. Public sector involvement is largely limited to providing a framework for the economy's regulation and expansion. The government's major contribution to economic growth has been to provide economic and social services, most notably to build highways, irrigation, and power facilities as well as to provide various incentives and financial assistance to promote private investments, export businesses and agricultural enterprises.

In 1993, total government expenditure was 15.8 percent of the GNP.

Infrastructural Support

Irrigation. During the period of the first two development plans, the irrigation service area increased from 1.5 million hectares in 1964 to two million hectares in 1974. By the end of 1993, the irrigated area was 4.24 million hectares which is 18 percent of the entire agricultural area. Most of the irrigation service areas are in the central and northern regions fed by tributaries of the Chao Phraya River. Areas in the Northeast irrigated by canals came to about 13 percent of the total.

About 3.4 million hectares have access to gravity irrigation, and 92,800 hectares of these are under an intensive on-farm development programme known as the Land Consolidation Project. Within gravity irrigation servicing areas, major structures such as reservoirs, diversion dams and main canals have been built.

Investment in on-farm development is generally required to enhance the effectiveness of the system.

Pumping irrigation is another important technique in the irrigation system. This technique was first implemented in 1973. In 1993 pumping stations serviced 500,000 hectares. The northeastern region benefits most from this service.

In addition, underground reserves provide a significant amount of irrigation water in certain areas. It is estimated that farmland irrigated by ground-water at present amounts to 1,600 hectares. Farm ponds are also used to supplement rainfall for many areas of the dry Northeast.

Public Utilities

The Electricity Generating Authority of Thailand (EGAT) is a state enterprise and the country's principal producer of electricity. Over the past few years, efforts to reduce the use of high-cost imported fuel oil for power generation by developing substitute domestic resources from natural gas and lignite have yielded satisfactory results.

The Metropolitan Electricity Authority (MEA) is responsible for the distribution of electricity in the Bangkok Metropolitan areas, while the Provincial Electricity Authority (PEA) handles the distribution to the rest of the kingdom.

Water supply to the capital city is the responsibility of the Metropolitan Waterworks Authority (MWA). It has successfully completed the first stage of a massive filtration and distribution scheme to double the city's potable water supply.

Key elements of the project were the construction of an enormous filtration plant capable of eventual expansion to 5.2 million cubic metres per day production and an underground network of transmission tunnels. Laser-directed "moles" were employed to dig and lay 3.86 metre-diametre pipes 20 metres below the ground in the world's first soft-earth tunneling project, a feat of considerable engineering ingenuity involving both Thai and foreign contractors.

Government Incentives and Financial Assistance

Agricultural Credit. The main concern of economic and social development has been to make additional short-and long-term credit funds available of farmers. There are two sources of institutional credit for agriculture: the publicly-owned BAAC and the commercial banks. Expansion of agricultural credit in the past few years has increased substantially. Increased agricultural lending has resulted from the Bank of Thailand's provision that 20 percent of total commercial bank deposits (up from five percent in 1975) be lent to farmers directly or through the BAAC. In addition, two percent of the total is to be lent to the agribusiness sector.

Industrial finance. One means of promoting industrial activity is to direct funds to further economic development. At present, major secondary cities in Thailand are adequately served by private banks. Up to 1975, 60 percent of the deposits made in the provinces were being channeled back to Bangkok, a situation which necessitated government guidelines requiring that at least 60 percent of the deposits be lent locally. Priorities of the Industrial Finance Corporation are to support industries which significantly increase the value-added worth of a commodity, generate employment, use domestic raw materials, produce export products, or locate their factories outside of Bangkok.

Industrial services. The technical assistance and training services provided by the Department of Industrial Promotion (DIP) serve to promote industrial development. DIP also has five regional centres in Chiang Mai, Khon Kaen, Songkhla, Chon Buri and Suphan Buri. The training and advisory services offered cover all aspects of industrial management, investment and joint-venture, industrial technology and industrial design.

Foreign Trade and Balance of Payments

In Thailand's open economy, foreign trade accounts for a major portion of the national product. Its importance has grown substantially over the past 20 years as its share in the national income increased from 34 percent in 1961 to 67 percent in 1993. As the economy becomes more open, it is increasingly susceptible to change in world economic conditions.

Exports. During 1988-1992 total value of exports increased at an annual average of 20.3 percent. Total value increased from about 18 percent of the Gross National Product in 1984 to approximately 29.5 percent in 1993.

There have been improvements in the structure of Thai exports value, most notably the diversification of export commodities. The share in total exports held by the country's seven major agricultural products, (rice, tin, rubber, maize, sugar, kenaf and tapioca) declined from about 54 percent in 1978 to 12 percent in 1993. Meanwhile, exports of manufacturing sectors increased from 65.8 percent in 1988 to 81.0 percent in 1993. An impressive rate of export growth has also occurred for textile and garment, electronic equipment, frozen squid, canned pineapple, fish meal and canned marine products, gems and jewellery.

Thailand's traditional export markets are concentrated in the East Asia region. In 1993, Japan took up 17.05 percent of total exports and three other countries in the region — Malaysia (2.8 percent), Hong Kong (5.29 percent), and Singapore (12.07 percent). With the high rate of growth in the East Asia region, as well as the growing economic interdependency between Japan, the newly industrialized countries in Asia and ASEAN, the prospect for future export expansion looks bright.

Imports. Thailand's import bill increased from 242,284 million baht in 1984 to 1,143,000 million baht in 1993. Most of the increase was experienced after 1986 when the country started a period of economic boom. Between 1961 and 1973, the portion of the total Gross National Product spent on imports stood at between 18 and 21 percent. During 1973-1982, the ratio increased to 28 percent as a direct result of substantial rises in the import price of petroleum. In 1993 expenditures on imports accounted for about 36.6 percent of the Gross National Product.

Import structure has changed in recent years. The proportion of consumption goods imports has continually declined from 23.7 percent of total import value in 1967 to only 9.6 percent in 1993 as a result of the government's industrial development policy oriented towards import substitution. At the same time, imports of raw materials and capital goods increased substantially to about 73 percent of total imports by the end of 1993.

Thailand relies on imports from certain major trade partners, particularly Japan and the United States. In 1993 imports from these two countries accounted for 42.3 percent of the total. Over the period 1978-1988, the proportion of imports from West Germany and the United Kingdom declined from 9.67 percent of the total to about 8.3 percent while imports from Saudi Arabia and Qatar, the major exporters of petroleum, increased substantially. During the period under review there has been no significant change in the direction of imports from ASEAN countries. Imports from Malaysia and Singapore totaled respectively 6 percent and 9 percent of the total in 1993.

Terms of trade. With the continuing increase in fuel prices, world-wide inflation, and the decline of primary product prices in the world market since 1975, the terms of trade have become less favourable. However, there was a significant improvement in 1992/1993 with the sharp rise in primary commodity prices in the world market.

Balance of payments. Thailand's trade deficit has been increasing gradually over the past two and a half decades. Trade deficit of 221,000 million baht was registered during 1993. The main reason for this deterioration was the huge demand for import of raw and semiprocessed materials, and capital goods created by the expanding industrial sector.

At the same time, the world price of many Thai export commodities continued to decline, resulting in a lower growth rate in export earnings. While the trade deficit grew bigger, income from services and foreign capital inflows were insufficient to offset the tremendous gap. Consequently, the balance of payments registered a record deficit of 13,298 million baht in 1978. Since then however, the situation has turned around, thanks to tight fiscal and external debt management, lower oil prices, and substantial increases in capital inflow, exports, and tourism. The balance of payments has registered a surplus since 1984. By the end of 1993, Thailand's official foreign reserves stood at US$ 25,438.8 million, equivalent to about seven months of imports.

Conclusion

Thailand has emerged from the 80s as one of the most promising developing nations in the world. The two digit growth rates of 13 percent, 11 percent and 10 percent, it achieved in 1988, 1989 and 1990 were the highest rates of growth. The initial main engines of growth have been external-led factors including export, tourism, and foreign investment, but lately, the domestic demand played more role in stimulating growth. This is due to several factors including high growth rate of the construction sector, increasing spendings by individuals benefiting from the current economic boom, and rising investment from both private and public sectors. However, the growth rates in 1991, 1992 and 1993 were lower at 8.2, 7.4 and 7.5 percent respectively, consistent with the long-term sustainable expansion. Increasing rate has been around 3 percent during recent year.

This fast-growth pattern is accompanied by rapid structural changes in three dimensions. First, there is a clear internationalization of the Thai economy. The share of exports to the Gross Domestic Product rose from 19.2 percent in 1982 to as high as 29.5 percent in 1993.

This internationalization of the Thai economy represented both challenges and opportunities since the increasing openness of the economy allows Thailand for wider access to the world market but, even though it opens the country to more unstable forces in the world arena.

Second, there is an increasing interdependency among countries in the Asia Pacific region (including Japan, NICs, U.S., Canada, Australia, New Zealand, China, and ASEAN). Massive relocation of export industries from the surplus economies, particularly Japan and the newly Industrialized Economies (NIEs), in Asia led to the increasing integration of Thailand into the Asia-Pacific industrial structure. During 1987 as much as 64 percent of the foreign investment seeking promotional priviledges in Thailand were from the Asia Pacific region and the share was still high at 62 percent in 1993.

Finally, there has been a new structural change as a result of the economic boom. Wage rate is rising and shortages are being felt in some critical technical man-power areas. Thus, the Thai economy is rapidly moving from a labour abundancy situation to one of more full employment. This allows for better income distribution as development impacts are being more dispersed in the kingdom. With adequate training and technical facilities, Thailand is ready to move up to a higher level of production structure with more value added to the economy, thus allowing other nations with cheaper unskilled labour to move into its place for an orderly development transition process in the region.

"Thai Khu Fah" Building, the Government House.

GOVERNMENT AND POLITICS

Thailand's present governmental structure has undergone gradual and practical evolution in response to the changing environment. The Kingdom of Sukhothai (1257 - 1378 A.D.) adopted the paternalistic system of government. The King, while enjoying absolute sovereign power, would, like a father, look after all his subjects and personally pay close attention to their well-being.

The Ayutthaya Kingdom inherited extensive Khmer traditions and customs, including their system of government with the kings as demigods. A major indigenous development in the governing system during the reign of King Barommatrailokanat (1448 - 1488) left behind a clear division between the civilian and military administration and a strong centralized government.

The succeeding Ratanakosin Kingdom established in 1767 in Bangkok also adopted the Ayutthaya system and government structure. Thus, for over three centuries, the basic pattern of the administration of the country was, by and large, carried out without drastic changes in terms of reorganization.

In face of the threatening advance of colonialism, King Rama V or His Majesty King Chulalongkorn the Great (1868 - 1910) carried out major reorganization of the central, regional and local administration, which formed the basis of the present system. His administrative reform and rapid drive for the country's modernization proved successful both in maintaining the country's independence throughout the turbulent years of the Western colonial threat and in providing a foundation for the modern system of government.

The Ministry of Interior.

King Rama VII granted the first constitution to the Thai people on December 10, 1932, which marked the first reign of constitutional monarchy.

Changes in 1932

The politics of Thailand took some significant turn on 24 June 1932 when a group of young intellectuals, educated abroad and imbued with the concept of Western democracy, staged a bloodless coup, demanding a change from absolute to a constitutional monarchy. Determined to avoid any bloodshed, His Majesty King Prajadhipok (Rama VII) agreed to the abolition of absolute monarchy and the transfer of power to the constitution-based system of government as demanded. To some, this demand was premature, but fortunately with the far-sightedness of King Prajadhipok and his predecessors in particular King Chulalongkorn the Great (Rama V) and King Vajiravudh (Rama VI), Thailand was not unprepared for this transition. While continuing the process launched by the two previous kings, King Prajadhipok had every intention of accustoming the Thais to the Western system of constitutional monarchy and had considered the eventuality of altering such form of government to the people at an appropriate moment. Popular readiness, the King believed, was an important ingredient to success for such transition. It was only a matter of waiting for the right time.

On 10 December 1932, His Majesty King Prajadhipok signed Thailand's first constitution and thus ended 700 years of Thailand's absolute monarchy. Despite the number of successive constitutions that followed in the span of just over half a century, the basic concepts of constitutional government and monarchy laid down in the 1932 constitution have remained unaltered.

Major Ingredients in Thai Policies

The first and foremost concept is the status of the monarch as Head of Armed Forces and Upholder of the Buddhist Religion and all other religions. Every constitution provides that the monarch is sacred and inviolable in his person. His sovereign power emanates from the people, and as Head of State, he exercises his legislative power through the House of Parliament, executive power through the Cabinet headed by the Prime Minister, and judicial power through the courts. The monarch is empowered with the right to be consulted, the right to encourage, and the right to warn whenever the government appears not to administer the state affairs according to the wished and for the good of the people.

The second concept concerns the legislative branch. The leaders of 1932 realized that the goal of popularly-elected government could not be

The cabinet room inside the Government House.

attained immediately, and that considerable experimentation and adaptation would be necessary before a balance could be struck. For this reason, the first constitution was a cautious document that created a bicameral National Assembly with two categories of members, half of whom were elected by popular vote as MP's or

The Government House.

Members of Parliament who serve a 4-year term in the Lower House, the other half were appointed by the King on the recommendation of the Council of Ministers (now called the cabinet) as Senators who serve a 6-year term in the Upper House or the House of Senate.

The third concept concerns the executive branch. Every constitution holds that the Prime Minister is head of government and head executive. A slight difference between the Thai Prime Minister and those in other countries is that, since the creation of the post of the Prime Minister in 1933, the Thais have often looked to their Prime Minister as a protective figure, possibly due to their tendency to extend family structure into the sphere of government.

The cabinet is responsible for the administration of 13 ministries, as well as the Office of the Prime Minister and the Office of State Universities. Each ministry is politically headed by a minister with one or more deputy ministers, all of whom will sit in the cabinet. A number of cabinet committees have been set up consisting of relevant ministers, such as the Cabinet Economics Committee and the Cabinet Social Committee, to coordinate major policies concerned. This development enables the government to ensure that no policies incompatible with other related ones are made. The committees may be assigned by the Prime Minister to examine the merits of each project or policy for the cabinet so that the latter will not have to go into such details before giving final approval or disapproval to that project or policy and spare itself time to consider other important matters.

Besides the ministers responsible for each ministry, there is a number of ministers holding the portfolio of "Minister Attached to the Prime Minister's Office." They take charge of various responsibilities undertaken by this office which in itself ranks as a ministry and is largely concerned with formulating the national policy. One of its primary subdivisions, the Budget Bureau, prepares the nations's annual budget. The National Economic and Social Development Board lays out longer term development planning. The Juridical Council provides expert assistance in drafting laws and gives ruling on questions concerning administrative law. It remains quite distinct from the Justice Ministry, which administers laws after they are promulgated. The Board of Investment (BOI), which provides incentives for investment, comes under the responsibility of the Prime Minister's Office, with the Prime Minister being the Chairman of the Board. Several other organization Office, the Technical and Economic Cooperation Department and the Office of the National Education Commission also fall under the responsibility of the Prime Minister's Office.

At a time when economic growth of the country is one of the highest in the region and the country is in the process of diversifying from agriculture to industry, the Ministry of Industry and the Ministry of Commerce play an important role in the government. The former's functions include the fomulation of manufacturing and mining policy, the licensing of factories and mineral leases, the formulation and supervision of industrial standards, the provision of technical assistance (especially to small-scale industries), and supervision of the Small Industries Finance Office.

The Ministry of Commerce facilitates external and internal trade. This includes control or supervision of prices for certain strategic commodities such as rice, temporary restraints on a narrow range of imports (in cooperation with BOI), and the provision of export promotion services.

The Ministry of Interior, to which all local administrators are attached, is one of the largest ministries. Its departments include Local Administration, Accelerated Rural Development, Public Works, Town and Country Planning, Corrections, Community Development, and Lands.

The **Police Department,** which forms a major part of the Interior Ministry, is one of the largest government ministerial departments. The Police Department is divided into three forces and a number of smaller units. The Metropolitan Police Force is concerned with crime prevention and suppression, traffic control and, through the Police Fire Brigade, with firefighting in the Greater Bangkok Metropolis. The Provincial Police Force is operated throughout the rest of the country. The third force is the Border Patrol Police, and elite force established in 1951 to prevent insurgent infiltration and maintain peace and security in border areas. The Police Department also includes the division responsible for matters concerning immigration and visas.

The **Ministry of Agriculture and Cooperatives** covers fisheries and forestry as well as farming. Its Co-operatives Promotion Department has gained increasing importance in recent years by providing farmers with opportunities to work together, pool resources, and take advantage of economies of scale.

The **Ministry of Transport and Communications** controls aviation, harbours, highways, land transport, post, telegraph and telecommunications (including satellite microwave transmission), and the national meteorological network.

The **Ministry of Education** standardizes elementary, secondary schools, and teacher training programme. In addition, it supports the non-formal education in rural areas to ensure an equal opportunity in education and educate those excluded from the school population. Moreover, the ministry is also incharge of Fine Arts and Religious Affairs, the latter being a very important assignment in a country where religion retains a major influence in public affairs.

The **Ministries of Defence, Finance, Foreign Affairs, Public Health, Science, Technology and Energy, Labour and Social Welfare** effectively keep pace with accelerating developments in their areas of authority.

In addition to the ministries mentioned above, these authorities are also given jurisdiction over state enterprises or public corporations which deal with public utility services.

The head of career civil servants in each ministry is the permanent secretary, who has administrative control over all the departments of the ministry, each of which is headed by a director-general, also a career civil servant.

The Armed Forces

The Thai Armed Forces are divided into three branches : the Royal Thai Army (RTA), Royal Thai Navy (RTN) and Royal Thai Air Force (RTAF). The Thai soldiers are composed of professional cover soldiers and those recruited by conscription. Every male aged twenty is subject to two years military service. Students are allowed deferment until they have graduated.

His Majesty the King is Commander-in-Chief of the Royal Thai Armed Forces and the Cabinet is the instrument through which national security policy is formulated. A National Security Council, composed of a number of ministers, is in charged with coordinating the maintenance of national security and peace.

The Ministry of Defence.

His Majesty King Bhumibol
Adulyadej joined the judiciary
in the court.

Judiciary and Justice Administration

The history of judiciary and the administration of justice in Thailand can be traced back into the Sukhothai period (1257 - 1378). According to a stone inscription recorded in the reign of King Ramkhamhaeng the Great, it showed the notion that the King was the "Fountain of Justice" who, sometimes, adjudicated the cases himself.

The modern judiciary and legal system in the formality as some Western countries was laid down in the reign of King Chulalongkorn the Great, the fifth monarch of the Royal House of Chakri (1868 - 1910). The Ministry of Justice was also established in 1892.

Presently, the Courts of Justice are divided into three categories, i.e., the Courts of First Instance, the Courts of Appeal and the Supreme Court. There are about 140 Courts of First Instance throughout the Kingdom. In Bangkok Metropolis, they are, for example, the Civil Court, the Criminal Court, the Juvenile and Family Court, the Central Labour Court and the Central

Tax Court, including Kwaeng Courts which have jurisdiction over minor civil cases and criminal cases with maximum punishment of imprisonment not exceeding 3 years or fine not exceeding Baht 60,000 or both. In the provinces, they are the Provincial Courts, and in some large provinces the Provincial Juvenile and Family Courts and Kwaeng Courts are included.

The Courts of Appeal consist of one Bangkok-based Court of Appeal and three Regional Courts of Appeal. There is one Supreme Court with jurisdiction to review and adjudicate all cases, and the Court's judgments are final. However, in criminal cases the accused may petition His Majesty the King for clemency.

There are also military courts which deal with military personnels in criminal cases.

To ensure their impartiality and independence, Thai courts adjudicate cases according to the laws in the name of His Majesty the King who is above politics in all aspects. The judges themselves are also protected from any political interference. Essentially, no new court shall be established with the purpose of trying any particular case.

Under Thai criminal proceeding, an injured person may institute a prosecution himself or lodge a complaint with the authorities concerned and have his case conducted by them. If the injured person lodges a complaint, the police inquiry officials will conduct an inquiry and file all facts and evidence for submission to the public prosecutor. After reviewing the file of inquiry, the public prosecutor may issue an order of prosecution and further the case to the court or issue an order of non-prosecution and release the alleged offender according to the evidence.

In a criminal case, the accused is guaranteed by the provisions of laws on the presumption of innocence and the right to defend himself, including the right to have a counsel and other standard treatment of human rights protection. No judgement of conviction shall be delivered unless and until the court is fully satisfied that an offence has actually been perpetrated and that the

The Criminal Court.

accused has committed that offence. In case of doubt, the benefit will be granted to the accused. In this regard, the Office of the Attorney General is responsible for the prosecutorial functions and the Department of Corrections is responsible for the persons convicted.

In a civil case, any person, whose rights or duties under the law are involved in a dispute or must be exercised through the medium of court, is entitled to submit his or her case to a civil court having territorial jurisdiction and competency over it. Civil proceedings in Thai courts are administered mainly by the Civil Procedure Code of 1934 and the following revisions.

In the course of today's business, however, the tendency to rely on the arbitration system seems to be on the rise due to its convenience, informality and saving of time, the Thai justice administration recognized this trend by adopting the Arbitration Act of 1987.

Owing to the rapid growth of modern transportation and communication, some crimes are frequently committed beyond one country's boundary. Thailand also actively involved with international community in fighting against transnational crimes. Therefore, many treaties on extradition, transferring of prisoners and mutual assistance in criminal matters have been entered by Thailand.

Democracy and Thailand

The changes brought about by the successive monarchs and the 1932 introduction of democracy and constitutional monarchy took a long time to gain the attention of the majority of the citizenry, as the kingdom encompassed such a vast area with millions of its population living in the countryside.

During almost six decades of constitutional democracy, the concept, initially alien to the majority of the people and remaining so for a few decades afterwards, has undergone a long process of refinement and reconceptualization in order to adapt the democratic system to the specific needs of the Thai nation. With the present civilian administration providing a unifying element for the country, Thailand's democratic system is thus being set on the right course of development stipulating a foundation for the political system of in which pre-eminent power is held and exercised by the people.

The House of Parliament.

Their Majesties the King and Queen of Thailand granting an audience to the President of the Lao People's Democratic Republic and Madame at Chitralada Villa during their State Visit to Thailand between 14-19 February 1995.

INTERNATIONAL RELATIONS

In order to understand the present Thai foreign policy, it seems beneficial to trace its evolution chronologically from the commencement of relations with European countries in the early part of the sixteenth century, the colonial era (nineteenth century) up to the present time.

Early Contact with the West

In the early sixteenth century, Siam's (as the country was known before the twentieth century) relations with Western countries was apparently marked by overseas trade and propagation of Christianity. In 1516, Siam concluded a commercial agreement with Portugal, the first of its kind between Siam and a European power. Later in the century, Siam entered into trade agreements with other European countries, namely, Spain, the Netherlands, England and France. After a ship of the first envoy Siam ever despatched to Europe was wrecked on the way to France, Siam, in 1684, sent her second diplomatic mission to forge friendly ties with King Louis XIV. In 1685, the French sent Chevalier de Chaumont to sign the Treaty of Friendship with Siam. In despatching a mission to King Narai, Louis XIV had two major objectives: to persuade King Narai of Ayutthaya to embrace the Catholic faith; and to obtain all possible

During the reign of King Narai of Ayutthaya, Siam enjoyed lively diplomatic exchange with several European countries. Of special interest was France under Louis XIV, which sent a diplomatic mission to this bustling capital.

commercial advantages. The French emissary was granted audience on 18 October 1685. Actually, the King of Siam looked for a friendly power to counterbalance the growing influence of the Dutch. As it turned out, King Narai himself diplomatically rejected the efforts to convert to Catholicism; but granted permission for Christianity to be propagated in Siam.

All in all, as a small country in the midst of burgeoning colonisation by Western powers at a time to exploit its rich resources, Siam still managed well to preserve her sovereignty and independence.

His Majesty King Chulalongkorn at Bernstorff Palace in Copenhagen, Denmark during a visit to Prince Wademar of Denmark on July 1, 1907.

The Colonial Era

At the height of European colonialism in the mid nineteenth century, survival as an independent nation was the preoccupation of Siam's conduct of foreign policy.

During that time, Thai Kings forged friendly relations with as many countries as possible while making all possible efforts to avoid confrontation in order to compromise with several European pressures and demands such as signing a number of unequal treaties, granting extraterritorial rights to European citizens, and, very reluctantly, granting vast territories to Britain and France. Painful as the sacrifices were for the time being, Siamese or Thai diplomacy led to the country's survival as the only independent country in the region.

In the face of external threats, the leaders realized that the country must be modernized in the shortest time possible. Thus, they began a thorough reorganization of its legal system, including the codification of its laws. Extensive general reforms, along with the accustomization to Western cultures and international norms, were also undertaken. During the reign of King Rama V (1868-1910), through his farsightedness and dedication to his people, Siam embarked on an ambitious and far-reaching modernization programme. Besides making state visits to observe modernization in several European countries, King Rama V sent his children to attend schools, universities and military academies in countries such as Russia, Germany, Britain, France and Switzerland. Upon returning to Siam, these Western-educated princes were subsequently responsible for modernization of Siam's bureaucracy. The Royal Court also hired many foreign technicians and advisers with relevant expertise to assist in

the process of modernization, some of whom were given wide responsibilities and were rewarded with noble titles.

In World War I, Siam supported the Allies who were victorious. Subsequently, Siam signed the Treaty of Versailles and became one of the founding members of the League of Nations. With a stronger foothold in the international arena, Siam began to renegotiate the revision of unequal treaties, concluded with the Western powers during the height of colonialism. In 1920, the United States became the first country to give up special trading privileges and extraterritorial rights except in certain legal cases. By 1937, all consular courts and other foreign privileges had disappeared, thanks particularly to the help of Dr. Francis B. Sayre, an American adviser in the Ministry of Foreign Affairs, who devotedly exercised his legal expertise to salvage Siam from disadvantageous treaties and agreements.

The Post World War II Era

Immediately after the Second World War, Thailand's position was quite vulnerable due to its occupation by Japan and its uneasy relations with the Axis powers during the conflict. A few European powers unjustifiably considered Thailand a defeated nation and thus made several unreasonable demands for compensation. Fortunately, the United States stood by Thailand and mitigated the pressure. The heroic and selfless activities of the Free Thai Movement in close cooperation with the United States and British governments during the war successfully supported the Thai argument of the invalidity of its declaration of war.

Prince Wan Waithayakorn.

In 1946, through diplomatic skills of the Thai leaders, Thailand was accepted as the 55th member of the United Nations. Since then, with its firm conviction that the United Nations is a viable forum in which the world community can work together to solve common problems, Thailand has been an active participant in various United Nations' activities. It has served on the Trusteeship Council, the Economic and Social Council (ECOSOC), and numerous specialized agencies of the United Nations, notably the United Nations Educational Scientific and Cultural Organization (UNESCO), the United Nations International Children's Fund (UNICEF), and the Food and Agriculture Organization (FAO). Thailand has also been the sites of many regional offices of United Nations agencies and other international organizations such as the Economic and Social Commission for Asia and the Pacific (ESCAP), the Food and Agriculture Organization (FAO), the United Nations International Children's Fund (UNICEF), and the Southeast Asian Ministers of Education Organization and Secretariat (SEAMEO and SEAMES).

In recognition of Thailand's active role in United Nations' activities, former Foreign Minister the late H.R.H. Major General Kromamun Naradhip Bongsprabandh (Prince Wan Waithayakorn) was unanimously elected to serve as President of the United Nations General Assembly in 1956. He was the second Southeast Asian to have been so elected since the founding of the United Nations.

Thailand in 1954 became a founding member, along with the United States, Britain, France, Australia, New Zealand, the Philippines and Pakistan, of the now defunct Southeast Asian Treaty Organization (SEATO). The apparent objective of this organization was to contain the spread of communism. The then widely-held domino theory suggested that if Thailand could be maintained as a strong and prosperous anticommunist bulwark, the growing communist threat in the region might be checked and contained.

The history of Southeast Asia had left behind a formidable obstacle to regionalism. It was a "balkanized" region which found its expression in the formation of the Association of Southeast Asia (ASA) in Bangkok in 1961 by the Federation of Malaya, the Philippines, and Thailand. This purely regional effort was stifled in September 1963 by regional disputes followed by the establishment of Malaysia, the conflicting territorial claim of the Philippines and the opposition of Indonesia. These conflicts led to a tense period of confrontation and military clashes.

Her Majesty Queen Elizabeth II visited Thailand in 1972.

Under such tense circumstances, Thailand, acceptable to all parties concerned, initiated the idea of forming another regional organization to replace the dormant ASA. As a result, the philosophy underlying ASA found a new expression on 8 August 1967 when the Foreign Ministers of Indonesia, Malaysia, the Philippines, Singapore, and Thailand affixed their signatures on the Bangkok Declaration at the Ministry of Foreign Affairs of Thailand. The signing marked the beginning of the Association of Southeast Asian Nations (ASEAN) with its wider and more solid participation than that of the frail ASA.

Their Majesties the Yang Di-Pertuan Agong and the Raja Permaisuri Agong of Malaysia during their State Visit to Thailand in 1973.

ASEAN was conceived in Southeast Asia by Southeast Asians. It was born out of the political will of the majority of nations in Southeast Asia with an aim to promote peace and to accelerate economic growth, social progress, and cultural development in the region through joint endeavour in a spirit of equality and partnership. The member countries began to learn about one another, to work together and to become more

responsible in determining the future of their region. Later on, the Sultanate of Brunei Darussalam officially joined the membership of ASEAN on 7 January 1984, thereby becoming the sixth member of this regional grouping. With the addition of Brunei Darussalam, ASEAN now has a population estimated at more than 300 million and a total land area of more than 3 million square kilometres.

1970's: Changing Realities

The advent of the 1970's marked drastic changes in regional and global political configurations which brought about new challenges for Thailand's policy makers. On the international front, world politics was transformed from bipolarization toward multipolarization with the return of China to the world arena and with Japan and Western Europe gradually resuming their political and economic roles.

On the regional level, the United States' withdrawal from Vietnam and the Nixon Doctrine, in which United States would continue to give Asian allies the material assistance they might need for their own defense, but the Asians themselves would have to supply the manpower needed to defeat external or internal aggression, created a vacuum of power as well as a sense of uncertainty and anxiety over United States defense commitments on mainland Southeast Asia. The communization of the three Indochinese states and the prediction of the falling dominoes represented a lurking danger to the security of the free nations in the region, and to Thailand in particular.

To keep pace with the changing international environment, Thai foreign policy has undergone at least three basic developments, which have had long-lasting effects today.

First, it adopted an omnidirectional policy trend by seeking diplomatic, commercial, and cultural relations with all nations, regardless of their political ideology and economic system. Notably, in 1975, Bangkok and

Beijing began full diplomatic recognition and exchanged ambassadors. Full diplomatic relations with the new state of Cambodia were also established in that year, while relations with Vietnam were normalized in 1976.

Second, regionalism has come to play a more significant role in Thai foreign policy. At the first summit meeting of the ASEAN countries' Heads of Government in Bali in 1976, ASEAN codified in contractual form the principle of Pacific settlement of disputes among ASEAN members. Subsequently, the spirit of the Bali Summit further solidified political and economic cooperation among ASEAN states to the extent that ASEAN today can be called a "diplomatic revolution" in Southeast Asia.

Since then, ASEAN has expanded its joint activities to conquer new horizons, encompassing the fields of trade, tourism, industry, energy, science and technology, finance and banking, transportation, cultural and social development. Recent initiatives include import tariff reduction among member countries and industrial complementation. These activities intertwine ASEAN's interests and have given further impetus to development of the region.

Furthermore, ASEAN also expanded its cooperative relations with other developed countries. By 1976, ASEAN established cooperative links with Australia, Japan, Canada, New Zealand, and the agencies of the United Nations through the UNDP and ESCAP, followed by the United States in 1977. The links with the European Community and Canada were formalized through the signing of Cooperation Agreements in 1980 and 1981 respectively. The ASEAN foreign ministers meet annually with the foreign ministers of these dialogue partners and the Com-

Photograph taken on the occasion of the State Banquet, at Chakri Throne Hall in the Grand Palace, in honour of Their Majesties the Emperor and Empress of Japan during the State Visit to Thailand between September 26 - 30, 1991.

missioner and the President of the EU Council of Ministers to discuss various international and regional issues of common interest and concern.

Third, Thailand has sought to promote even more its non-aligned foreign policy. With regard to its relations with major powers, it has sought to forge an "equidistant" policy, that is, a more equal relationship based on more balanced interests with all of them. The declaration of the concept of Southeast Asia as a Zone of Peace, Freedom, and Neutrality by ASEAN in 1973 is but one example of this.

Flexible responses to the evolving international events are among other things that enable Thailand not only to be the domino that did not fall but also to be more stable, with a firmer foothold in the international community.

Thailand in 1980's

The Vietnamese invasion of Cambodia in 1978 and its occupation thereafter, followed by an armed confrontation between Vietnam and China, shattered the hope of regional peaceful coexistence. The Soviet's military presence in Vietnam further complicated the security equation of the region. In the face of this challenge, the Thai stance on the Cambodian problem has been guided by the principles of neutralisation externally and self determination internally. In the search for a lasting peace in the region, Thailand and its ASEAN partners have put relentless effort in bringing this problem to the world attention through the United Nations.

As a frontline state which had to bear the brunt of adverse consequences of war in Cambodia, Thailand played an instrumental role in finding a comprehensive political settlement to the Cambodian problem. Through cooperation and support from the international community, strategies have been devised to put political and economic pressure on Vietnam while leaving room for political negotiation.

As evidenced by the overwhelming votes supporting ASEAN-sponsored resolutions on the Cambodian problem in the United Nations General Assembly every year, the legitimacy of ASEAN's pursuit has won worldwide acclaim and support. Eventually, Vietnam announced unilateral troop withdrawal from Cambodia by September 1990, paving the way for a negotiated settlement among the Cambodian parties under the leadership of Somdech Prince Narodom Sihanouk.

In recognition of Thailand's active role in and support for the noble causes of the United Nations, Thailand was, on 22 October 1984, elected to serve as a non-permanent member of the United Nations Security Council during 1985-1986. Thailand's election marked the first time ever that it has served on the Security Council since joining the United Nations in 1946. Throughout this eventful tenure as non-permanent member of the United Nations Security Council, it was with great pride that Thailand was able to contribute towards the resolution of conflict and the enhancement of development in many parts of the world.

Thai Foreign Policy in the global context

Back in 1986, when the Cold War was still very much a reality, Thailand, at the United Nations, called for "a new world order of peace and justice". A few years later, the world did indeed change, the Cold War ended and the President of the United States came to the fore front and also called for "a new world order".

Now in the 1990's, Thailand has continued to be active in the international arena. Whenever appropriate, Thailand would serve as a peace-maker, a bridge between two or more adversaries. Thailand continues to be a firm supporter of the United Nations. Thailand has been one of the early advocates of United Nations' role in preventive diplomacy. Realizing that preventive diplomacy cannot work without timely and accurate information with analysis on global situations, Thailand,

Foreign Minister Kasem S. Kasemsri presiding over the Opening Ceremony of the Thai Ambassadors and Consuls General Seminar, Bangkok, August 1995.

again back in 1986, called for the creation of "an early warning system" for the United Nations. Such a system is now high on the United Nations Secretary-General's agenda. In addition, Thailand has contributed military as well as civilian personnels to the United Nations peace-keeping operations around the world, including Namibia, Iraq/Kuwait, and closer to home, Cambodia. Indeed, several battalions of the military engineers risked their lives to clear the minefields, placed by warring factions inside Cambodia, to safeguard lives, peace and opportunities for infrastructural developments of Cambodia.

Thailand in 1990's

The final decade of the twentieth century saw, for the first time, the rising hope for regional peace and the expansion of democracy throughout the world as the Berlin Wall was pulled down and the collapse of Communism in Eastern European countries. The Soviet Union and the United States entered into an unprecedented stage of cooperation to arrest the nuclear arms race and resolve regional conflicts throughout the world.

The end of the Cold War and the new wind of change had favourably been conducive to a search for peace in Cambodia. Vietnam withdrew its troops from Cambodia as its leaders in Hanoi realized that the time had come for their government to concentrate on economic development and the improvement of the well-being of the Vietnamese people. Countries, which once were hostile to one another, began to seek friendship, understanding and cooperation.

To prepare for Thailand's greater role in the world arena, Thailand has successfully won unanimous acceptance as observer to the Non-Aligned Movement during the NAM (Non-Allied Movement) Summit in Jakarta in September 1992. Soon afterward, Thailand, formally, applied for NAM membership to be approved by the year 1995. Hence, Thailand's contribution to economic cooperation among developing countries will further be enhanced and intensified.

Thailand is also committed to intensifying its economic cooperation at multilateral fora, in particular at GATT to achieve a comprehensive and balanced package of the new trade order under the Uruguay Round. Thailand has also been an active member of the Asia-Pacific Economic Cooperation (APEC) whose aim and objective is to enhance free trade and prosperity in the Asia-Pacific region and beyond.

Cambodian Problem

In a continuing effort to find a lasting peace in Cambodia, it was Thailand which tried to bring the Cambodian parties together. The Pattaya informal meeting among the warring factions led to the historic signing of the Paris Accord on 23 October 1991. The peace accord entrusts the United Nations Transitional Authority in Cambodia (UNTAC) to supervise the transitional government and arrange the general election in May 1993.

Long before Western donor governments, the Thai Government was the first to provide concrete and substantial assistance to the reconstruction of Cambodia through highway repairs and construction, establishment of schools and rural development. These constructive endeavours represent the largest aid outlay to Cambodia of any country. They are undertaken for the benefit of

Foreign Minister Thaksin Shinawatra leading foreign ambassadors on a visit to the Thai-Cambodian border on 9 January 1995.

the long-suffering people of Cambodia and for facilitating the operations of the United Nations mission in that country. More than 350,000 Cambodian displaced persons, who had stayed in various camps in Thailand for more than 13 years, were able to make a journey home with dignity in order to participate in the UNTAC-Supervised elections in May 1993. It was the Thai military which extended full cooperation and facilities for UNTAC troops to move in and out of Cambodia.

When the United Nations Security Council decided to impose trade sanction to persuade the Khmer Rouge to return to the peace process, it was Thailand which would be affected most and yet the elected Government of Prime Minister Chuan Leekpai decided to comply fully with the UN resolution despite the commercial losses of Thai traders who earlier had entered into business contracts with all Cambodian parties.

The Government recognizes Cambodian government formed by the winning parties.

Thailand and Southeast Asia

Thailand firmly believes that the key to genuine stability and prosperity for the whole of Southeast Asia lies in creating greater economic interdependence among the countries in the region, based on commonality of interests and mutual benefits. This will not only lead to an increased prosperity for all, but also decrease the likelihood of regional conflicts. Such interdependence can be achieved through an expanding network of formal and informal linkages, at the bilateral, multilateral, and regional levels.

It would be in Thailand's best interest if her nieghbours are prosperous and at peace. In 1992, the Thai Government expanded its economic and technical assistance programme to an unprecedented budget level of 203 million baht in fiscal year 1993, to provide bilateral aid to her less fortunate neighbours in Indochina and elsewhere. Through this programme, Thailand hopes to help her friends build up their physical infrastructure, particularly roads, railways and waterways. At the same time, it hopes to assist in human resources development to acquire the skills essential for improving the countries' competitiveness in the international market.

On a sub-regional level, Thailand has taken serious steps to strengthen her cooperation with Vietnam, Laos, Cambodia and Myanmar. In addition to having a strong cultural affinity, the five countries are joined together by the Mekong River, which forms an essential lifeline for all these riparian states. Talks and studies are being conducted to also link southern China with northern Myanmar, Laos and Thailand together by roads to enhance people-to-people contacts, and cooperation in trade and tourism. Thailand, sharing a long border with Myanmar, would like to see positive changes in Myanmar. That is why it believes isolating Myanmar would be counter-productive. Thus, it should extend constructive cooperation to enable Myanmar to play a more constructive role in a family of nations in Southeast Asia.

Thailand and ASEAN

One cannot, of course, engage in any discussion about a peaceful and prosperous Southeast Asia without

Deputy Foreign Minister Surin Pitsuwan with his Burmese counterpart at the signing ceremony of the Thailand-Myanmar Friendship Bridge, Yangon 17 October 1994.

THE 27TH ASEAN MINISTERIAL MEETING
AND POST MINISTERIAL CONFERENCES
BANGKOK, THAILAND
22-28 JULY 1994

The 27th ASEAN Ministerial Meeting and Post Ministerial Conferences held in Bangkok between 22-28 July 1994.

mentioning the instrumental role played by ASEAN. Ever since its inception over a quarter of a century ago, ASEAN has played a leading part in promoting peace and prosperity in Southeast Asia. It is therefore most appropriate that this organization should serve as the nucleus in this direction.

ASEAN has already moved boldly to strengthen its intra-regional economic cooperation. At its Fourth Summit Meeting in Singapore in January 1992, the ASEAN Heads of government agreed to establish an ASEAN Free Trade Area (AFTA) by the year 2008. AFTA has the full and firm backing of the Thai government. Prime Minister Chuan Leekpai has expressed confidence that ASEAN could realize the goal of AFTA much earlier than the 15-year time frame. Thailand's commitment to AFTA has thus far been based on a solid record. Thailand's exclusion list, for instance, contains the smaller number of products compared to Brunei Darussalam, Indonesia, Malaysia and the Philippines while the level of participation in the fast track programme is high. Thailand firmly believes that AFTA will be beneficial to Southeast Asia as a whole. Parallel with AFTA, Thailand has been in close consultations with Malaysia and Indonesia to turn the concept of triangular growth area into a reality. The growth area, where barriers, regulations and impediments to economic growth are to be removed, will supplement AFTA substantially. Success in this endeavour would consolidate ASEAN's position as an important economic grouping and enable it to serve as the anchor for stability and progress in this region through the twenty-first century.

Foreign Minister Kasem S. Kasemsri at the Opening Ceremony of the Exhibition on the Cooperation between Thailand and the United Nations to Celebrate the 50th Anniversary of the United Nations, at the U.N. Conference Centre, Bangkok, 15 August 1995.

All in all, Thai foreign policy in the early 1990s has been driven by a strong desire to seek peace, progress and prosperity especially in Southeast Asia. With its remarkable economic growth sustained over the years and a steady path toward democracy at home, Thailand is ready to play a more engaging role in Southeast Asia. As the dawn of the next century is imminent, Thailand is determined to contribute to the cause of world peace and development with confidence and purposefulness.

Dr. Suvit Yodmani, Regional Director For Asia and the Pacific United Nations Environment Programme (UNEP), delivering an Opening Address on behalf of UNEP at the Official Opening of the International Conference of Asian Parliamentarians on Environment and Sustainable Development. Malaysian Prime Minsiter, the Honourable Professor Dr. Prasop Ratanakorn, Senator also in attendance.

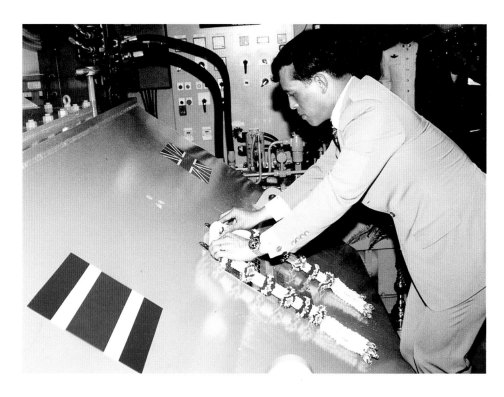

*His Royal Highness Prince Maha Vajiralongkorn presiding over the
Opening Ceremony of Mae Toei Hydro-Electric Power Plant at
Omkoi District, Chiang Mai Province.*

ENERGY AND NATURAL RESOURCES

Past and projected energy consumption profiles for Thailand can be summarized as follows:

Energy Consumption
(in percentage)

	1986	1991	1996	Annual Growth
Oil & Oil Products				4.0
Imported	46.0	36.4	41.5	-
Domestic	5.1	5.7	2.2	-
Natural Gas	0.5	15.6	18.3	8.9
Hydro electricity	9.5	4.0	4.3	3.1
Lignite and Coal	2.4	8.5	7.9	9.5
Traditional Energy	36.5	29.8	25.8	1.4
Total,%	100.0	100.0	100.0	**4.7**
Million barrels of oil equivalent	143	238	279	

Traditional energy in the above table includes firewood, charcoal, bagasses, and rice husk. Assessment of non-commercial use of firewood and charcoal is very approximate. Non-commercial uses of solar and wind energy in salt production, drying of agricultural products, etc. are not included. From the above table, energy consumption per capita in 1991 was about 665 litres of oil equivalent.

It should also be noted that the projected consumption in 1996 is based upon an annual growth rate of 4.7 percent. However, the actual growth of total energy consumption in 1988 was more than 13 percent and in 1991 was 5.4 percent owing mainly to the rapid expansion of the industrial and transportation sectors. As a result, development of domestic energy sources such as natural gas, oil, lignite, biomass, etc., has already been accelerated.

Mineral Resources

Natural Gas and Oil

The potential production for natural gas and oil in Thailand is quite substantial. In 1992 the natural gas reserve in Thailand is estimated at about 544,775 million cu.m., comprising 23 fields off-shore and 3 fields on-shore. Recoverable reserves have been estimated at about 455,630 million cu.m., of which 243,380 million cu.m. is proven reserves. In 1991, total natural gas production was 8,075.2 million cu.m. Most of the gas reserves are located in the off-shore gas fields in the Gulf of Thailand. At present, natural gas production from the Gulf of Thailand is about 19.5 million cu.m. per day. Methane, ethane, LPG, and condensate are separated in gas seperation plants and used for electricity generation, as raw materials for the petrochemical industry, and as cooking gas and vehicular fuels.

The crude oil reserves have been estimated at about 1,150 million barrels. It is expected to have a recoverable reserve of 498 million barrels, of which 236 million barrels is proven reserves. In 1991, total crude

oil production was 8,934,900 barrels. Most of the crude oil reserves are located at Sirikit oil field in Kamphaeng Phet Province. Current production from Sirikit oil field is about 23,000 barrels per day equivalent to 93.96 percent of total crude oil production. New oil field were recently found in Suphan Buri and Sukhothai Provinces. The actual production is about

The Map Ta Phut Gas Separation Plant is the largest of several plants
constructed on the Eastern Sea Board to exploit natural gas from the
Gulf of Thailand.

The Electricity Generating Authority of Thailand (EGAT)'s Mae Moh Power Plant in Lampang Province is the largest lignite-fired plant in the country.

527 barrels per day. In addition, more gas and oil fields are expected to be found in Thailand, both off and on-shore.

Lignite

Lignite deposits have been scattered around in Thailand in 72 basins. In 1992 the estimated lignite reserve for the whole country is about 2,069.2 million tons, of which over 80 percent are located in the North. The significant reserves in the North are about 1,598.3 million tons equivalent to 77.2 percent of the total reserves of the country. Recently, large lignite deposit has been identified at Saba Yoi District, Songkhla Province, with a reserve of over 400 million tons. In 1991, the production of lignite is 15 million tons, of which 12 million tons were used for generation of 2,059 Megawatt of electricity.

Utilization of lignite in industry has been actively promoted. The amount of lignite consumption by industry increased from 1.3 million tons in 1988 to 2.8 million tons in 1991. At present industrial uses of lignite occur mainly in the cement industry and also in small and medium size factories around Bangkok.

Boilers used in power stations and industry emit sulphur dioxide and NO_x directly into the atmosphere. With the increasing uses of domestic lignite and imported coal for electricity generation and industry stream production, a better pollution control on the use of this energy source is being considered.

It has also been estimated that geological reserves of lignite could reach 2,600 million tons, from which the recoverable amount is quite considerable.

Oil Shale

Exploration of oil shale in Thailand commenced in the northern part of the country in 1935. In 1991, 21,000 million tons of oil shale have been identified with a shale oil reserve of about 6,700 million barrels. Recoverable reserves at Tak Province deposits have been estimated at about 18,600 million tons. The kerosene content in Thai oil shale is relatively low, below 10 percent on the average. Though several processes for shale oil extraction have been developed, mainly in the U.S., at the present level of oil prices the exploitation of shale oil in Thailand would not be competitive. However, the oil shale reserves represent a large domestic source of energy for the future.

Renewable Resources

Hydro Electricity

Hydro power has been developed for power generation since 1964. In 1991, the total hydroelectric potential in Thailand is estimated at about 10,626 Megawatt. A larger potential on two international rivers, the Mekong River on the eastern border and the Salween River on the western border, are capable of generating 28,340 Megawatt. The Current generation capability of domestic hydroelectric dams is at 4,458 Gigawatt-hour per year. Domestic rivers' hydro potential still exists and can be further utilized when a few environmental issues can be solved in the future.

Once the biggest dam in the region, the Bhumibol Dam in Tak Province has recently been outstripped by the Sri Nakarindh Dam in Kanchanaburi Province.

As a part of the rural electrification programme to bring electricity to 95 percent of all villages in Thailand by 1990, 29 small hydropower sites have been identified as economically suitable for more accurate cost estimates and detailed engineering work. It should be noted that the thorough feasibility study of a small hydropower project tends to indicate that the cost of electricity generated from a suitable site can be more economical than electricity generated from a set of photovoltaic plants. One way to further reduce the capital cost of a small hydropower plant is to run a commercially available pump as a turbine.

Biomass

In 1991, the total biomass supply and the total biomass production including fuel wood, paddy husk, and bagasse was equally about 10,858 kilo tons of oil equivalent, represented 24.7 percent of total energy supply and 42.9 percent of total energy production. During the last decade, the total modern energy production from lignite, crude oil, natural gas, and hydroelectric grew at 40 percent per annum and the total biomass production decreased at a rate of 0.27 percent per annum especially in the use of fuel wood. In the past, fuel wood production has caused deforestation. Recently, to avoid serious environmental and economic damages, reforestation programmes by both public and private sectors have been implemented and have had good success. In 1991, the total consumption of the biomass is about 7,281 kilo tons of oil equivalent or 23.9 percent of total energy consumption. More than 62 percent of total biomass consumption are used by residential sector and more than 94 percent of total residential sector consumption are in rural area. Several agriculture residues have been used as fuels in rural industries. Most of the bagasse is used as boiler fuel in sugar mills. Rice husk is used as boiler fuel in rice mills. Palm oil wastes consisting of fibre, shells, and empty bunches are also used as boiler fuel in palm oil mills. Other agricultural residues such as straw, maize stalks, cassava stalks, coconut shells and husk also have potential as energy resources for rural areas.

The picture depicts a gasifier for rice husk and other biomass to produce energy from residues. (A biomass thermal processing project at AIT).

It is realized that some types of industrial waste waters can be utilized for biogas production. Laboratory scale tests were conducted on several types of such waters such as tapioca waste, canning food waste, and dairy waste in order to determine their potentials for this purpose. A pilot study of biogas production from pineapple waste has been successfully conducted and an industrial plant is built at a pineapple canning factory. Several breweries in Thailand now generate biogas from their wastes. Liquid wastes from sugar mills and palm oil mills are also being considered for biogas generation.

Solar and Wind Energy

Thailand is fairly well endowed with solar radiation at 17 MJ/m2 per day on the average, though about 50 percent of the global radiation appears as diffuse radiation. Equipment using direct radiation is therefore hardly economical. Solar energy has been used non-commercially in the country for centuries. Its use in salt production from sea water has been estimated to be as much as the equivalent of 20 million barrels of oil. Sun drying of about 15 million tons of paddy rice per year requires solar energy equivalent to about half a million barrels of oil. Sun drying has also been widely used for other agricultural and marine products, though there has been no official attempt to estimate the amount of non-commercial solar energy utilization.

A solar water heating industry has been established in Thailand for a decade or more, with solar collectors installed in hospitals, hotels, and private homes. Current domestic production of solar collectors is over 10,000 sq.m per year. Development of solar dryers has also been very active in the country and a few designs of free convection dryers have been commercialized with some success. Several designs of solar panel have been developed, including vertical surface solar panels, and installation of large solar panels for demonstration is being planned.

Generation of electricity by photovoltaic cells has been developed rapidly in Thailand. A large number of demonstration projects for telecommunication, lighting, and water pumping have been set up, with a combined peak output of about 400 kilowatt. Semi-conductor laboratories in two academic institutes conduct research and development on solar cell materials and fabrication. Photovoltaic modules are locally produced in two factories.

In general, the potential of wind energy in Thailand is not very promising as the average wind speed in the country is only about 2 m/s, which is rather low for economical utilization. However, high wind speeds exist in some coastal areas, and windmills have been used for water pumping in salt farms and rice fields in Samut Sakhon, Chon Buri, and other provinces. Recently, it has been shown that traditional sail-type windmills used for water pumping in salt farms are more economical than diesel-driven water pumps. Demonstrations of wind electric power systems have also been conducted.

Thailand has attempted to utilize its solar and wind energy for diverse purposes, from salt production to sophisticated photovoltaic electricity generation.

Energy Conservation

Recently the Royal Thai Government has introduced the demand side management for energy consumption. For example, the peak and off-peak electricity rates has been introduced, resulting in some energy savings. In addition, the Energy Conservation Fund has been introduced in order to promote usage of

energy efficient equipments by providing financial support to both the public and private sectors. Furthermore, the Energy Conservation Centre of Thailand has also been set up to investigate and demonstrate usage of energy efficient equipments. The Centre is also promoting energy saving habit for households and industries.

Conclusions

The energy security of the country has been achieved through development of the main domestic resources, namely natural gas, oil, and lignite. It is expected that more natural gas and lignite reserves will be identified and that dependency on imported energy will be further reduced.

Biomass will still remain the main energy resource in rural areas of Thailand for the decades. Plantation of fast-growing trees can provide an alternative source of energy and help decrease deforestation. The large potential of hydro-power from domestic and international rivers can be utilized once environmental and political constraints are removed.

Domestic lignite and imported low sulphur coal and gas appears to be the most viable alternative sources of energy for electric generation and industry, in addition to imported electricity and gas from neighbouring countries. Technologies for pollution controls on their uses are already available. Large domestic reserves of oil shale can also be utilized when the proven shale oil extraction processes become economical in the future.

Domestic resources of solar energy and biomass, especially agricultural and industrial wastes, have high potentials for utilization and viable technologies are being identified and developed. During the next decade, it may be stated with confidence that Thailand will have adequate energy supply for the development of the country.

AGRICULTURE

Prior to 60 years ago, the Thai agriculture was traditionally under the feudal system growing rice as the staple food of the economy. During the mid 1930s agriculture was then opened up to a trade system. This was a pre-development stage of the agriculture sector in Thailand. It followed that, after the First-Five-Year National Economic and Social Development Plan being launched (1961-1966), the agriculture sector diversified its production into economic crops, fruit and tree crops, livestock and fisheries. Over 30 years of national development, six development plans have been implemented with a development priority given to agriculture.

The agriculture sector has an important role in contribution to growth of the economy since the historical time. It has been a major source of food supply, farm workforce and employment generation, national income and foreign exchange earnings. However, as the non-farm sector, namely industry, has been growing at a rapid rate during the past decade, agriculture has gradually declined its importance to the share of economic growth. Despite this, agriculture remains its vital role in ensuring national food security, as well as being the basic source of labour force to facilitate growth of the non-farm sectors, particularly the agro-industry.

Agricultural Development

During the past three decades of national economic and social development in Thailand, six national development plans have been implemented. The GDP of the agriculture sector increased from 23,111 million baht in 1961 to 284,489 million at constant prices in 1991, a forty time increase. Nevertheless, the share of GDP by agriculture compared to the total GDP of the whole economy declined from 39.19% in 1961 to 12.43% in 1991, an approximate 16% decrease. This was due to a decrease in crop production, the largest component of GDP in agriculture.

In terms of growth, the agriculture growth has shown a declining trend at the rate of 7.6%, 4.2% and 2.5% in the First, Second and Third, and the Sixth Plans respectively. For the Seventh Plan (1992-1996), the agriculture growth rate is targeted to be 3.4% per annum.

Agricultural Resources

Land

Thailand has the total area of about 320.7 million rai, of which about 65% is engaged in agriculture. In 1988, about 148 million rai were agricultural land, of which about 74.19 million rai were paddy land, 32.72 million rai growing upland crops, and 19.53 million rai for fruit and tree crops. Over the past three decades, land use in agriculture was tremendously increased through deforestation. Despite farmland expansion, land productivity remains stagnant and declines, whereas land quality has been rapidly deteriorated. In addition, the existing agricultural land has been partly shifted to non-farm use in response to urbanization and expanding industrial zones. Land development policy, therefore, puts emphasis on accelerating land reform, improving productivity, and conservation.

Water Resources

Water Resources in Thailand are obtained from two main sources : surface water and ground water. These include rainfall, river basin, lakes, canals, swamps, irrigation water, and underground water. Among all, rainfall is the most important water source for agriculture as about 80% of agricultural areas are under rainfed condition. Thailand receives rainfall at an average volume of some 752 billion cubic metres annually. The most important and the largest river basin in Thailand is the Chao Phraya Basin covering nearly all the areas in the northern and central regions. Groundwater resources exist throughout the country but their quantity and quality vary according to local hydrogeological conditions. Water resource development began over 700 years ago. It was during the reign of King Rama V, however, that water resource development activities such as building canals for cropping and waterway transportation in the central region were more clearly apparent. Later on, several large-scale irrigation projects were constructed by the Royal Irrigation Department (RID) and the Electricity Generating Authority of Thailand (EGAT). It was not until the Fourth and the Fifth National Economic and Social Development Plans that small-scale projects were emphasized. At present, the most developed irrigation systems are found in the Central Plain. Nevertheless, due to economic growth and hence, increasing demand for water resources, there remain important issues in relation to water resource development: the maintenance of irrigation systems; the efficient use and optimal allocation of existing water.

Fishery Resources

Fishery Resources in Thailand are harvested from the Gulf of Thailand, the Andaman Sea, rivers, lakes, streams, canals and reservoirs. The harvest includes fish, crustaceans, molluscs and other marine fauna and flora. Fishery resources can be divided into three groups : fresh water fishery resources, brackish water fishery resources, and marine fishery resources. During the past three decades the country's marine fisheries have been rapidly developed, contributing to an average output of some 2 million tons. This has placed Thailand to the top ten marine fishery product producing countries worldwide.

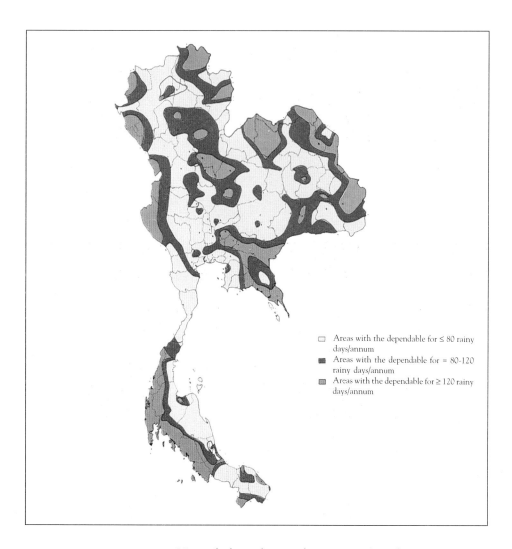

Areas with the dependable for ≤ 80 rainy days/annum

Areas with the dependable for = 80-120 rainy days/annum

Areas with the dependable for ≥ 120 rainy days/annum

Map showing Areas with Dependable Precipitation (with the amount ≥ 10 mm.).

Nevertheless, the proclaimation of Exclusive Economic Zone (EEZ) by neighbouring countries in 1980 has resulted in loosing about 800,000 square kilometres of Thai fishing grounds as well as bringing about frequent fishing conflicts. To resolve the problems, the Thai government has promoted the joint-fishing ventures with other coastal states in recent years.

Forest

Forest resources in Thailand can be classified into five types: evergreen forest, mixed deciduous forest, dry dipterocarp forest, pine forest, and mangrove forest. Of these, the dominant type of evergreen forest is tropical rain forest covering 43% of total forest area. Its concentration lies in the highest rainfall zone, i.e. in the southeast, east coasts, and along the peninsula. Over the past three decades, Thailand's once abundant forests were excessively utilized through illegal logging, land encroachment and shifting agriculture. As a consequence, the country's forest area was reduced from 273,628 square kilometres (53% of total area) in 1961 to 143,417 square kilometres (28% of total area) in 1989, a 47.58% decrease during the 28-year period. Forest destruction also led to disaster consequencies as withered by the flood and land-sliding in southern Thailand. This forced the Thai government to ban forest concession nationwide. The national forest policy target has been set in the current Seventh Development Plan (1992-1996) to devote 25% of land area as conserved forest land, and to manage 15% of land for economic forests in order to maintain the country's forest land of 40% of total area.

At present the Royal Thai government is implementing at least 2 major reforestation projects.

(1) Royal Forestry Department's project to reforest 160,000 rai a year (64,000 acres) in FY 2536-FY 2537 utilizing the government budget.

(2) The reforestation of 5 million rai (2 million acres) to honour the king's 50 years of reign in 1996, to be supported by both the public sector and private sector. Many major Thai companies already accord their supports to the project. The project will last for 3 years from 1994-1996.

Target (Million Rai)

FY 2537 (1994)	1.5
FY 2538 (1995)	1.5
FY 2539 (1996)	2.0
Total	**5.0**

The reforestation will protect water resources and soil erosion. Furthermore, since 1989, there is a complete ban on logging of natural forests.

Farmers' Socio-economics

Most of Thailand's population is located in the countryside. Agriculture population accounts for 35.85 million in 1991, or 62% of the total population in the country. Agricultural active labour force is taken by 19.48 million in the same year, or approximately 67% of the total labour force.

Between the First and the Fifth Plans, agricultural population and the number of farm families were steadily increased at a slower rate. A typical Thai farm family consists of 5 persons and extends beyond the nucleus of parents and their offspring to include grandparents, cousins, or other relatives. Within the household, 67% of the total family members devotes to active labour force, the remaining is elderly and young members. About 50% of the active labour engages in farming and employs off-farm income during the off season. Most of the family members finish their compulsory education only up to the 6th grade.

Agricultural Technology

It was inevitable that Thai development in agricultural technology was initiated from the rice monoculture which was the cornerstone of the Thai economy. During the reign of King Rama V, the first rice cultivars contest was originated in 1907 at Thanyaburi.

Continually selective sustenance assured the seed technology improvement. Fifty years later, plant breeders rendered more science and technology to develop plant breeds. Bio-genetic engineering has also played the most vital role in breeding in the recent years. The subsequent development of breeding stocks and fisheries has been conducted with great success. Of all livestock raised for the market, cross and pure bred chickens and artificial insemination have been applied since 1939. Likewise, other indigenous breeds of livestock have been improved through the embryo transferring technique, as well as the stimulating of tiger prawn production by eye-ablated technique.

Moreover, several important factors for agricultural development, namely:chemical fertilizers, pesticides, and agricultural equipments and tools, have contributed to the nation's reputation as one of the largest food exporter in the world. The evidence is witnessed by the increase use of imported fertilizers, although the application rate is relatively lower than the neighbouring countries. Notwithstanding the on-farm crises on labour shortages and pest infestation, large volumes of labour saving tools and agro-chemicals are added to farm activities. This can be showed by the growth rate of agricultural machinery procured by the farmers, which was 5.80-23.37% per annum during 1978-1987, according to the types and as high as 10.31% growth for agro-chemical use during the period of 1973-1988.

Crop Components

Rice

Rice is the most important food crop grown in all regions of Thailand. Over 50% of the Thai farmland is devoted to rice, yielding about 20 million tons of paddy annually. About 60% of rice is for domestic consumption as staple food and the rest is for export accounting for about 20% of total agricultural export earnings. Currently, Thai rice exports to more than 100 countries and takes the lead in the world market sharing 40% of the volume.

Maize

Maize is the important feed grain concentrated in the north, the northeast, and the central regions of Thailand. More than two-third of the annual production is absorbed domestically by the feed industries and the rest is exported by taking the account of 7% of world market share. Maize exports contribute substantial foreign exchange earning to the country. In recent years, rapid expansion of the livestock industry has triggered the demand for maize and begun to curtail grain export availability.

Sorghum

Sorghum, a relatively minor coarse grain, grows in the North and the Northeast which account for 45-50% of the planted area. In the past, sorghum was produced primarily for export. In recent years an expansion of the livestock industry has given rise to domestic demand for sorghum, accounting for 90% of total sorghum production.

Basmati

Basmati, a high-priced-scented rice crop, has been introduced into Thailand since 1973. The current area of concentration of Basmati is in the North. Basmati rice for export has been currently promoted under the Public-Private Coordination for Agriculture and Agro-industrial Development Programme. Major exporting markets for Thai Basmati rice are the Arabian countries. Thai Basmati exports account for 2% of the world market share.

Cassava

Cassava, a drought-tolerant cash crop, contributes major income to farmers in the Northeast. Cassava products are mainly exported as animal feed to the EC market, the largest buyer. Cassava roots are processed in the forms of chips, pellets, flour and starch, and sago. About 90% of cassava products for export is in the form of pellets. However, since 1983, cassava exports to the EC have been restricted under the voluntary export restrained agreements. Despite this, there have been rising demands for cassava exports outside the EC market in recent years. The current cassava development emphasizes variety improvement rather than planted area expansion.

Mung bean

Mung bean is concentrated in the lower north, the central and the northeastern parts of Thailand. Mung bean is mainly grown for export to Japan, India, China, the United Kingdom, and the Saudi Arabia.

Sugarcane

Sugarcane, the essential raw material for the sugar mills is concentrated in the central region accounting for over 50% of both planted area and production. About one-third of the annual production is consumed domestically and the rest is exported in the forms of raw and refined sugars. Thailand ranks the third of the world's largest sugar exporters.

Cotton

Cotton, fibre cash crop concentrated in the north and the central regions, has increased its importance as the raw material for the expanding textile industry in Thailand. Despite the recent increases in market demand for cotton, cotton production is still relatively low due to the lack of improved seed varieties, the high production cost, and the unstable cotton price. To meet the expansion of the textile industry, part of cotton deficit has been made annually through imports.

Kenaf

Kenaf, fibre crop important to the northeast farmers, is used as raw material for gunny-bag industry. Most of the kenaf output is consumed domestically and some for exports. The recent production and planted area of kenaf show a decreasing trend as there is an increase in the use of synthetic fibre substitutes.

Sericulture

Sericulture has been practised in Thailand for more than 90 years. Nevertheless, raw silk production remains relatively low despite the increasing demand particularly from overseas for Thai silk fabric and products in recent years. Low silk production is due to the short-comings of improved strain of silkworm eggs and the less developed sericulture. It, hence, gives rise to import demand for raw silk.

Soybean

Soybean is mainly grown in the north and the northeast regions. Domestic consumption of soybean increases annually due to the expansion of livestock and animal feed industries. As local production of soybean is not sufficient to supply the rising demand, soybean cake is usually imported from China and India.

Groundnut

Groundnut, mainly grown in the North, and the Northeast, is mostly consumed domestically. Only 10% of annual output is exported. However, Thailand also imports sizable groundnut cake as raw material for the domestic feed industry.

Oil palm

Oil palm is widely grown in the south of Thailand, with current total planted area of 0.8 million rai and annual fresh fruit bunch production of 1.5 million tons. The palm oil is mainly for domestic consumption.

Rubber

Rubber planting, originated in the South, has been currently expanded to the Northeast and the East.

Rubber production in Thailand has been well developed through improved varieties. In 1991, Thai rubber output reached the highest of the world record. Major export markets for Thai rubber consist of Japan, USA and China.

Coffee

Coffee, Robusta variety, is widely grown as a cash crop in the South. Planted area of coffee tends to increase as the crop yields a high income to farmers. Coffee exports steadily increase annually, however, export value may fluctuate depending upon the world production and trade.

Cocoa

Cocoa is a new cash crop which has a good marketing potential. Although cocoa production has been currently promoted by the Government, cocoa import tends to increase annually to meet domestic consumption demanded by the two cocoa processing plants.

Cashew

Cashew planting, originally concentrated in the South, has been expanded into the northeast region under the Crops Diversification Programme promoted by the Minsitry of Agriculture and Cooperatives. Cashew nut exports are in the forms of unshelled nuts to Asian countries, contributing substantial foreign exchange earnings each year.

Longan

Longan, a fruit crop, has been grown in Thailand over 100 years with area of concentration in the North. About 80% of the fruit production is consumed domestically as fresh longan and the rest is exported as fresh and canned longan.

Lichee

Lichee, a fruit crop grown in Thailand over the same period as of longan, has its major producing areas in the North. The famous varieties are *Hong-huai*,

Ohia, and *Kim Cheng*. Thailand exports fresh and canned lichee to Hong Kong, Malaysia, Singapore and the United States.

Grape

Grape has its suitable growning location in the West with area of concentration in Ratchaburi province. Most of grape produced is consumed domestically with a small quantity for export as fresh and canned fruit. Thailand exports fresh grape to Malaysia and raisin (dry grape) to Singapore.

Mango

Mango is grown in all regions but area of concentration is in the Northeast. At present, mango production has greatly been developed through improved varieties to meet the consumers taste and preference. Overseas demand for Thai mango has steadily increased both in the forms of fresh and canned fruit.

Mangosteen

Mangosteen, queen of the fruits, is limited to the South and the East due to the suitability of climatic conditions. Its production is mainly for domestic consumption. Mangosteen is also exported as fresh and frozen fruit to Hong Kong and Japan.

Tangerine

Tangerine, a famous citrous crop, has its area of concentration in the central part of Thailand. The most famous and tasteful variety of tangerine is grown in Bang Mot district, the suburban Bangkok Metropolitan area. Nowadays, tangerine is grown more at Rangsit in Pathum Thani Province, north of Bangkok. Tangerine is mainly consumed domestically, whereas a minor amount exported to Laos and Malaysia.

Durian

Durian has its reputation as king of the fruits grown in Thailand for over a century ago. The original area of famous durian was in Nonthaburi Province, close to Bangkok. Nowadays, the major durian producing areas concentrate in the east region. The popular varieties are *Mon Thong*, *Chani*, and *Kan Yao*. Durian exports as fresh and frozen fruits to Malaysia and the United States.

Pineapple

The major pineapple producing area is located mostly in the central region where processing plants were centred around. Currently, Thailand becomes the world's leading fresh pineapple producer and canned pineapple exporter. Pineapples for exports are processed into canned, juice, frozen, dehydrated, and paste products.

Pomelo

Pomelo, a citrous fruit, is generally favourite to consumers for its taste and high nutritional value. Pomelo has good market potential since the fruit is of low perishability and thus, allowing for distant transport to overseas consumers. To increase export competitiveness, however, more research and development are aimed to variety improvement and pest resistance.

Asparagus

Asparagus has been introduced to farmers since 1973 under the Royal Initiative Project implemented in Hup Kraphong Cooperatives, Petchaburi Province in the central region. Production and marketing potentials of asparagus have been rapidly developed for export as fresh and canned vegetable.

Baby Corn

Baby corn is consumed domestically and also exported as fresh and canned vegetables. Its major producing areas are in the Central, the North and some provinces in the Northeast. The export competitiveness of Thai baby corn could be increased through improving product quality.

Sweet Bamboo

Sweet bamboo was introduced to Thai farmers over 80 years ago. About 60% of bamboo shoot production goes to processing plants for export to Japan, Singapore, Hong Kong and European countries.

Tomato

Tomato is widely grown in all regions but concentrated in the central and northeastern regions. In addition to be consumed as fresh fruit, tomatoes can be processed for export in the forms of canned fruit, concentrated juice, sugar preserved and dried fruit, earning export incomes for over a billion baht annually.

Pepper

Pepper has its major producing area in Chanthaburi Province of the eastern region, accounting for 80% of the total area planted. Thailand exports ground and whole peppers to the United States, the Netherlands, Germany, and Singapore. Export price of pepper varies, however, depending upon the world situation.

Cut Flowers and Ornamental plants

Cut flowers and ornamental plants have increased their roles both as commodities for export, and import substitutes. Today domestic demands for cut flowers and ornamental plants quickly gain popularity due to an expansion of the hotels and condomeniums. Major cut flowers for exports consist of orchids, roses, chrysanthemum, and gerbera, etc. Exports of orchids, in particular, contribute about 90% of the total export value of Thai cut flowers and ornamental plants annually.

Livestock Component

Cattle

Cattle are raised primarily for draught with meat production as a by-product. Most of farm family own a small herd, either water-buffalo or cattle, using low-cost production technology based on open access resources such as agricultural residues and farm labour. The major animal herding areas are in the Northeast. In recent years, there have been increasing imports of live cattle for breeding. Cattle product imports are also increased in response to an expansion of the leather industry.

Dairy Cow

Dairy Cow is mainly raised for milk production. The commercial production of dairy cow in Thailand began after the establishment of the dairy farm and herd training centre granted by the Danish Government in 1962. Dairy production was then developed through the subsequent establishment of the Dairy Farming Promotion Organization of Thailand, a state-own enterprise under the Ministry of Agriculture and Cooperatives in 1971. The present major dairy cow raising areas are Saraburi, Ratchaburi, Nakhon Pathom, Chiang Mai. About 49% of milk production is processed for ready-to-drink fresh milk, and the rest for recombined milk. Currently, milk production is insufficient to meet the rising demand generated by population growth and better standard of living. Dairy products, particularly in the form of milk powder, are thus imported. As for exports, Thailand exports only a small quantity of milk products to neighbouring countries such as Singapore, Laos, and Myanmar.

Swine

The largest swine production area is the Central Plain, accounting for about 36-40% of the total production. This area consists of provinces around Bangkok such as, Nakhon Pathom, Ratchaburi and Chachoengsao. The Northern ranks second, accounting for 26-30% of the total production. Commercial production of swine in Thailand has developed slowly due to the instability in the market price of pigs, feed costs, and government regulations. Most production is consumed domestically through meat processing which consists of two types : (1) a varieties of traditional meat products such as Chinese sausages, roasted pork, etc. (2) continental meat products such as ham, bacon and baloney. A small number of live pigs and frozen piglets are exported to Hong Kong and Singapore.

Poultry

The poultry production consists of broiler, hen-layer, and duck-layer. Among these, the broiler industry has experienced a rapid expansion through the

increase in the number of commercial farms during the past decade.

The major zone of broiler production is in the Central Plain where more than 35% of all broilers are raised. The largest chicken-raising provinces are Chacheongsao, Nakhon Pathom, and Chon Buri. Chicken farms can be classified into three types : (a) backyard farms in which most variety raised are native chickens, (b) independent commercial farms of which growers employ modern farm management to grow their broilers and do their own marketing, (c) contract farms of various types such as price guarantees, hire-to-grow (wage) contracts and open-account contracts. In addition to be domestically marketed, chicken meat in the forms of part and frozen one is also exported to Japan, which accounts for Thailand's largest market share.

Native duck has long been raised in Thailand for meat and egg consumption. The major raising duck areas are located in Chachoengsao, Chon Buri, Nakhon Pathom, Suphan Buri and Ratchaburi of the central region. Due to growing domestic demand, the Department of Livestock Development has introduced, in particular, the breeds with high feed conversion from abroad emphasized on commercial duck farms. Since then export market opportunity has opened to Thai frozen duck meat and egg, although the value has considered relatively insignificant. The overseas markets include Hong Kong, Singapore, Japan and Germany.

Fishery and Product Components

Shrimp and Prawn

Shrimp and prawn are major export commodities contributing to a large amount of foreign exchange earnings annually. Shrimp and prawn exports are processed into chilled, frozen, dried, boiled, and canned products. Thailand's important markets of frozen shrimp and prawn are Japan, the United States, Singapore and France.

Squid

Squid, a marine product, ranks the second to shrimp and prawn. Squid products processed into frozen and dried squid contribute to considerable export earnings. Major importers of Thai squid are Japan, Italy, France and Switzerland.

Fishmeal

Fishmeal, an essential source of protein, is processed mainly from trash fish. Most fishmeal production is consumed domestically. Domestic demand for high quality fishmeal has been rapidly increased in response to the expansion of livestock and shrimp farmings. Part of the high grade fishmeal requirement can be met by imports.

Canned Tuna

Canned Tuna accounts for the most important marine product export item contributing to export value of 10 billion baht each year. Production of canned tuna in Thailand has steadily expanded in response to the increasing overseas demand. At present, there have been 22 fish canning plants in Thailand. Canned tuna exports to the United States, the United Kingdom, Germany and Canada.

Source: *Agriculture in Thailand*, Ministry of Agriculture and Cooperatives, 1992.

Their Majesties the King and Queen during a visit to preside over the Opening Ceremony of "BOI FAIR'95" at Laem Chabang Deep Seaport, Si Racha District, Chon Buri Province.

MANUFACTURING

Development and Diversification

Traditionally, Thailand's economy has been based on agriculture. It is only relatively recently that the manufacturing sector has begun to play a significant role.

This transformation, over the last 30 years, has been dramatic. The agricultural share of the Gross Domestic Product (GDP) has declined steadily from 40 percent in 1960 to 11.2 percent in 1994. At the same time, the manufacturing sector has expanded rapidly, with its share of GDP increasing from 13 percent in 1960 to 42 percent in 1994. The sector employs more than 3 million people, over 10 percent of the entire labour force. While manufacturing is increasing in regional areas, industrial activities are still highly concentrated in the central region.

The industrial sector grew at an average rate of 9.5 percent per year during the 1970s. Its share of GDP increased from 15.9 percent in 1970 to 22 percent in 1979 and production of manufactured goods continued to increase and diversify. By 1980, these developments had changed the structure of Thailand's manufacturing sector. The relative importance of processing industries had diminished in favour of labour-intensive exports (which had risen to 11 percent) and intermediate and capital goods.

Through 1982, the contribution of manufacturing to GDP was still slightly below that of the agricultural sector. However, since 1983, the contribution of manufacturing to the GDP has exceeded that of the agricultural sector. By the latter part of 1980s, especially since 1987, manufactured products increased dramatically to become the leading sector of the Thai economy. The growth of manufactured products reached 12.6 percent in 1987.

Since 1990, the industrial sector has undergone a rapid diversification process. Industrial production was more evenly spread between a number of sectors, including consumer goods, component parts, and intermediate capital goods. Other growth industries include computers, automotive and autoparts,

An assembly line producing magnetic parts for floppy disc drivers.

electronics, heavy industries and huge projects in steel, petrochemicals, and communications. There is an increasing number of industrial products, with new entrants seen every year as the economy adjusts its production structure to take advantage of new opportunities.

The electronics industry produces high-quality goods.

In 1993 and 1994, both domestic and export production of manufactured goods showed strong growth, with total manufacturing output expanding by more than 11 percent each year. Domestically, strong growth occurred in beverages, tobacco, and construciton materials.

Further growth in manufacturing is expected in the late 1990's, with the expected brisk recovery in the major industrialized countries coupled with sharp rises in domestic consumption, and the favourable investment climate in Thailand. Some adjustment in the structure of manufacturing output is expected in the 90's in favour of higher technology and higher value-added products, such as those in the electrical and electronics sectors. Projects involving very high technology, bringing with them huge investment, such as the wafer project (electronic parts), pig iron project, and copper cutthroat project will be on stream.

Capacity Utilization of the Manufacturing Sector

Since 1990, the manufacturing sector has expanded annually at an average of 13.3 percent. A survey of 1994 capacity utilization covering 40 types of manufacturing industry (representing about 39 percent of total manufacturing activity), indicates an upward trend in capacity utilization from 76.1 percent to 78.7 percent of full capacity. The increase reflects production expansion to meet the increase in domestic demand and exports.

Comparing the current situation with the situation in 1990, when the rate of capacity utilization reached 84 percent, and the cement industry operated at 100 percent capacity, this year's high level of capacity utilization is not expected to exert significant pressure on domestic prices, provided economic growth in 1995 does not exceed the projected 8.5 percent. Consumer goods, steel products, vehicles, plastic pellets and electrical

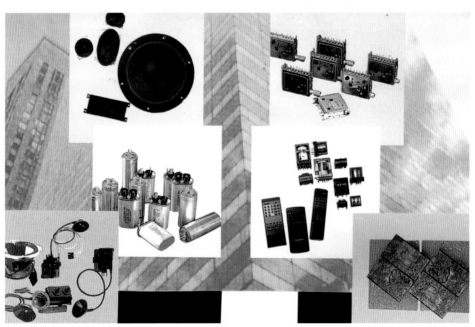

appliances still have excess capacity due to recent investment expansion.

Workers canning pineapples, one of several processed fruits and vegetables.

Exports and Imports of Manufacturing Goods

Thailand has moved from being heavily dependent upon the export of agricultural commodities (less than 3 percent of exports being manufactured products) in 1960, to its current position, where over 80 percent of its exports are manufactured goods, and the export sector is the principal engine of growth for the Thai economy.

Thailand's exports have experienced double-digit annual growth due to the dynamism of the sector itself, combined with consistent government policies promoting free trade and fair competition. These policies have paid off.

Thailand's present export structure reveals a greater diversity (in terms of both products and markets) than most of her competitors, including the East Asian dragons. Thailand is the world's largest source of precision ball bearings, for example, and will soon become Honda's largest production base for worldwide export. In agricultural products, Thailand is the world largest exporter of frozen shrimp, canned seafood, tapioca and canned pineapple. The top twenty export items include a growing number of industrial products and new entrants are seen every year.

Throughout the late 1980s and early 1990s, Thailand's exports have increasingly included electrical products, integrated circuits, and computers and their components. In 1990, electrical consumer goods registered growth of over 54 percent, while computers and components grew by more than 44 percent.

In 1993, manufactured exports (which accounted for over 80 percent of total export value) expanded at a 17.7 percent to 747 billion baht, an increase of 17.7 percent from the previous year.

In 1994, exports grew faster than anticipated, with export earnings exceeding 1,000 billion baht, claiming a market share of more than 1 percent of the world's exports for the first time. The growth rate of around 19 percent was observed in all categories. Manufacturing and fishery exports, in particular, grew by 20 percent and the continued development of the production efficiency for new manufactured items was evidenced by an exceptional increase in exports of products requiring high technology, such as vehicles and parts, electrical appliances and computers and computer parts.

The United States continued to be Thailand's largest market, with overall exports growing more than 9 percent. More than 80 percent of exports to the United States were manufactured products, and major items which recorded significant increase were textiles, computer parts and components, electrical circuit breakers, integrated circuits and parts. The second most important export market was Japan. Over 60 percent of exports to Japan were manufactured products, with major exports being electrical appliances, furniture and parts, electrical circuit breakers and integrated circuits. Export to ASEAN countries expanded at more than 30 percent in 1993.

Exports of Major Items

	1992			1993 (million baht)		
	Volume	Value	Growth	Volume	Value	Growth
1. Manufactured Products	-	634,390	14.7%	-	752,557	18.6%
Garments	-	86,688	0.0%	-	89,529	3.3%
Computers and parts	-	55,384	19.3%	-	62,744	13.3%
Electrical appliances	-	42,908	22.5%	-	62,634	46.0%
Precious stones and jewellery	-	36,582	1.9%	-	41,030	12.2%
Plastic products	-	15,272	17.9%	-	39,453	158.3%
Integrated circuits	-	28,619	11.1%	-	35,550	24.2%
Footwear	-	25,639	7.7%	-	27,936	9.0%
Base metal products	-	15,523	5.0%	-	19,261	24.1%
Fabrics	-	17,540	12.8%	-	18,601	6.0%
Televisions and radios	-	17,448	38.8%	-	18,488	6.0%
Furniture and parts	-	15,069	10.6%	-	16,738	11.1%
Canned fish	309,973	16,275	-13.6%	317,938	16,658	2.4%
Vehicle parts and accessories	-	8,730	26.8%	-	13,227	51.5%
Sugar	3,757,348	18,290	28.0%	2,218,986	12,185	-33.4%
Canned crustaceans	63,127	10,339	21.3%	61,424	11,436	10.6%
Rubber products	-	9,151	28.6%	-	11,373	24.3%
Telecommunications	-	7,266	-0.8%	-	9,646	32.8%
Travel goods	-	7,782	14.4%	-	8,974	15.3%
Spinning	-	7,613	3.9%	-	8,542	12.2%
Toys, games	-	8,780	12.6%	-	7,928	-9.7%
Clocks, watches and parts	-	8,533	12.9%	-	7,266	-14.8%
Canned pineapple	491,368	8,274	13.9%	502,835	7,190	-13.1%
Others	-	168,473	26.8%	-	206,168	22.4%
2. Agricultural Products	-	123,810	13.3%	-	110,695	-10.6%
Rice	4,899,387	36,214	18.7%	4,778,404	32,947	-9.0%
Rubber	9,104,522	29,611	21.5%	7,342,150	29,180	-26.6%
Tapioca products	1,463,599	28,925	15.9%	1,492,795	21,736	0.9%
Frozen fowl	180,242	10,830	2.8%	163,274	9,294	-14.2%
Others	-	18,230	-3.5%	-	17,528	-3.9%
3. Fishery Products	-	48,793	11.6%	-	55,689	14.1%
Shrimp, fresh and frozen	140,435	31,696	18.8%	148,886	37,843	19.4%
Fish, fresh and frozen	291,918	8,072	-0.8%	281,584	8,195	1.5%
Others	-	9,025	1.6%	-	9,651	6.9%
4. Others	-	17,655	-9.3%	-	16,921	-4.2%
5. Total Exports	-	824,644	13.6%	-	935,862	13.5%

Notes: Volumes in metric tons: values in million baht
Sources: Bank of Thailand: Customs Department

On the import side, the rapid growth of the manufacturing sector has created a large demand for a growing range of intermediate goods. Thailand currently imports large quantities of capital goods, raw materials, and intermediate goods each year. From 1988, when total imports reached about 501.4 billion baht, (a record increase of 46.6 percent), imports have seen consistent growth reaching 1,337 billion baht in 1994.

The value of imported capital goods increased substantially throughout the late 1980s. The import values of raw materials and intermediate goods increased by 50.1 percent, with prices rising by 24 percent and volume increasing by 21 percent. Import values of basic metals grew by 75 percent, with imports of iron and steel rising by 72 percent. Imports of raw materials used in the production of consumer goods also increased significantly. Import values of chemicals grew by 34.5 percent and precious stone imports jumped by 74 percent.

In 1992, the value of exports registered substantial growth to approximately 824 billion baht, and the value of imports also rose considerably to about 1,033 billion baht. In line with the buoyant expansion in economic

activities, imports in 1994 rose by 17 percent, with a volume growth of 15.6 percent.

Reflecting the acceleration in domestic expenditure, the imports of capital goods and consumer goods increased markedly, while the import of raw materials and semifinished products grew in line with the expansion of manufactured exports. Other imports, particularly fully-assembled automobiles and parts, moderated after rapid growth in 1993.

Due to the rapid growth of exports relative to imports, the trade deficit rose slightly to 240.5 billion baht but declined as a proportion of GDP for the fourth consecutive year to 6.7 percent; Thailand's trade deficit is due primarily to the import of capital goods and raw materials used for investment and increasing the country's production capacity in the future. However, recognizing this dependence on foreign supplies, the government encourages investment in capital goods and intermediate products which add value to the basic raw materials that are exported. Throughout the 1990s, export-oriented business will continue to display strong performance and increasing sophistication.

Imports by Economic Classification

million baht

	1980	1990	1991	1992	1993
Capital Goods	46,075	327,684	385,493	426,035	501,086
(share in total imports)	24.4%	38.8%	40.2%	41.2%	43.0%
Machinery and parts	31,608	254,230	303,395	312,948	382,746
Nonelectrical	20,402	153,629	186,560	184,898	213,084
Electrical	11,206	100,601	116,835	128,050	169,662
Metal manufactures	3,142	17,054	21,074	24,683	29,420
Fertilizers and pesticides	4,225	14,352	13,139	15,863	16,738
Scientific and optical instruments	2,290	16,088	20,781	23,015	26,925
Construction materials	1,612	545	618	873	891
Other	3,198	25,415	26,486	48,653	44,366
Intermediate Products and Raw Materials	45,312	285,044	329,592	331,327	349,398
Chiefly for consumer goods	28,182	191,818	231,736	223,250	231,398
(share in total imports)	14.9%	22.7%	24.2%	21.6%	19.8%
Chemicals	14,962	65,345	68,627	80,876	88,007
Textile fibre	3,175	15,715	18,787	17,943	14,607
Paper and paperboard	2,114	9,273	10,983	12,977	14,862
Tobacco leaves	1,019	1,431	1,261	1,309	1,296
Textile yarn and thread	786	7,669	8,291	9,497	10,050
Other	6,126	92,385	123,787	100,648	102,576
Chiefly for capital goods	17,130	93,226	97,856	108,077	118,000
(share in total imports)	9.1%	11.0%	10.2%	10.5%	10.1%
Iron and steel	10,335	65,381	71,870	79,483	80,662
Other base metals	5,900	25,054	21,403	23,784	30,243
Other	895	2,791	4,583	4,810	7,095
Consumer Goods	19,286	71,672	82,774	103,651	114,421
(share in total imports)	10.2%	8.5%	8.6%	10.0%	9.8%
Nondurable goods	12,257	31,829	36,163	45,207	48,848
Food and beverages	6,182	16,977	19,322	24,458	26,293
Clothing and footwear	3,037	5,868	6,359	7,490	7,945
Medicinal and pharmaceutical product	2,130	5,316	6,253	8,062	8,357
Other	908	3,668	4,229	5,197	6,253
Durable goods	7,029	39,843	46,611	58,444	65,573
Household goods	2,266	12,476	15,127	19,475	21,784
Electrical appliances	2,887	21,732	24,599	30,689	34,143
Cycles, motorcycles, carts	931	3,380	4,201	4,883	6,230
Other	945	2,255	2,684	3,397	3,416
Other Imports	78,013	160,048	160,973	172,229	201,687
(share in total imports)	41.3%	19.0%	16.8%	16.7%	17.3%
Fuels and lubricants	58,733	78,346	87,662	83,758	86,457
Vehicles and parts	6,912	55,722	47,288	58,363	82,658
Other	12,368	25,980	26,023	30,108	32,572
Total Imports	188,686	844,448	958,832	1,033,242	1,166,592
Merchandise imports (C.I.F.)	190,025	832,604	963,879	1,015,496	1,137,064

Sources: Bank of Thailand

Government Policies Pertaining to the Manufacturing Sector

Over the past 35 years, the government has prepared seven National Economic and Social Development Plans. The broad policy directions of the Thai government have been laid out in these and evaluation of the specific policies towards industrialization been made according to the economic situation. The plans have increasingly reflected the importance of industrial development in the overall development of the country.

For over three decades, successive governments have consistently held to two basic policies, which can be traced back to the earliest industrial development efforts of the government. The first of these policies was that the private sector would be the motivating force behind industrial development and that the government would not make industrial investments which were in competition with the private sector. The second was that the state would provide support to industry in the form of physical infrastructure, technological resources and manpower development.

These basic policies are found in each of the national development plans and confirm the commitment of the government to a mixed economy. The major changes in the government's orientation towards industrial development involve the direction of the development, the structure of the sector and the role of industry in the overall economy.

One of the main objectives of the Seventh Economic and Social Development Plan (1992-1996) was to maintain economic growth rates at levels that would ensure sustainable growth and stability. The industrial sector, targeted to grow at 9.5 percent per year, is driven by growth in the petrochemical, engineering, electronics and basic industries. This should occur as a result of the continuing trend of Japan and the East Asian newly industrialized countries (NICs) to relocate their industrial bases to this region to take advantage of competitive labour costs, and opportunities to reap the benefits of Thailand's increasing domestic purchasing power.

The annual growth rate targets under the Seventh Plan in percent are:

- GDP growth: 8.2
- Industrial growth: 9.5
- Export growth: 14.7
- Private investment growth: 8.8

Economic policy-making during the Seventh Plan has been based on the conviction that liberalization is the key to enhancing the competitiveness of the Thai economy. Industrial policies are designed to encourage competition, reduce restrictions on the private sector, and transform the government's role from one of control to one of support and supervision.

In an increasingly competitive international environment, Thailand can sustain its growth potential only by competing successfully in the world market. In this respect, it is the government policy to create an environment conductive for private businesses, to invest and upgrade production to higher level, and to use higher production technology to enable the industries to compete successfully in new products.

To accomplish this, the government has launched measures to reduce the cost of raw materials, lower labour costs, increase the supply of skilled labour, and upgrade production standards to international levels. Other areas which have become increasingly important to industrial policy-making in the 90's include environmental protecting, R & D, and the supporting industries. Measures have been established to speed up supporting industry development in areas which help upgrade technology, increase the industrial capability of the country and encourage industry to grow and develop efficiently.

Growth in manufacturing will also be supported by government efforts to develop trade and investment with the countries of Indochina: Lao PDR, Cambodia, and Vietnam, as well as Myanmar and southern region of the People's Republic of China. As they develop, these countries will demand manufactured goods, such as basic construction materials and consumer goods.

Open Investment Policy

Since the end of 1986, Thailand has been a favourite location for foreign firms escaping appreciating currencies and escalating labour costs. The flow of foreign firms has been matched by local investors who, stimulated by lower interest rates and a booming economy, have also increased investment activities.

Manufacturing has been the longest recipient of FDI. Despite a decline in other sectors, FDI in manufacturing continues to expand, with the petroleum sector attracting the largest amount of FDI.

The government continues to take a very positive stance towards foreign direct investment in the manufacturing sector. The Thai government has consistently welcomed foreign investment, recognizing the important role played by foreign technology, management and marketing skills as dynamic forces contributing to Thailand's economic development. Investment is encouraged whether from domestic sources or abroad. The emphasis is on increasing the role of the private sector in Thailand's economic development.

Since 1990, the government has been exploring a variety of measures to promote the supporting industries. Sub-contracting activities are actively encouraged and a special incentive package has been implemented to promote their development to facilitate the growth of the electronics and other industries. As a result, Thailand's supporting industries have grown rapidly in the past five years.

The private sector has played (and will continue to play) a crucial role in the industrial development of Thailand, while the government has played a promotional role to construct and create the physical and institutional infrastructure and to design measures to support the growth in the industrial sector. However, the private sector needs to join with the government to

co-operate in solving economic problems and tackling development problems.

Consequently, the Joint Public-Private Sector Consultative Committee was set up in 1981 to mobilize the private sector to work together with the government in addressing a wide range of economic and social issues.

The Board of Investment as a Business Partner

The Board of Investment is the government agency responsible for administering incentives and providing services with a view to encouraging investment in priority areas. It comprises two bodies: The Board itself and the Office of the Board of Investment.

Chaired by the Prime Minister, the Board is responsible for administering the investment promotion law and establishing overall policy guidelines. In response to the changing situation in the economy, the BOI has designated a range of select investment categories for promotional privileges and incentives under the Investment Promotion Act.

The general guidelines used by the BOI in granting approval are derived directly from national development priorities. Accordingly, the BOI gives special consideration to investment projects which are export oriented, support resource development, substantially increase employment, locate in the provinces, establish or develop industries which form the base for further stages of industrial and technological development. Projects which carry out significant R & D activities, or establish basic transportation, networks, public utilities and environmental protection systems are considered priority projects and are eligible for special incentives.

The BOI aims to supplement and strengthen the domestic resources by encouraging foreign businesses which allow technology transfer, encourage Thai participation in ownership and management, help upgrade the product quality of Thai suppliers and subcontractors. For those companies and industries

enjoying promoted status, the basic incentives offered by the BOI include tax incentives such as corporate income tax holidays, exemption or reduction of import duties on imported items, and exclusion from taxable income of dividends during the tax holiday, etc...

To prevent unfair competition from imports, temporary tariff surcharges or bans may be imposed on imports. To ensure security of investment, the Investment Promotion Act also guarantees against nationalization, state competition, and state monopolization. Furthermore, the investor is granted permission for foreign ownership of land and for entry, employment of foreign nationals, and to remit foreign currency abroad.

In recent years the BOI has been shifting its emphasis towards a more services oriented role. The general activities of the BOI have been streamlined and project processing time reduced by 40 percent. In addition, they provide investment information, investment opportunity surveys and identify potential joint venture partners. The BOI also assists promoted companies in obtaining the permits and licenses that are required for starting up operation and also facilitates work permits and visas for foreigners working on promoted projects or carrying out feasibility studies.

In order to support the governments decentralization policy, the BOI began overhauling the criteria for granting privileges on September 1, 1987, with the most recent revisions becoming effective on April 1, 1993. The new provisions grant promoted status to existing projects if they relocate to regional areas. Promoted projects receive privileges according to the Zone they are located in. Promoted projects which are located in Zone I receive the least benefits while those in Zone III obtain the maximum benefits.

These promotional privileges, however, are non-compulsory requirements for investment in Thailand. Investors may exercise the option of developing their projects on a non-promoted basis.

Environmental Management and Industrial Development

The rapid economic growth resulting from industrialization and export promotion has been accompanied by a deterioration in environmental quality. Waste discharge has serious effects both

within and outside the factories' premises. Recognizing that a deterioration environment may impact both economic development and the quality of life of the Thai people, the government made provisions in the Sixth National Development Plan to integrate the needs of environmental protection and conservation with the needs of the expanding industrial economy.

Water treatment plants serve the needs of environmental production.

The Seventh Plan set definite targets to improve environmental quality throughout the country. This was a departure from previous plans on a number of accounts. Most significant was the recognition that the task ahead was beyond the scope of government alone. The formulation of this plan was intended to be a consensus -building exercise. It relied on the cooperative effort of all sectors, including government agencies, state enterprises and universities, the private sector, and non-government organizations.

There are many laws and regulations pertaining to the environment. In June of 1992, a new National Environmental Quality Act replaced the 1975 National Environment Act, creating a stronger foundation for a system of national environmental management.

In April 1992, a new Hazardous Substances Act introduced a comprehensive control framework for the possession, use and handling of all substances considered mutation-inducing, infectious explosive flammable and corrosive. Later that year, a new Factories Act retained the basic restrictions of the former one but included strict pollution regulations and tougher penalties. Firms proposing investments in industries, such as petrochemicals, industrial estates, steel industries which might harm the environment, are required to perform an environmental-impact study prior to receiving permission to set up factories.

There are also several agencies which deal with various aspects of environmental regulation and management in the country, including divisions of the Ministry of Industry, the Ministry of Science, Technology and Environment, the Ministry of Public Health, the Ministry of Interior, and the Ministry of Transport and Communications.

Government Agencies: The Investment Promotion Drive

To promote investment in Thailand, in addition to BOI, the government has set up several specialized agencies and institutions to help with the physical implementation of industrial projects.

Industrial Estates

To cope with the problems of major cities and to fulfill regional development objectives. The Industrial Estate Authority of Thailand (IEAT) was established in 1979 as a state enterprise. The government aimed to accelerate industrialization and urban development planning through implementation of well-equipped industrial locations as a way to help solving the problems of urban deterioration.

Industrial estates provide a wide range of public utilities and facilities such as roads, sewers, central waste-water treatment plants, electricity, and

telecommunications together with necessary services such as post and telegraph offices, banks, residences, and oil service stations. There are two categories of industrial estates: a General Industrial Zone (GIZ), intended for industries or other business beneficial or related to industries, and an Export Processing Zone (EPZ), designated for export manufacturing industries.

Bird's eye view of projects along the Eastern Seaboard.

Firms located in an EPZ are exempt from import duties on machinery, equipment, inputs needed for the manufacture of exports, and export duties. Custom officials are stationed at the EPZ to monitor the imported raw materials and exported finished goods, and firms in the EPZ do not have to put up any form of guarantee.

Industrial estates were initially the almost exclusives domain of the Industrial Estate Authority of Thailand, but now the private sector and joint-ventures with the IEAT can establish industrial estates. There are now more than three dozen industrial estates in all regions of Thailand, and more are under construction. The vast majority of these industrial estates have received promotional privileges from the Board of Investment and must comply with strict standards with regard to factory facilities and utilities. So, investors

Map Ta Phut Industrial Zone, southeast of Bangkok.

seeking factory facilities are faced with a growing number of choices.

The Eastern Seaboard Development Programme, which was launched in 1981, has the aim of promoting industrial development and decentralizing the economy. This project is comprised of two principal locations, Map Ta Phut, and Laem Chabang.

Map Ta Phut, a designated industrial zone with an area of 6,000 rai, located about 200 km. southeast of Bangkok has become the centre of a fully-integrated petrochemical complex based on a supply of natural gas from the Gulf of Thailand. The zone will also have a deep-sea port and serve as an industrial estate for capital and technology-intensive concerns and all are in occupied.

Laem Chabang, located in Chon Buri Province with an area of 3,556 rai, 155 km. southeast of Bangkok and about 15 km. north of the resort town of Pattaya, will have a deep-sea port, a general industrial zone and an EPZ, as well as commercial areas. Industries set up here will be principally light, labour-intensive, and non-polluting. The land is still available for rent in EPZ only.

Industrial Standardization

Standardization is an essential tool for the development of the economy and industry of the country. Realizing the importance of standardization, the Ministry of Industry promulgated the Industrial Product Standards Act in 1968 which established the Thai Industrial Standards Institute (TISI) as the national standards body responsible for standardization activities in Thailand. The objectives of TISI are to increase the reliability and the popularity of the local products, to provide a basic of fair trade and fair practice environment, to eliminate barriers to trade, to guarantee the safety and protection of the people and public property, and to save resources and cost in production while keeping pace with the development of industry.

The Institute, in its capacity as the national standards body, represents Thailand as member of various international organizations (both regional and global) to participate in the formulation of opinions and rulings on issues that may affect the country's economy.

In 1991, the Institute announced the adoption of TIS/ISO 9000 series as National Standard for Quality Systems. This is, in every aspect, similar to the international ISO 9000 series established by the International Organization for Standardization and to the European Standards EN 29000. With this world class standard, the industry of Thailand will become more competitive in the international market.

The Institute has formulated many standardization issues concerning environmental protection and the enhancement of the quality of life. It has also overseen the promulgation of a Royal Decree requiring many products to conform to standards. To enforce this law, the Institute works in close cooperation with other government bodies. The industrial standards of Thailand have now achieved international acceptance.

Selected Sector Investment Opportunities

Electronics

Thailand's electronics industry has made major strides in the past decade and now produce many types of electronics equipment, subassemblies and components. The electronics industry has played an increasingly important role in the manufacturing sector, particularly with product manufactured for export. Among the leading industrial and professional electronics products are hard disk drives for computer, keyboards and telephones. Thailand also has become a major manufacturing and assembly base for a number of electronic and related components, including integrated circuits, printed circuit boards, miniature ball bearings, computer cards and cables. During the rapid economic growth of 1986-1994, higher value-added and higher technology products such as facsimiles and cellular telephones began to be produced. Firms that manufactured components for export gradually started supplying parts and components to be assembled into export products.

Some of the most promising investment opportunities in Thailand's electronics industry are in the areas of consumer electronics, computers and peripherals, communication equipment, electronic assemblies, and supporting industries such as molds and dies, metal plating, transformer winding.

Automotive Industry

Thailand's automotive industry has performed spectacularly since 1988, tripling production from 145,000 units to almost a half a million units in 1993. Production is projected to reach 1 million units by 2,000. The kingdom is currently Southeast Asia's largest and most dynamic auto market and the world's second largest pickup market.

Thailand is well positioned to join the small global group of automotive "tigers," whose performance

places them a notch below the automotive giants (Japan, North America and Europe), but well ahead of other developing countries.

Automobiles are now being made in Thailand for export.

Thailand initiated its diversification drive in 1991 by allowing competition from imports for the first time in 20 years. In 1992 alone Thailand imported 22,000 vehicles or 20 percent of the passenger car segment. Under pressure from imports, domestic producers cut prices by up to 25 percent, with the result being more people can afford cars, government revenues are up and Thailand's industry is now more productive. Further diversification through import duty reductions are in the offing.

A second tool for diversification in promotion of new vehicle assembly operations. The Board of Investment has re-opened promotion privileges to automotive assembly projects for export, aiming to make Thailand a regional automotive production centre. This is encouraging North American, Korean, and European firms to enter a market that has been near-exclusively owned by Japanese manufacturers.

Thailand effectively implemented local content requirements in the 1980s and 1990s to achieve basic component assembly and delivery capabilities. In its quest to enhance its global competitiveness, Thailand is now making industrial deepening a priority as it courts new investments in components and supporting industries. Established automakers are expanding their investments and setting up supply lines within the country; this is considered a strong indication of the profitability of such operations.

Industrial deepening will transform the automotive assembly industries into pillars of the economy, which will integrate raw steel into metal-bending into finished body panels. Ventures which promise additional value-added work in Thailand are favoured.

Thailand's auto industry means to get globally competitive. Look for Thailand to pursue market diversification and industrial deepening to achieve competitive targets in 2000. Well-managed, progressive foreign companies should seize ensuing opportunities and take their share of Asia's fastest growing automotive market.

Engineering Plastics and Synthetic Fibres

Engineering plastics, with their superior properties, are finding increasing uses in applications demanding higher performance than commodity plastics. Engineering plastics include polyacetal nylon, polycarbonate, and thermoplastic polyester molding compounds. Now only nylon is produced in Thailand mainly for the synthetic fibre industry. Thailand has been exporting an ever larger part of its synthetic fibre production.

Engineering plastics have seen excellent growth over the past few years and the Board of Investment announced in April 1994 that it will begin granting special investment incentives for the production of engineering plastics as part of its strategy to encourage growth in Thailand's supporting industries.

Investment opportunities for engineering plastics include polyacetal, nylon, PET, and PBT. Production of

these compounds is promoted by the BOI. The growing demand for PBT at around 1,500 to 2,000 tons a year is a possible investment opportunity.

The expansion of production facilities for the three main synthetic fibres (polyester, nylon and acrylic) for domestic and export markets is being met by new investments. New investment opportunities will depend entirely on the export market and it is expected that foreign investment will play an important role in this development.

The Chemical Industry

The chemical process industry in Thailand is one of the country's foundation industries. Its products find uses as raw materials in the chemical process industry itself, in other industries, and as final industrial and consumer items.

The chemical process industry in Thailand has two key advantages: the country's population of just under 60 million means a good-size domestic market, and its location in Southeast Asia suggests a potential distribution hub.

Thailand also has significant natural resources such as natural gas, lignite, and other mineral resources already used raw materials in the industry. Growth in this key industrial sector has been stunted for some years but, with the establishment of a petrochemical complex along Thailand's Eastern Seaboard, the situation is changing.

This complex industry, with its numerous subsectors, poses several problems in terms of a development strategy. Highly capital and technology intensive, it is also highly polluting and must serve a complex array of subsectors and cross-subsector applications.

Environmental Markets

Environmental markets in Thailand are set to develop during the 1990s with investment opportunities emerging in a number of sectors. Public awareness and stronger legislation are going hand in hand, paving the way for sustainable economic development.

On the investment promotion side, the BOI unveiled criteria in April 1992 identifying projects that promote "restoration and conservation of the environment" as worthy of special investment privileges. The BOI also insists that all promoted projects include adequate environmental protection systems. In certain areas, particularly industrial and municipal waste water treatment and management of hazardous substances, there is a window of opportunity for foreign equipment suppliers and service companies.

In the next decade, municipal water and solid waste treatment, hazardous substance management, vehicle emission control equipment, clean technologies for the power industry, and pollution control should be industries with major growth opportunities. Additionally, there should continue to be opportunities in services such as monitoring and laboratory services, environmental systems management training, consulting services and range of niche markets.

Metal-Working and Machine Tools

At the core of Thailand's industrialization are two basic support industries: metal working and machine tools.

Demand for metal-working and machine tool products is directly dependent on the success of a handful of down stream manufacturing and assembly industries, in particular the automotive, electronics, and construction industries.

In the 1990s, BOI will continue to provide generous investment incentives and service support to start up metal-working and machine tool operations. In 1993, casting, forging, and mold and die firms became eligible for increased promotion incentives because these industries encourage technical transfer. The BOI's BUILD programme will assist firms in matching demand and supply and will help small-and medium-size Thai metal-working firms reach international standards.

Overall, Thailand's rapid industrialization, and the high potential for the future, signal a ready market opportunity for foreign metal-working and machinery firms seeking a profitable operating position. Additionally, Thailand requires assistance in developing several segments of the metal-working industry. Chief among them are casting and forging, molds and dies, precision parts, machinery parts, and metal finishing.

Telecommunications

The Thai telecommunications industry has extraordinary growth potential. There is not only a strong demand for existing services, but also for an array of new services as Thailand commits itself to meet international competition head on.

The country knows that an adequate and reliable telecommunications network is a basic social and business necessity. Thailand is joining the Information Age, and with projected private and public sector investments of US$ 24 billion between 1992 and 2001, Thailand is likely to emerge as a major telecommunications player in Southeast Asia.

Now, and for at least the next decade, Thailand will have a high demand for telecommunications services, equipment, and components. The Office of the Board of Investment (BOI) is actively promoting a parts and components networking facility.

Demand will be particularly high for cellular telephones, key telephones, facsimile machines, modems, telephone sets, office PBX, pagers, and satellite dishes and receivers.

Thailand is an ideal regional base of telecommunications projects. Neighbouring countries, such as Cambodia, Laos, and Vietnam are keen on improving their telecommunications infrastructure, and foreign and Thai companies are investing in the region's telecommunications industry.

Supporting Industries

The rapid growth of the Thai economy has been accompanied by a dramatic increase in manufacturing activities and a significant diversification of the structure of exports. However, this process has depended primarily on the exploitation of inexpensive labour. The deepening of the industrial structure and the development of the technological capability that will sustain Thailand's growth in the medium term has only just begun.

This crucial sector is receiving increased attention and support from the government. Not coincidentally, the major industrial push into the provinces has, in large part, come from supporting industries. The two major manufacturing trends are, in fact, the increase in supporting industries and investment in the provinces.

The clear need to increase the sophistication of the manufacturing sector opens up a wide range of investment opportunities in the engineering and supporting industries. These opportunities range from basic metal-working activities to the provision of testing and R & D services. Foreign participation in these areas is being actively encouraged. The growing domestic market and increasing experience in this field makes Thailand a prime investment site for this type of activity.

The BOI has recently increased incentives to supporting industry activities such as mold and die, jig and fixture, and forging and casting. These industries promote technical transfer and help build up the industrial structure. More incentives are currently being considered.

To help develop this type of investment, the Board of Investment approved a proposal to establish a National Supplier Development Programme (NSDP). The purpose of this programme is to step up the growth of small and medium supplier enterprises in Thailand.

Investment in the supporting industries offers the greatest potential, as they are somewhat less developed than either the assembly or component industries. They require substantial capital investment to start up operations, but once facilities are in place and operation begins, investors can reap the benefits of "getting in on the ground floor". Thailand needs assistance in expansion or technological improvements in several support industries, including metal-working, electronics and machine tools. Such investment can also benefit from the increasing demand in other sectors such as electrical and electronics, from machinery and other consumer products.

Agro-Industry–The Potential for Biotechnology

In Thailand, agriculture continues to play an important role in the Thai economy. The majority of the Thai population still earns its living in the agricultural sector and many of the new export markets that Thai entrepreneurs have tapped are related to agriculture in one way or another. One trend that has been observed involves the use of technologies new to Thailand to enhance the quality and value-added of agricultural products. Examples of biotechnological projects include transformation of tapioca slurry into modified starch to support the paper and chemical industry, the improvement of aquaculture technologies to increase yields and quality, and the development of new chemicals to enable the increasing use of natural rubber.

It is generally accepted that Thailand's scientific base in the biotechnology area is relatively strong and many of the advances referred to above have contained significant local content. Unlike the development of most other industries, which tend to be led by the private sector, biotechnology activities in Thailand have been carried out mainly by the public sector, particularly the R & D centres of the major public universities. Good prospects for investment and commercial gain in applied biotechnology products and processes exist in several key economic sectors. Examples of the sort of projects that should find a market include development of disease-resistant agricultural plants, improved quality livestock and aquaculture, specialty chemicals such as those used in food processing, pharmaceutical development, and utilizing micro-organisms for pollution control.

Thailand: Standing Out in Asia

The basic ingredients for a successful investment project can be found in Thailand. The country is strategically located in the Pacific basin and enjoys political stability. The industrial structure is well diversified and can therefore respond quickly to changes in international demand patterns or increases in protectionism.

The Thai economy is resilient and dynamic, with continuing high growth rates, favourable export performance and financial stability.

Thai economy took off into double digit growth in 1988 with GDP increasing by more than 13 percent –the highest in Asia. This performance was repeated in 1989 and 1990, with growth of 12.3 percent and 11.5 percent respectively. The economy has slowed down somewhat, registering 7.5-8.5 percent growth in 1991-1994.

The country has a highly-productive labour force, approaching 32 million workers, with the majority being under 30 years old. In comparison with other countries in the region such as Indonesia, China and Vietnam, Thailand's labour force can no longer compete in terms of cost alone. However, when taking into account

Gas pipe lines form part of Thailand's industrial infrastructure.

trainability and efficiency, the Thai labour force is among the most "cost effective" in the region. The minimum wage rate is just around US$ 5-6 a day and Thai workers have established a solid reputation among foreign investors for their diligence and adaptability. Each year about 800,000 join this force and the literacy rate is above 90 percent. More than 15,000 students are presently enrolled in engineering programmes at universities and about 76,000 students graduate each year from vocational schools around the country.

Land and other basic facilities are inexpensive and there exists extensive infrastructure for industry. However, in 1994, specific emphasis is firmly on developing Thailand's infrastructure at all levels.

In 1992, the private sector was contracted to expand the telephone system in Thailand. Through April of 1995, over 1 million new lines have been added within Bangkok, and an additional 600,000 lines have already been installed in the provinces, with more on the way. Fibre Optic Submarine Cable Network Projects are expected to be completed by the end of 1997 and two communications satellites have been launched.

Construction of new roads has been a major priority both in Bangkok and the provinces. Several elevated roads and fly-overs to address congestion in Bangkok are well underway and two mass transit projects are under construction.

To help in the overall government policy of decentralization, 1994's budget earmarks US$ 8.4 million to upgrade infrastructure throughout the country and to accelerate industrial distribution in rural areas. This account for over 30 percent of the total budget and represents a 25 percent increase over 1993. Much of the new infrastructure investment is expected to be carried out by private sector consortia.

Of specific interest to investors are measures which have eliminated tax clearances, made work permits easier to secure, facilitated the establishment of regional offices, and lifted restrictions on foreign ownership of condominiums.

Thailand's Economy at a Glance

	1989	1990	1991	1992	1993	1994
A : General						
Population (million)	55.9	56.3	57.0	57.8	58.5	59.3
Labour Force (million)	30.4	31.2	31.8	32.4	33.1	34.0
Unemployment Rate	3.6%	3.9%	3.1%	3.1%	3.2%	n.a.
(% of labour force)						
B : Economic Growth						
GDP at Current Prices						
(billion US$)	72.2	85.6	98.2	110.4	123.7	138.8 1/
Sectoral shares of GDP (%)						
Agriculture	16.8%	14.3%	14.2%	13.4%	12.7%	12.0% 3/
Manufacturing	26.7%	27.2%	28.3%	28.3%	29.1%	30.0% 3/
Construction	5.5%	6.2%	6.6%	6.6%	6.6%	6.7% 3/
Services and Others	51.0%	52.3%	50.9%	51.7%	51.6%	51.2% 3/
GDP at Constant 1988 Prices	68.1	76.3	82.7	89.4	96.7	104.7 3/
(billion US$)						
Growth rates (%)						
Overall	12.2%	11.6%	8.1%	7.6%	7.9%	8.2% 2/
Agriculture	9.3%	-2.5%	6.1%	4.1%	2.4%	3.0% 2/
Manufacturing	16.0%	16.0%	11.8%	10.6%	11.3%	11.5% 2/
Construction	28.3%	22.0%	11.9%	3.5%	7.9%	9.6% 2/
Services and Other	9.8%	13.0%	6.1%	7.3%	7.4%	8.2% 2/
Share of Gross Domestic Investment in GDP	35.1%	41.1%	42.0%	40.1%	n.a.	n.a.
Share of National Savings in GDP 31.6%		32.6%	33.7%	34.3%	n.a.	n.a.
GNP per capita (US$)	1,292	1,508	1,698	1,880	2,085	2,309 1/
C : Price Indicators						(Jan.-Mar.)
Consumer Prices (% Change)						
Whole Kingdom	5.4%	6.0%	5.7%	4.1%	4.6%	5.0
Bangkok and Metropolis	6.3%	6.6%	5.4%	3.9%	5.4%	5.7
Producer Prices (% change)	4.6%	3.4%	6.9%	0.2%	-0.5%	n.a.
D : External Account						(Jan.-Mar.)
Exports (billion US$)	19.8	22.8	28.2	32.1	36.4	9.5
(% change)	27.7%	14.5%	23.5%	13.1%	13.1%	16.8%
Imports (billion US$)	25.3	32.8	37.9	40.2	45.1	12.2
(% change)	29.9%	29.0%	15.4%	5.5%	12.0%	12.4%
Trade Balance (billion US$)	-5.5	-10.0	-9.7	-8.1	-8.7	-2.7
Current Account Balance						
(billion US$)	-2.5	-7.3	-7.6	-6.4	-6.8	-1.9
(% of GDP)	-3.5%	-8.5%	-7.7%	-5.7%	-5.5%	n.a.
Net Capital Movements						
(billion US$)	5.6	9.7	11.3	9.9	11.6	3.1
Balance of Payments						
(billion US$)	4.0	3.8	4.1	3.0	3.9	0.8
(% of GDP)	5.5%	4.4%	4.2%	2.7%	3.2%	0.6%

	1989	1990	1991	1992	1993	1994
Official Reserves						
(billion US$)	10.5	14.3	18.4	21.2	25.4	26.7
(in months of imports)	5.0	5.2	5.8	6.3	6.8	6.6
Total Debt Service						
Ratio [4][5]	10.6%	9.1%	9.8%	10.5%	10.2%	n.a.
Public	5.8%	5.0%	4.2%	3.7%	3.7%	n.a.
Private	4.8%	4.1%	5.6%	6.8%	6.5%	n.a.
E : Money and Banking						(Jan.-Mar.)
Money Supply (MZ)						
(billion US$)	47.0	59.8	71.9	83.2	99.0	97.1
(% change)	26.2%	26.7%	19.8%	15.6%	18.4%	13.8%
Private Domestic Credit						
(% change)	29.8%	33.3%	21.0%	20.6%	23.1%	23.8%
Commercial Bank Deposits						
(% change) [6]	26.8%	27.5%	21.4%	16.2%	19.2%	14.5%
Interest Rates (end of period)						
Prime Rate :						
Minimum overdraft rates						
(MOR)	12.5-13.5	16.50	14.00	11.50	10.50	10.25
Minimum loan rates						
(MLR)	12.50	16.25	14.00	11.50	10.50	10.00
Deposits :						
Savings deposits	7.25	10.00-12.00	8.50	6.00-6.50	7.00	7.00-7.25
F : Public Sector (Fiscal Year)						
Government Revenue						
(billion US$)	12.0	15.5	18.2	19.6	22.1	25.2
Government Expenditure						
(billion of US$)	9.7	11.4	13.4	16.6	19.5	23.0
Fiscal Balance						
(billion US$) [1]	2.3	4.1	4.8	3.0	2.6	2.2
(% of GDP)	2.0%	4.8%	4.9%	2.7%	2.1%	1.6%

	1990	1991	1992	1993	1994p	1995e
G : Exchange Rate (Jan.-Apr.)						
(baht per US$)	25.59	25.52	25.40	25.32	25.15	24.83
H : Investment : (Jan.-Mar.)						
BOI Project Applications						
No. of projects	1,015	630	444	1,255	1,538	312
Investment						
(million US$)	20,529	11,063	8,373	11,062	23,522	5,186
BOI Projects Starting UP						
No. of projects	415	433	438	375	311	33
Investment						
(million US$)	3,051	2,933	3,757	5,101	4,036	1,185
Investment Index						
(end of period)	134.2	108.3	91.0	115.3	115.1	120.1

	1989	1990	1991	1992	1993	1994
Corporate Securities (end of period)						
SET Index	613	711	893	1,683	1,360	1,217
No. of quoted companies	214	276	320	347	389	403
Average monthly turnover (million US$)	2,045	2,593	6,091	7,244	7,004	4,650

I : Tourist Arrivals

	1989	1990	1991	1992	1993	1994
Number of Tourists (in thousands)	5,299	5,087	5,136	5,761	6,167	6,700
(% change)	10.2%	-4.0%	1.0%	12.2%	7.1%	8.5%
Total Revenue (million US$)	4,322	3,918	4,846	5,048	5,774	7,129

J : Net Foreign Direct Investment (million US$)

	1989	1990	1991	1992	1993	1994
Total 2,447	2,019	2,112	1,654	595	n.a.	
By Country						
U.S.A.	241	232	463	305	164	n.a.
Taiwan	280	108	87	61	94	n.a.
Japan	1,093	612	337	381	122	n.a.
U.K.	44	10	126	162	44	n.a.
Germany	45	33	24	32	30	n.a.
Hong Kong	275	454	572	175	128	n.a.
Singapore	240	245	264	225	-114	n.a.
Others	230	316	239	313	127	n.a.
By Sector						
Industry	1,213	935	686	805	512	n.a.
Trade and Services	916	535	432	238	396	n.a.
Construction	129	130	571	152	70	n.a.
Mining and Quarrying	45	81	123	125	52	n.a.
Agriculture	30	23	-6	13	-6	n.a.
Financial Institutions	177	268	258	138	-460	n.a.
Others	211	209	48	183	31	n.a.

K : Economic Prospects for Asia and Australia

	GDP 1994	Growth 1995	Inflation 1994	Inflation 1995	Currency/US$ 1994	Currency/US$ 1995 (Jan.-Apr.)
Japan	0.6	1.7	0.5	0.7	101.74	93.09
S.Korea	8.3	7.3	6.3	5.9	806.0	781.7
Taiwan	6.2	6.4	3.8	4.1	26.3	25.8
China	10.5	8.0	27.0	30.0	8.51	8.51
Hong Kong	5.5	n.a.	8.4	8.0	7.70	7.74
Vietnam	8.5	n.a.	14.5	n.a.	10,800	11,000
Thailand	8.2	8.4	3.3	5.0	25.15	24.83
Malaysia	8.5	8.5	4.0	4.3	2.61	2.53
Singapore	8.7	7.6	3.7	3.0	1.51	1.43
Indonesia	6.5	6.9	8.2	8.5	2,151	2,221
Philippines	3.5	4.5	11.0	8.5	27.02	24.82
India	5.0	5.3	8.5	11.0	30.37	31.25

	GDP 1994	Growth 1995	Inflation 1994	Inflation 1995	Currency/US$ 1994	Currency/US$ 1995 (Jan.-Apr.)
Pakistan	3.3	5.0	10.3	9.8	30.37	30.84
Sri Lanka	6.0	6.1	10.0	10.0	49.39	49.66
Australia	3.7	3.3	2.3	3.0	1.38	1.34
New Zealand	4.0	3.8	1.4	2.0	1.71	1.55

Sources : Various Embassies; _The World in 1995_, The Economist; National Economic and Social Development Board; Bank of Thailand; Department of Business Economics, Ministry of Commerce.

Notes : Figures are real growth rates in %, unless stated otherwise; Inflation refers to consumer prices Exchange rates of local units to U.S. Dollar; Inflation, Interest rates, Jobless rates are year averages

Notes : P = provisional; e = estimated; n.a. = not available; * = Jan. '95 - Feb. '95
1/ estimated by NESDB
2/ estimated by The Brooker Group Ltd.
3/ Includes short-term debt
4/ Payment of interest plus principal divided by the value of exports
5/ Excluding foreign and interbank deposits
6/ Comprises the government's budgetary and non-budgetary deficits

Sources : Bank of Thailand; Board of Investment; National Economic and Social Development Board; Tourism Authority of Thailand, Compiled by The Brooker Group Ltd.

Future Prospects

From the mid-90s until the beginning of the next century, all economic forecasts put Thailand on a steady upward course with annual growth remaining strong around 8 percent and inflation well under control at approximately 5 percent. Stronger emphasis on sustainable development and science and technology are evident as Thailand joins the ranks of Newly Industrialized Economies. As of 1994, Thailand has a domestic market of around 60 million people, with rapidly increasing purchasing power (per capita income US$ 2,500, and is projected to reach $ 3,860 by the year 2000).

Continuing liberalization of the tax and tariff structures, an open door policy towards foreign investment, and macroeconomic stability will keep Thailand a favoured investment location. Increasing political stabilization and a trend towards regional cooperation within ASEAN and the countries of the Greater Mekong Sub-Region will attract more worldwide attention to the region as a whole.

Thailand's role in this new regional order will be crucial, as its strengths evolve beyond being merely a cost-effective labour platform to greater industrial capability, diversity, and depth, and its entrepreneurial leadership develops.

Thailand is well-positioned to serve as a regional base for investment in the emerging economies of the region. The government is actively forging linkages with the countries of the Greater Mekong and Thailand's newly-established offshore banking facility, the Bangkok International Banking Facilities (BIBF) will further enhance trade and investment between Thailand and her regional neighbours.

With the successful completion of the Uruguay Round of GATT negotiations, the country is on course to continue as an export powerhouse; its rapidly growing domestic market is also gaining importance as an attraction for foreign investors.

As Thailand begins its ascent up the value-added ladder, it is starting to produce, domestically, a greater share of the capital goods, parts, and components that fuel the manufacturing engine. Tremendous investment opportunities are implicit in this process.

The new model for what is possible in Thailand may be seen on the country's Eastern Seaboard, where one of the developing world's most ambitious integrated development plans is currently being implemented. By the year 2000, access to two new airports, three deep seaports, a global transpark, and rail system will support investments in a full range of industrial activities. Now that the large scale investment in a number of basic industries such as petrochemicals and steel

manufacturing are on stream, supporting industries and services are rapidly following.

As Thailand consolidates its current phase of development, its position in the new economic world order is stronger than ever before.

Source: The Board of Investment (BOI), 1995.

King Mongkut (Rama IV), the "Father of Science in Thailand".

SCIENCE AND TECHNOLOGY

Thai people have realized the benefits of science and technology for many centuries. In the ancient capital of Sukhothai, artisans possessed the technological skills necessary to produce fine glazed ceramics as well as superb bronze images of the Buddha. Moreover, engineers of the period constructed a number of sophisticated dikes to control water and prevent floods and also built an aqueduct to bring water from the mountains for the people of the city.

Other branches of technology came to Thailand during the Ayutthaya period, when relations were established with many Western countries. From there came knowledge in such fields as astronomy, ship-building, gun-powder production, and advanced concepts of metalurgy. The flood of new ideas continued in the Bangkok period with the introduction of steam engines, locomotives, and electricity. At the same time, Thais began to understand that without a proper knowledge of science it was not possible to develop a useful and advanced technology.

Perhaps the first Thai to realize this crucial fact was King Mongkut (Rama IV). While in the monkhood before becoming king, he studied English, mathematics, and sciences, mastering astronomy to such an extent that he was later able to accurately

King Mongkut paid special attention to astronomy and could predict accurately the occurence of a total eclipse at Wa Ko, Prachuap Khiri Khan Province in 1868.

Injection moulding, used by some 3,000 plastic factories.

predict the occurence of a total eclipse at Wa Ko, a sub-district in Prachuap Khiri Khan, on August 18, 1868. Therefore in 1982, the year in which the Bangkok Bicentennial was celebrated, the Thai government designated him as the "Father of Science in Thailand." Thai scientists, in turn, have decided on August 18 as Thai National Science Day; on this day a national science exhibition is held and an outstanding scientist of the year is honoured.

At present, science and technology are playing a vital role in various industrialization processes. Since Thailand possesses a limited number of natural resources, some of which have deteriorated because of poorly conceived exploitation, productivity improvement is essential. To enhance such efforts, and thereby ensure stable, long-term growth of the Thai economy and steady improvement of the national life, it is crucial that the development of science and technology be promoted.

The Ministry of Science, Technology and Energy (MOSTE) was established on March 24, 1979 with the responsibility of undertaking the development of the country's science and technology. Before the establishment of this ministry, activities in these fields were carried out independently by many agencies without proper coordination, resulting in overlapping in functions, operations, and plans. Moreover, there were no effective plans or policies for the development of science and technology. All of these gave rise to many problems such as a lack of continuity of activities and a waste of human resources.

Some of the major functions of the Ministry of Science, Technology and Energy include:

(1) To lay out policies, plans, and projects related to science, technology, energy, and environment;

(2) To develop technology within the country that will assist in production and marketing;

(3) To study, analyze, and do research that will produce significant data for science, technology, energy, and environment; and

(4) To collect, compile, and propagate the results of research and development related to these fields.

In the past, national development programmes placed little emphasis on the role of science and technology. It was only during the period of the Fifth National Plan (1982-1986) that some attention began to emerge. The Sixth Plan (1987-1991), by contrast, has assigned high priority to this topic in recognition of the growing importance of science and technology in national development. Under this plan, foundations are being laid for developing production and processing capabilities in order to elevate the country's status to a level equal to or higher than that of the newly industrialized countries.

Implementation of development in science and technology consists of the following activities:

– Support of systematic management of science and technology in order that they may play an increasing

Modern technology in use at factories.

Close attention at every step of working.

Cargo liners being loaded with heavy containers.

role in national development. This concentrates on those branches which are of primary importance in future national development and on developing manpower in science and technology corresponding to future economic needs.

– Development of a basic structure for science and technology. This includes the development of appropriate organizations and the revision of various laws, rules, and regulations that have hindered previous development.

– Development of manpower for science and technology. This will seek to increase efficiency by emphasizing qualitative improvement and maximizing benefits from employment. Support is given to the production of manpower in those areas where there is a shortage of personnel such as electronics, petroleum, biotechnology, and material science.

– Promotion of national research and development. This is carried out by formulation appropriate policies and allocating funds to areas of research in need of immediate assistance.

– Increase in effectiveness of technology transfer from abroad. Foreign investment in the development of science and technology is encouraged while education is improved for better technology transfer.

– Development of data and information systems. In particular, an information network has been set up to derive and science and technology indices for use in determining appropriate policies and plans.

– Promotion of the role of the private sector in developing and using technology. Tax incentives are given to encourage the private sector to invest in the development of science and technology.

This factory is a pilot project for an R&D programme promoting the development of manpower and the biochemical engineering research field.

Five Technological Policies

To strengthen the country's scientific and technological capabilities, the Ministry of Science, Technology and Energy has formulated certain guidelines and policies. The Ministry has a policy to improve scientific and technological know-how in four areas, namely: technology transfer, scientific and technological information, research and development, and upgrading scientific and technological personnel. These areas will lead to the implementation of five technological policies, as follows:

1. Implementation for industrial development. The emphasis here is on fundamental industries such as chemical, metal, and electronic, in order to improve the quality of the products and promote high-level industries. For example, fundamental industries are used to pave the way for development of a steel industry, or the production of zinc oxide as a raw material may promote the development of the paint industry.

2. Implementation for agricultural development. The use of new agricultural technology, agricultural engineering, biotechnology, and genetic engineering will lead to the increase of agricultural products and research to develop new strains of crops and animals as well as

improved agricultural equipment. Examples of this are the application of new agricultural technology to crop selection, the production of a seedless water melon, the production of improved bacteria for industrial processes, and the use of insects in pest and weed control.

3. Implementation for energy development. Further research is being done into alternative and cheaper forms of energy such as hydroelectric power, solar and wind energy so that the country's dependence on imported energy sources will be lessened.

4. Implementation for environmental and resource management. Standards have been set up for environmental protection, while serious work is being done to protect the country's environment. Future planning to solve environmental problems will be in harmony with the overall development of the country.

5. Implementation for the development of national defence. The Ministry of Science, Technology and Energy has been working closely with the Ministry

of Defence in the application of various technologies, particularly the development of armaments and communications to strengthen the national security.

Princess Chulabhorn Research Centre

Her Royal Highness Princess Chulabhorn is well-known among scientists for her devotion and ability in promoting scientific research in Thailand. Since obtaining her doctorate degree in chemistry from Mahidol University in Bangkok, Princess Chulabhorn has led several important research projects related to chemistry, natural products, medicinal plants, and polymers. During her intensive involvement in these projects, she found that it is difficult for Thai researchers to obtain funding or financial support in their work. As a consequence, she conceived the idea of establishing a research centre which will act as a fund raising agency as well as providing opportunities for Thai researchers to exchange ideas and research results.

The Princess Chulabhorn Research Centre was established within Mahidol University and was officially inaugurated by Her Royal Highness Princess Maha Chakri Sirindhorn on July 4, 1988. Since the inauguration the Centre has undertaken a number of projects, among them the following:

H.R.H. Princess Chulabhorn posed for a photo with foreign lecturers and scientists during the symposium on "Bioactive Compounds from Plants" co-organized by the Ciba Foundation and the Chulabhorn Research Institute.

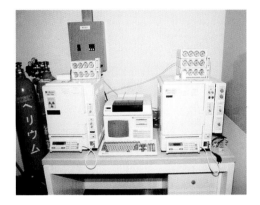

Laboratory equipment.

– Drug resistance research which aims at finding suitable chemical and natural drugs which can cure malaria patients with minimum drug resistance.

– Research related to natural products such as ginger which can relieve motion sickness and several other medicinal plants which may be used as anti-tumor drugs.

– Research on polymers to develop plastic sheets which can be used to protect top soil in the drip irrigation process.

Besides awarding funds to researchers, the Princess Chulabhorn Research Centre also provides post-graduate education as well as post-doctorate degrees.

Human Resources in Science and Technology

An important problem faced by a developing country like Thailand is developing the human resources necessary to create new technology as well as to adopt and adapt imported scientific and technological skills to the prevailing socio-economic environment of the country. Although Thailand has a number of researchers working in various universities, government departments, and private organizations, the number is lower than in other more technologically advanced countries. There are two aspects of human resource development in Thailand which aim to increase the scientific and technological manpower to a more satisfactory level.

The first aspect involves the types of research being conducted in the country. Although many Thai researchers conduct original and basic research to extend the boundary of scientific knowledge a large number work only on the use of imported technology and

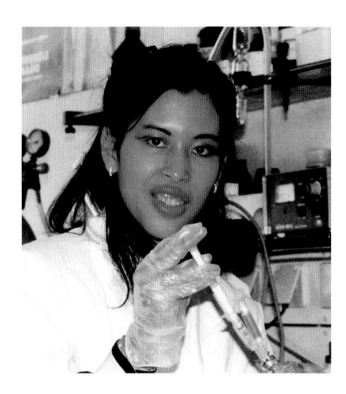

Princess Chulabhorn.

equipment. It is obvious that dependence on such technology from abroad without attempting to modify or enhance it will prevent the country from developing its own potential. Several government offices are trying to promote original and basic research by providing financial support to Thai researchers in universities as well as other sectors. It is foreseen that during the last decade of the century this will result in great improvement in the quality of Thai researchers and scientists.

The second aspect concerns changes in the Thai economic structure from agriculture towards industry and changes in the development concept away from increasing production volume towards improving efficiency and quality. These changes require more modern and complex production processes and management. This is especially true of new industrial projects in petrochemicals, fertilizers, electronics, and the like, which require manpower with a high level of scientific and technological competence.

Table 1

Numbers of students in state educational institutions
in various fields, 1993

Field	No. of students	Percent
Humanities	24,919	3.80
Education	51,237	7.82
Fine Arts	2,682	0.41
Social Sciences	340,831	52.01
Law	103,052	15.73
Engineering	30,145	4.60
Natural Sciences	37,235	5.68
Medical and Health Sciences	43,625	6.66
Agriculture	20,287	3.10
Others	1,254	0.19
Total	**655,267**	**100.0**

Source : Ministry of University Affairs

Several universities put more effort into producing social science graduates in the 1990's, as can be seen in Table 1, which shows the numbers of students in various fields within state educational institutions.

Manpower development in science and technology in the country is the responsibility of the educational institutions of the government, especially at the university level. At the vocational level, the target is mainly to develop practical skills in manipulating equipment and machines. Vocational school graduates are expected to be a major part of the work force in industry, while university graduates in science and technology are expected to be the developers and implementors in the country.

Due to the high demand for graduates in science and technology, in 1988 the government increased the number of students admitted in major fields such as engineering and technology by five percent. At the same time, the Ministry of University Affairs also permitted several private universities to expand their engineering courses under the strict scrutiny of the Engineering Curriculum Committee to ensure the quality of the graduates.

In the recent past, it was difficult to encourage students to study sciences because Thailand did not have many research institutions and it was thought that science graduates had little option but to become science teachers. Some science graduates found jobs outside their fields and only a few wished to work for the government.

A group of engineers at their work place.

In order to attract good students and to encourage graduates in science and technology to work in the government universities and research institutions, the government has launched a project called the Development and Promotion of Science and Technology Talent (DPST). The main objective of this project is to provide financial support to exceptionally good students, starting from the Bachelor's Degree and going on to advanced degrees. The project was initiated in 1984 with a modest plan, as shown in Table 2, but quickly won wide acceptance. Each year about 5,000 high school students apply for the scholarships offered by the project, though only about 30 can be awarded them.

Quality control using chemical, physical and microbiological methods is conducted on finished products before shipping them to the markets or consumer standards.

Table 2
Numbers of students in DPST Project

Year	Secondary			Bachelor's				Master's		Doctoral			Total
1984	30	-	-	-	-	-	-	-	-	-	-	-	30
1985	30	30	-	30	-	-	-	10	-	-	-	-	100
1986	30	30	30	30	30	-	-	10	10	-	-	-	170
1987	30	30	30	60	30	30	-	10	10	5	-	-	235
1988	30	30	30	60	60	30	30	10	10	5	5	-	300
1989	30	30	30	60	60	60	30	15	10	5	5	5	340
1990	30	30	30	60	60	60	60	15	15	5	5	5	375

Technology Transfer and Cooperation with Other Countries

Thailand realizes that science and technology are the property of mankind and are not limited to any particular country. At the same time, the country recognizes the rights of intellectual property and is a member of the Berne Convention on copyrights.

Thailand has been importing technologies for industrial production for more than 60 years from major countries such as the U.S.A., Japan, Great Britain, the Federal Republic of Germany, France, Italy, etc. In the past such transfer was arbitrary and any company was free to purchase equipment and technological know-how which were considered profitable. This resulted in unnecessary loss of money and the technology purchased might not fit the desired technological growth. Recently, therefore, the government has established a Technology Transfer Division within the Ministry of Science, Technology and Energy to help promote more effective transfers and provide guidelines on how one can get better profit through suitable technological transfer.

Table 3
Technology fees classified by industry

Industry	m. baht			
	1982	1983	1984	1985
Chemicals and chemical products	48,870	42,035	50,896	68,067
Electrical appliances	132,414	124,276	194,597	178,143
Cosmetic	157,188	143,097	154,224	138,006
Petroleum products	37,558	56,546	11,962	47,849
Batteries	6,911	10,359	10,466	7,481
Pharmaceuticals	133,111	100,990	108,557	109,198
Rubber products	72,306	37,785	82,163	74,915
Transport equipment	167,810	170,862	280,088	259,999
Paints	9,060	16,063	12,009	26,886
Textiles	89,840	111,737	119,690	158,135
Food and beverages	150,164	222,209	247,913	257,410
Others	487,897	534,442	721,259	718,740
Total	1,493,129	1,570,401	1,993,824	2,044,829

The values of payments for technology transfer remitted through the Bank of Thailand are shown in Table 3.

The increase in percentage of technological fees over the last decade was 28 percent. Technology is, of course, a kind of commodity whose value varies with economic expansion. Since it is impossible for any country to develop all fields of technology at the same time, it is natural that the suppliers are the price makers. Thailand is aware of this situation and is trying to develop its own technology with the cooperation of more advanced countries as well as international organizations.

Advanced Science and Technology for National Competitiveness

The National Science and Technology Development Agency (NSTDA) is a funding and research organization established under the "Science and Technology Development Act of B.E. 2534" on December 30, 1991. As an autonomous organization operating under the policy guidance of its board, chaired by the Minister of Science, Technology and Environment, NSTDA supervises three national research centres, namely National Centre for Genetic Engineering and Biotechnology (NCGEB), National Metal and Materials Technology Centre (MTEC) and National Electronics and Computer Technology Centre (NECTEC). These centres are major driving forces for rapid science and technology development in support of national economic and social policies.

NSTDA supports both public and private sectors through research funding, information services, institution-strengthening programmes, human resource development through a substantial number of scholarships both local and overseas, technical and consultancy services, and training courses. Apart from these activities, NSTDA is setting up a Science and Technology, Research and Development Park (STRDP), to start construction in 1994 at Rangsit, north of Bangkok. The Park aims to attract high-value

THAICOM, Thailand's first national communications satellite project.

international and local investment, and to develop networking to provide benefits to the private sector as well as to educational and research institutes.

While a government agency like NSTDA is trying hard to establish advanced science and technology foundation, several activities in advanced technology take place in the private sector. On December 18, 1993 Shinawatra Computer and Communications Company launched a communication satellite, *Thaicom 1*, to its orbit. This satellite has ten C-band transponders and two Ku-band transponders and will be used for television, telecommunications and computer processing purposes. The launching of *Thaicom 1* has stimulated many activities in science and technology especially in development of telecommunication industry and information technology.

The receiving dish at the THAICOM main control station located on Rattanathibet Road in Nonthaburi Province.

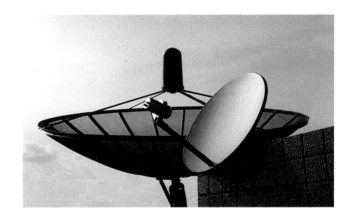

-THAICOM's C-Band transmissions include much of East and Southeast Asia. -Ku-Band transmission is focused only on Thailand and adjacent countries in Indochina.

C-BAND

Ku-band

Science and Technology for Rural Development

Science and technology are not only involved with advanced computer-integrated manufacturing, aerospace research, and genetic engineering. They also play an important role in rural development. Poverty in some remote villages of Thailand is caused by a lack of energy resources, improper soil conditions, lack of knowledge about suitable crops, health, and sanitation, and marketing and financial problems. Thanks to a good transportation system and stable financial institutions, the latter problems are less severe than before, but it is now time to use science and technology to help solve the others.

Through various departments, the Thai government has initiated a number of projects to apply science and technology to the development of rural areas. One of these is a project to improve soil conditions in Samut Songkhram, a small province west of Bangkok. This province is close to the Gulf of Thailand and has suffered from salt water intrusion to such an extent that it is no longer possible for farmers to grow rice. The Science and Technology Research Institute of Thailand and the Land Development Department have cooperated in using scientific and technological knowledge to prevent salt water intrusion and introduce suitable chemicals to recondition the soil.

Another project at Chumphon, a coastal province in the south of Thailand, aims at developing agricultural products on the sandy soil. This includes experimenting with different types of crops which can not only survive but give high yields in the coastal areas. The project has been very successful and has become a demonstration site where other villagers can come to study and learn to use the same techniques on their own farms.

In Narathiwat Province, close to the border of Thailand and Malaysia, yet another large project involves a swamp area where the people have much difficult in growing crops because of the acid soil. His Majesty the King is very interested in using modern

THAICOM *satellite has been placed into an orbit 35,786 kilometres above the Earth in the equatorial plane.*

technology to improve this land and through Her Royal Highness Princess Maha Chakri Sirindhorn the project was initiated in the mid-80's. It involves the use of new technology such as remote sensing to map the area, locate water resources, study the swamp area, and classify the land. A computerized geographic information system has been developed to record the pertinent data for monitoring land use and crops. Chemists and environmental engineers work closely together to improve the soil conditions through reduction of acidity, while at the same time the Irrigation Department has constructed a dam to reserve water for agriculture and household consumption.

A major effort in rural development is called the Green Isan Project, the word *Isan* referring to the northeastern part of Thailand. This part of the country was once rich with thick forests and wild animals, but in recent decades many roads have been built to enable the farmers to transport their crops to Bangkok and other areas. Unfortunately, the roads also brought in a serious problem of illegal deforestation and without the forests soil conditions became steadily worse. The Thai government has therefore launched a national project which brings in the best brains from all sectors to help solve the problems.

Experience in many rural development projects has shown that while science and technology may not be sufficient in themselves to solve the varied problems, they can be valuable components in the over-all development process.

GULF OF THAILAND

*Remote sensing and geographic information systems are used in
assessing the environmental conditions in several areas such as the
Songkhla Lake Basin, shown above.*

Expressway network in Bangkok.

TRANSPORT AND COMMUNICATIONS

Thailand enjoys a modern, up-to-date and sophisticated transport and communications system as a result of careful planning and the continued efforts of the government. Carriage of goods by road is an important means of transport. In 1992, road freight traffic originating and terminating in Bangkok alone exceeded 38,000 million ton-kms. There are now more than 54,388 kilometres of national highways and more than 135,000 kilometres of rural roads in the country. In 1992, there were 3.3 million motor vehicles, excluding motorcycles registered throughout the country.

Passenger transport is served by 633 interprovincial routes, while some 2 million passengers within the Bangkok area are served daily by some 188 bus routes.

Rail transport involves about 8 million tons of freight and 86 million passengers carried annually. The rail network extends 3,981 kilometres nationwide with all main lines originating from Bangkok. Of the three main lines, one terminates in Chiang Mai in the North (752 kms), one in Nong Khai and Ubon Ratchathani in the Northeast (1,092 kms) and the other near the Malaysian border at Padang Besar and Sungai Kolok (1,200 kms).

The Thai economy relies on its ports as gateways to prosperity. In 1992, Thailand exported approximately 34 million metric tons of goods by sea while importing more than 50 million tons. There were approximately 6,800 callings of vessels of all types at Bangkok Port in the same year.

Bangkok Port is a river port which provides facilities for general cargoes, bulk cargoes and petroleum products. Containers are handled at a modern terminal

1) TEUs = 20-foot
   Equivalent Unit.
2) DWT = deadweight
   tons.

with 6 berths, fully equipped with gantry cranes as well as a few private berths within the Bangkok Port area. Currently the annual container import and export turnover through Bangkok amounts to 1,303,309 TEUs[1]. Laem Chabang Commercial Port and Map Ta Phut Industrial Port are deep sea ports on the Eastern Seaboard. Laem Chabang, which commenced operation since early 1992, has been designed to provide services to large container ships and bulk carriers which cannot be accommodated at the Bangkok Port. The Port of Map Ta Phut which started to operate in March, 1992 has three terminals, comprising one general cargo terminal and two liquid bulk cargo terminals. Other deep-sea ports in southern Thailand are the Songkhla Port in the Gulf of Thailand and Phuket Port on the Andaman sea. Songkhla Port facilities include 2 multipurpose berths and 1 container berth for vessels of 20,000 DWT[2]. Phuket Port has 2 berths for vessels of 20,000 DWT. These two deep-sea ports are designed to serve the need of shippers in the southern part of Thailand and to promote the export of products of the region.

Bangkok is now an aviation hub of Southeast Asia, serving an average of more than 18 million passengers and 563,058 tons of freight annually. At

Bangkok Port.

present, 73 countries have air services agreement with Thailand and 69 airlines operate more than 500 scheduled flights to Bangkok or other international airports such as Chiang Mai, Phuket and Hat Yai. Furthermore, in 1993, more than 1,070 chartered flights arrived in the country. Thai Airways International or THAI, the national flag carrier, is reputed to be one of the world's best airlines in terms of services. It also provides domestic services to 21 destinations. Government policy has now been extended to include commercial helicopter services. At present, private persons are allowed to own fixed-wing aircraft.

In 1992, there were 1.79 million telephone lines in the whole of Thailand. The Government has since mid-1991 launched a 5-year programme to install 3 million additional telephone lines, improving proportion from 2.88 lines to 10 lines per 100 population. It has been projected that by 1995 there will be a total of 5 million new telephone subscribers in the country. The Telephone Organization of Thailand and the Communications Authority of Thailand have been using the most modern technology in response to private and commercial requirements. These include the introduction of IDD, SPC, ISDN, satellite communication, radio paging services, cellular telephone services, fibre optic submarine cable networks and microwave networks. In December 1993, Thailand launched its first domestic communication satellite, "the Thaicom". A private company also plans to join a low earth orbit communication satellite system.

The launch of the Thailand's first satellite, "Thaicom".

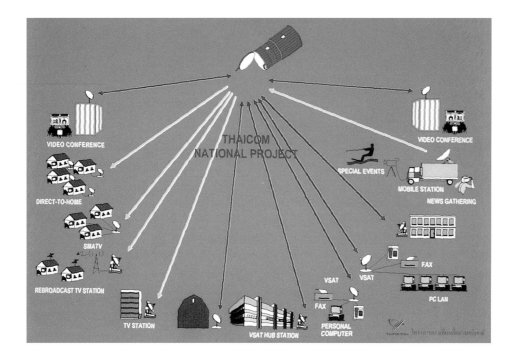

To cope with the fast growing demand for transport and communications infrastructure which has been a result of rapid economic expansion, the government has encouraged the private sector to participate. Thai and foreign investors have been invited to build and operate public utilities on a concession basis. Already in operation is the personal paging service. Contracts have also been concluded for an elevated expressway connecting the city and Bangkok International Airport as well as for northbound, southbound and eastbound multi-lane highways which are under construction. Also planned are a number of highways, commuter rail services and container terminals at Laem Chabang Port. The government hopes that this strategy will permit it to meet the immediate and future needs of the business community. Furthermore, the government has plans to liberalize some telecommunication services by amending the Telegraph and Telephone Act, 1934 to allow greater participation by the private sector in the provision of telecommunication services in Thailand.

Source : Ministry of Transport and Communications.

Laem Chabang Commercial Port.

The Eastern & Oriental Express carrying tourists from Singapore to Thailand via Kuala Lumpur and Penang.

TOURISM

Thailand has long been renowned among foreigners as the Land of Smiles and has become a popular tourist destination because of its many attractions located in various parts of the country, the friendliness and hospitality of its people, an efficient network of communications and transportation and other tourism-related infrastructure, as well as a high standard of service. All the above factors have contributed to the success tourism development of Thailand during 1990s.

Variety of Attractions and Culture

Thailand possesses a wide range of geographical features which vary from region to region. The North is a land of hills and mountains, the West is noted for its limestone caves, quiet river scenery, and waterfalls, while the eastern and southern regions are rimmed

by fine beaches and lush tropical islands, and the northeastern region is home to ancient Khmer ruins. The country has a long proud history and a vibrant culture which have left their mark in the many ancient religious edifices which are to be found in all regions. Throughout the country, there are more than 700 places of particular interest to tourists.

The North, for centuries an independent kingdom and a centre of culture and religion, is dotted with many ancient historical sites and monuments, among them the *Sukhothai Historical Park,* the *Doi Suthep Shrine* in Chiang Mai, and the *Phra Phuttha Chinnarat Image* in Phitsanulok. Northerners celebrate such festivals as *Songkran* (the traditional Thai New Year) and *Phao Thian Len Fai* (the candle festival), to name but two. The North is also home to a patchwork of hilltribes — the Musers, Yao, Meo, E-kaw, and Karen — who each possesses their own distinctive culture and way of life. The lowland northerners are noted as a gentle and hospitable people. In addition, the region abounds with many natural attractions such as mountain scenery, caves, waterfalls, and lakes. Other attractions include bargain hunting for local and tribal handicrafts in the bazaars and markets, while in the major towns Western-style night entertainment is widely available.

The Northeast was a centre of culture dating from prehistoric times through the Khmer period in the 12th and 13th centuries. The majority of tourist attractions in this region are historical sites which include the Khmer sanctuaries at Phanom Rung and Phimai, the *Phra That Phanom Shrine,* and Ban Chiang — site of a bronze-age culture dating back more than 5,000 years. Northeasterners celebrate their own festivals such as the *Bun Bang Fai* (rocket festival), the *Khao Phansa* (rains retreat) candle festival, and the *Prasat Phung* (wax castle festival). Local products of interest to tourists include handwoven cotton cloth, *mudmee* silk, wickerwork, and pottery.

The western and eastern regions are famed for their mountain scenery, caves, waterfalls, sandy beaches, and seaside resorts on the Gulf of Thailand, stretching from Rayong in the east to Prachuap Khiri Khan in the south. There are also many places of historical and religious interest, including the Grand Palace, the Temple of the Emerald Buddha, and many others in Bangkok and the *Phra Pathom Chedi* in Nakhon Pathom. Bangkok is a fascinating cosmopolitan city offering a variety of shopping and entertainments, while Pattaya, just over an hour away, is Thailand's premier seaside resort which combines the attractions of sun and sea with a dazzling nightlife scene. Local products of interest in this region include large variety of tropical fruits, seafood, spicy dishes of Thai cuisine, and Thai sweets.

The South, which is flanked on two sides by the Andaman Sea and the Gulf of Thailand, is lined with sandy beaches and palm-fringed islands lying just offshore. Many islands in the South are famous for picturesque coral reefs and fishes. They are ideal for scuba and skin diving, windsurfing and parasailing. Some of the finest beaches in the country are to be found in Phuket, Samui, and the islands in Phang-nga Bay, while inland are mountain scenery, caves, waterfalls, and steamy tropical jungles. The region was once a part of the mighty *Srivijaya Empire*. Many significant ruins dating from that period have been discovered, such as the *Chedi Wat Phra Mahathat* in Nakhon Si Thammarat, more than a thousand years old. The South is rich in culture and festivals such as the *Chak Phra* (pulling Buddha statue) and Tenth Lunar Month festivals. Unique to the region is the sport of bull fighting, while local products of interest include ornaments made from sea shells, pearl oysters, and hand-woven cloth.

Apart from natural resources, Thailand is also rich with various tourism activities. For example, exquisitely designed golf courses scatter in all regions. Several international competitions like marathon running, kite flying, and boat racing are held throughout the year. Besides, three of Thailand's various attractions: Ayutthaya Historical Park, Sukhothai Historical Park, and Huai Kha Khaeng Wildlife Sanctuary has recently been declared world heritage by UNESCO.

Contributions of Tourism

For 1994, visitor arrivals increased 7.05 percent with the total arrivals of 6.17 million and the country earned 145,211 million baht in tourism revenue with average length of stay mounting to 6.98 days and tourist expenditure per person per day equivalent to 3,373 baht. The government's policy is to spread the benefits of tourism to the provinces as widely as possible. As a result, the number of tourists making trips outside Bangkok has grown at a significant rate and the trend is towards even higher growth. It is also the government policy to facilitate the immigration process, such as visa on arrival and duration of stay, so as to foster more tourist arrivals as well as the average length of stay.

The development of tourism has helped preserve local customs and culture and has spurred on the work of restoring ancient monuments since these are of interest to tourists. By causing a demand for various handicrafts, tourism has also helped keep alive many traditional occupations which would otherwise have died out. The end result of all this activity is that the public is more aware of the nation's long history; seeing tourists coming to admire their country and what it has to offer has made Thais even prouder of their cultural heritage.

The tourist industry is composed of many sectors, among them hotels, transportation, travel agents, restaurants, and souvenir shops. In addition, many others are concerned indirectly with tourism such as souvenir manufacturers, food suppliers, and entertainers. Therefore, the income generated by tourism trickles down to all these areas. According to the study on "Labour Force in Tourism Industry 1992" conducted by the School of Applied Statistics, National Institute for Development and Administration (NIDA), Thailand's tourism industry has grown at a very high rate. As a result, the industry employs 1,693,005 people nationwide or 5.1 percent of Thailand's total labour force in 1992. It provides direct employment for 923,822 people while 769,183 people are indirectly employed. In terms of direct employment, hotel industry accounts for 37 percent of the total, followed by restaurants and food shops at 26 percent, and leisure and entertainment at 11 percent. The remaining 26 percent is in souvenir industry, transportation, tour operator and others.

Convenient Transportation

About 70 percent of all visitors to Thailand arrive by air through Bangkok's International Airport. From Bangkok, visitors fan out to all major provinces either by air, rail, car or coach. The country has a good system of highways stretching in every direction. Popular resorts and other tourist destinations are served by regular and reliable coach and bus services from the capital. Travel between provinces is also safe and comfortable, as there are good connecting highways. The State Railway of Thailand operates services to all regions of the country: the northern line to Chiang Mai; two northeastern lines, to Ubon Ratchathani and Nong Khai; the eastern line to Aranyaprathet; and the southern line which goes to Songkhla, connects with the Malaysian rail system and continues on to Singapore. For visitors with limited time, travel by air is also convenient since there are scheduled flights from Bangkok to more than 20 tourist destinations; Chiang Mai, Chiang Rai, Mae Hong Son, Lampang, Phrae, Nan, Phitsanulok, and Mae Sot/Tak in the North; Hat Yai/Songkhla, Phuket, Surat Thani, Nakhon Si Thammarat, Trang, Pattani, and Narathiwat in the South; and Nakhon Ratchasima, Khon Kaen, Udon Thani, Sakon Nakhon, Ubon Ratchathani, and Loei in the Northeast. As for travelling by water, boat trip to the floating market and river cruise to Ayutthaya are very notable. Pleasure cruise in dam's reservoir and rafting in the North are two other exciting activities while sea cruise to beautiful islands of the South, in the Gulf of Thailand and amid the Andaman Sea, is available all through the year. Visitors therefore have a wide choice of transportation and can plan their itineraries accordingly.

Bangkok is a commercial air hub for Southeast Asia and is served by 70 scheduled airlines. Travel to Thailand from any continent is thus fast and convenient.

Moreover, many new routes have been opened, while flight frequencies have also been increased. In addition to scheduled flights, there were more charter flights to Thailand from countries in Asia and Europe such as Hong Kong, Japan, People's Republic of China, Taiwan, Korea, Germany, France, United Kingdom, the Netherlands, Denmark, Switzerland, and Spain. Some of these charter flights landed directly at Phuket, Surat Thani and Chiang Mai, while others came to Bangkok. In 1994, there were 1,212 charter flights which carried 162,454 visitors to Thailand.

The government, meanwhile has carried out improvements on several airports, including the expansion of Bangkok's new domestic terminal and has installed modern navigation equipment at several provincial airports to conform with international standards. Improvements to Bangkok International Airport were completed at the end of 1988, increasing its efficiency and convenience for air travelers. The airport can now handle a peak load of 3,500 arrivals, 4,500 departures, and 4,500 transit passengers per hour. The apron can accommodate around 70 aircrafts. Modern facilities installed for the convenience of passengers include moving sidewalks, 56 immigration counters — 30 for inbound and 20 for outbound passengers, and 10 customs counters. Other facilities include duty-free shops, restaurants, foreign exchange counters, and both pay and toll-free telephone. The limousine and taxi services are available, while there is adequate level of bus and train services to the airport. There is ample parking for private cars. At the same time, the government planned to build another international airport at Nong Ngu Hao, which was expected to open in 2,000. At the moment, it is being under the study of detailed design.

Concerning the development of the transportation to new tourist destinations, the government agencies concerned are making plans and preparations to develop land, water and air routes to link tourist destinations along the borders of Thailand-Indochina-Myanmar-southern China into a new tourist region, with potential to draw a larger number of tourists to the area. Tourism agreements are being forged between Thailand and the neighbouring countries to lay the foundation of joint tourism development in the future.

Accommodations and Services

In 1994 Thailand has more than 4,850 hotels and other types of accommodation with over 246,113 rooms nationwide. The hotels range in quality from deluxe and first-class, with swimming pools, sports centre, conference facilities, and ballrooms, to low-budget guest houses and hotels providing just the basics in comfort and security. Hotel reservations can be made through a travel agent or through the Thai Hotels Association (THA) when booking any of its 200 members in Bangkok and the provinces. The THA also maintains a counter at Bangkok International Airport where visitors can make their bookings. Most local travel agents have connections with overseas agents in major markets. Therefore, visitors can plan their itineraries and make their hotel reservations before they leave home. Thai travel agents provide a friendly and professional service and most also offer good tour coaches and multi-lingual guides. The Thai Government has already promulgated the Tourist Business and Guide Act B.E. 2535 as a supplementary measure to protect tourists's benefits and to control the tour guides' operation to be in order. At the same time, the Tourist Police has been upgraded from the Sub-Division to the Division. Some more branches of the Tourist Police have been established in the major tourism cities throughout the country with a main aim to help the local police solve the tourists' problem of unsafety in their belongings and lives.

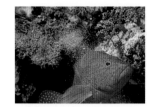

Tourism Resource Management

Several stages are required for the development and management of tourism resources. If a preliminary survey of the site indicates a good potential for development, a detailed follow-up study will be made to determine such factors as the economic condition of the

area, the available infrastructure and facilities, and how prepared the area could be for tourism development. The next step is to draw up a master plan to study in detail the tourism demand and supply, as well as to determine land use and infrastructure development in the area. The next step is a feasibility study to determine the economic rate of return on each project. Funding is obtained through either the government budget, or joint investment with the private sector, or entirely by private investment. The government negotiated for 1,100 million baht loan from the Japan Overseas Economic Cooperation Fund for use in the development of tourist-related infrastructure such as access roads to tourist sites, restoration of ancient monuments, development of national and historical parks, and so forth. These projects, scattered in all parts of the country, were implemented during 1988-1993.

The development of tourist attractions always has some impact on the environment which, if negative, will result in a decrease in popularity. The government is well aware of this and has attempted to limit or control development as well as stressing various measures for conservation of the environment in the tourist area.

Conclusion

Thailand has achieved considerable success in the development of its tourism industry. Government policies and guidelines have been drawn up for the systematic development of tourism, designed to sustain the long-term growth and at the same time raise the quality of tourism services. The government has also endeavoured to maintain diversity of visitors from various markets so that the country does not become dependent on any particular market, and this policy has paid considerable dividends. There has also been increased cooperation among government agencies as well as with the private sector to achieve greater efficiency. At the same time, the government has not neglected the social, cultural, and environmental impact of tourism and has formulated ways and means of preventing or alleviating these problems. It has also paid special attention to upgrading the skills of workers in the tourist industry so as to comply with international standards, as can be seen from the proliferation of institutes offering training in tourism skills.

To sum up, Thailand's tourism industry has thus been set on the right course of growth and is expected to remain the top income earner for many years to come, providing jobs for thousands of people and contributing to the equitable spread of income.

EXOTIC

Thailand

DISCOVER THE TREASURES OF A KINGDOM

THE TOURISM AUTHORITY OF THAILAND

Additional Tourist Information

More tourist information on Thailand can be available at the 17 TAT overseas offices scattered in the major cities around the world such as New York, Chicago, Los Angeles, London, Paris, Frankfurt, Rome, Tokyo, Osaka, Fukuoka, Seoul, Taipei, Hong Kong, Singapore, Kuala Lumpur, Vientiane and Sydney. Or contact the TAT Head Office as the following address:

Tourism Authority of Thailand (TAT)
372 Bamrung Muang Rd.,
Bangkok 10100, Thailand
Tel: (662) 226-0060, 226-0085
Fax: (662) 224-6221

LOOKING TO THE FUTURE

What will Thailand be like in the 90's ? This is a question to ponder, having witnessed how rapidly Thailand has transformed itself from a purely agricultural country into an agro-industrial one. The answer is, it seems, in the eye of the beholder.

For those looking at Thailand with economic foresight, a new decade opens up a new horizon of growing prosperity. New industries such as petrochemicals, pulp and paper, and large-scale garment manufacture develop alongside agriculture. Potash plants ensure the cheap production of chemical fertilizer which will benefit Thailand as an agro-industrial nation. The industrial development on the Southern Seaboard will bring wealth to the region. Yet with all this industrial development, Thailand still prides itself on its agriculture as it applies modern technology in the fields. A better infrastructure is now really underway and will speed development to accommodate pressing demands for a fast, effective and reliable communications network. One foresees high incomes but, at the same time, inevitably higher prices and inflation, a situation not unique to Thailand.

Those who keep watch on Thailand's rapid development out of an educational concern will wish to see more emphasis on education for the long-term development of human resources to serve the increasing demand for quality in all its aspects. The expansion of basic compulsory education from 6 to 9 years will be put into effect in the near future. There is a vital emphasis on science and technology at the tertiary level, in tune with the country's overall technological development.

Those who see Thailand's role from the global angle will also notice a tendency for Thailand to take a more prominent international and regional stance, looking towards the time when ASEAN becomes a common market with international standards, common rules and regulations to be observed, mutual understanding, and good will to be shared.

But any development at great speed and on a vast scale is bound to have an impact on social conditions. Those with a social conscience will be aware of the massive rural migration from all directions towards Bangkok in search of employment as result of the rapid growth of the nation's wealth. Although a labour force is essential for a newly industrialized nation, the government is faced with countless aggravation social problems caused by this migration of workers from rural areas; these call for sympathy, support and improved social welfare. Thailand is certainly aware of these problems and efforts are being made to find appropriate solutions.

Another effect of the outcome of rapid development is the environment, which finally seems to be a matter of increasing public concern. Lessons must be learnt from the past and measures taken to ensure that the environment will not be sacrificed to any form of development or modernization.

Altogether, the picture of Thailand in the 90's is a fascinating blend. As history tells us, the Thais have absorbed various foreign influences without losing their identity. Similarly, a number of changes may have taken place in the process of industrialization. Nevertheless, little has changed beyond recognition. At the heart of the nation, the monarchy remains a unifying force, the source of Thailand's political stability, and everywhere in Thailand, traditional ways of life can still be found. The modern art of the present day reflects Thailand's prestigious cultural heritage, merging past, present and future into one.

APPENDIX

Thailand's Economic Profile in Figures

A. Production and Investment

	1985	1986	1987	1988	1989	1990	1991	1992	1993	1994
Real GDP growth -Total	4.6%	5.5%	9.5%	13.3%	12.3%	11.6%	8.4%	7.9%	8.4%	8.7%
- Agriculture	4.5%	0.4%	0.1%	10.5%	9.7%	-3.7%	5.9%	4.2%	-1.7%	3.2%
- Manufacturing	-1.4%	9.8%	16.0%	17.9%	15.0%	16.0%	12.2%	11.3%	11.5%	11.5%
- Construction	-0.2%	1.5%	9.8%	12.7%	28.3%	22.0%	13.6%	5.1%	12.1%	10.2%
- Services & Others	8.0%	5.9%	9.8%	12.1%	9.8%	12.9%	6.5%	7.4%	8.7%	8.1%
GDP at current prices (bil.baht)	1,056	1,133	1,300	1,560	1,856	2,191	2,520	2,833	3,161	3,602
Bank of Thailand Investment Index	70.5	90.1	136.9	178.2	147.5	134.1	108.3	91.0	115.3	115.5

B. Population

	1985	1986	1987	1988	1989	1990	1991	1992	1993	1994
Population (mil.persons)	51.6	52.5	53.4	54.3	55.2	55.8	56.6	57.3	58.0	58.7
GDP per capita (baht)	20,473	21,576	24,332	28,716	33,615	39,238	44,543	49,447	54,491	61,349
Labour force (mil.persons)	26.1	27.0	28.0	29.7	30.8	31.0	31.3	32.5	32.3	32.6

C. External Sector

	1985	1986	1987	1988	1989	1990	1991	1992	1993	1994
Exports - value (bil.baht)	191.7	231.5	298.1	399.2	509.9	583.2	720.5	815.2	921.4	1,102.5
- growth	10.5%	20.8%	28.8%	33.9%	27.7%	14.4%	23.5%	13.1%	13.0%	19.7%
Imports - value (bil.baht)	253.3	245.7	341.4	500.1	649.7	838.6	967.8	1,020.6	1,143.1	1,343.0
- growth	4.60%	-3.0%	38.9%	46.5%	29.9%	29.1%	15.4%	5.5%	12.0%	17.5%
Trade balance (bil.baht)	-61.6	-14.2	-43.3	-100.9	-139.8	-255.4	-247.3	-205.4	-221.7	-240.5
Current account balance (bil.baht)	-41.9	6.5	-9.3	-41.8	-64.4	-186.2	-193.6	-161.3	-178.4	-213.8
(as percent of GDP)	-4.0%	0.6%	-0.7%	-2.7%	-3.5%	-8.5%	-7.7%	-5.7%	-5.6%	-5.9%
Net capital inflow (bil.baht)	51.4	11.4	27.6	94.1	144.5	247.8	288.2	251.6	284.6	361.8
Overall balance of payments (bil.baht)	12.5	33.6	24.1	62	102.3	97.2	105.8	77.1	98.8	104.8
Official reserves (bil.US$)	3.0	3.8	5.2	7.1	10.5	14.3	18.4	21.2	25.4	30.3
(in months of imports)	3.9	4.9	4.7	4.3	5.0	5.2	5.8	6.3	6.8	6.8
Total outstanding debt (bil.US$)	14.7	16.0	17.5	17.9	19.4	25.1	33.3	37.4	45.7	53.7
Debt service ratio - public **	11.1%	10.7%	9.4%	7.7%	5.8%	5.0%	4.2%	3.7%	3.7%	3.3%
- private **	11.6%	9.9%	7.7%	5.2%	4.8%	4.1%	5.6%	6.8%	7.0%	6.9%

D. Money and Prices

	1985	1986	1987	1988	1989	1990	1991	1992	1993	1994
Consumer price change (1990=100)	2.4%	1.9%	2.5%	3.8%	5.4%	6.0%	5.7%	4.1%	3.4%	5.1%
Growth of money supply (M2)	10.3%	13.4%	20.2%	18.2%	26.3%	26.7%	19.8%	15.6%	18.4%	12.9%
Growth of domestic credit (all)	12.3%	11.9%	17.4%	20.4%	28.8%	26.8%	19.9%	18.5%	19.7%	17.6%
Growth of deposits (all commercial banks)	11.6%	13.4%	20.2%	18.7%	26.9%	27.8%	21.0%	15.1%	18.6%	12.5%

E. Public Sector (Fiscal Year)

	1985	1986	1987	1988	1989	1990	1991	1992	1993	1994
Government revenue (bil.baht)	159.2	165.3	202.4	258.2	328.2	411.7	462.5	511.7	575.1	680.6
Government expenditure (bil.baht)	197.5	204	211.2	222.1	262.9	304.7	362.1	440.4	519.6	578.8
Fiscal deficit(-) surplus(+) (bil.baht)	-38.3	-38.7	-8.8	36.1	65.3	107	100.4	71.3	55.5	101.8
(as percent of GDP)	-3.6%	-3.4%	-0.7%	2.3%	3.5%	4.9%	4.0%	2.5%	1.8%	2.8%

F. Exchange Rate

	1985	1986	1987	1988	1989	1990	1991	1992	1993	1994
Baht/Dollar exchange rate (average selling rate)	27.16	26.30	25.78	25.34	25.75	25.64	25.57	25.45	25.37	25.2

Note: * GDP and other data from the National Economic and Social Develop
           ** payments of interest plus principal divided by the value of
              as of July 1995
Source: Bank of Thailand (except where noted)

Economic and Social Indicators

NATIONAL INCOME ACCOUNTS 1989-1994
GDP at Constant 1988 Prices

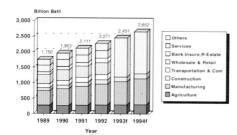

Billion Baht

Legend:
- Others
- Services
- Bank,Insure,R-Estate
- Wholesale & Retail
- Transportation & Com
- Construction
- Manufacturing
- Agriculture

Values: 1,750 (1989), 1,953 (1990), 2,111 (1991), 2,271 (1992), 2,451 (1993f), 2,652 (1994f)

Year

Source: National Economic and Social
Development Board (NESDB)

GDP BY SECTOR, 1993
Total 3,131.8 Billion Baht
At Current Prices

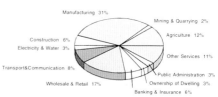

- Manufacturing 31%
- Mining & Quarrying 2%
- Agriculture 12%
- Construction 6%
- Electricity & Water 3%
- Other Services 11%
- Transport&Communication 8%
- Public Administration 3%
- Wholesale & Retail 17%
- Ownership of Dwelling 3%
- Banking & Insurance 6%

Sources: NESDB and Bank of Thailand

POPULATION BY AGE GROUPS, 1995
Projection, Medium Fertility Assumption

Age Groups

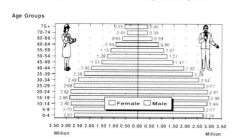

Female / Male

Million

Source:
Human Resources Planning Div.
NESDB

LABOUR FORCE SURVEY
1983-1995
Medium Fertility Assumption

Million Persons

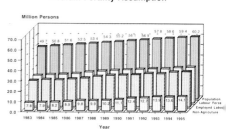

Year

Legend:
- Population
- Labour Force
- Employed Labo
- Non-Agriculture

Source: Human Resources Planning Div.
NESDB
Note: 1993-95 figures are projections.

MONEY SUPPLY and PRICE MOVEMENTS
1988-1994
M1, M2 and Consumer Price Index

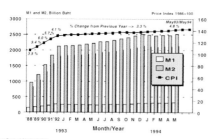

M1 and M2, Billion Baht — Price Index 1986=100

% Change from Previous Year --> 3.3 %

Legend:
- M1
- M2
- CPI

Month/Year

Source: Bank of Thailand and
Dept. of Business Economics

PER CAPITA GNP 1985-1994
at Current Prices

Thousand Baht — US.Dollar

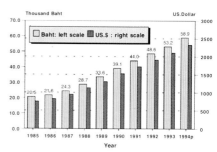

Baht: left scale / US.$: right scale

Values: 20.5 (1985), 21.6 (1986), 24.3 (1987), 28.7 (1988), 33.6 (1989), 39.1 (1990), 44.0 (1991), 48.6 (1992), 53.2 (1993), 58.9 (1994p)

Year

Source: NESDB

External Indicators

EXPORTS CLASSIFIED BY SECTORS
1980-1994

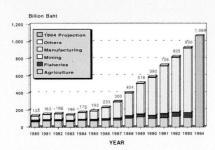

Source: Customs Dept.Ministry of Finance

EXPORTS BY COUNTRY
1993 Total 930,085 Million Baht

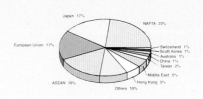

Source: Customs Dept.Ministry of Finance

IMPORTS BY ECONOMIC CLASSIFICATION
1980-1994

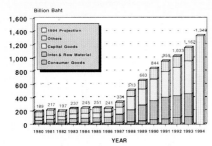

Source: Customs Dept.Ministry of Finance

IMPORTS BY COUNTRY
1993 Total 1,169,311Million Baht

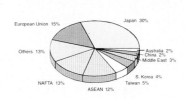

Source: Customs Dept.Ministry of Finance

EXTERNAL BALANCES
and Official Reserves
1985-1994

Source: Bank of Thailand

EXTERNAL DEBT SERVICE RATIO, 1977-93
and Long Term External Debt Outstandings

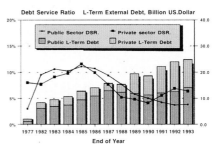

Source: Bank of Thailand
DSR = Debt Service Ratio

Domestic Indicators

INVESTMENT UNDER BOI PROGRAMMES
Total Investment Values 1991-1994

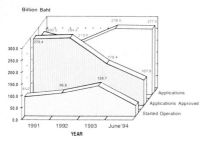

Source: Board of Investment (BOI)

Net Flows of Foreign Direct Investment
Classified by Country of Investor, 1993
Total 38,988 Million Baht

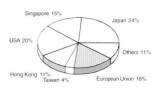

Source: Bank of Thailand's Estimation

BANKING SECTOR 1987-1994
Commercial Banks' Loan and Deposits

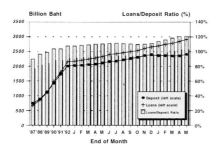

Source: Bank of Thailand

STOCK MARKET PERFORMANCE 1991-94
Securities Exchange of Thailand (SET)

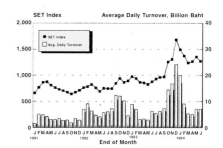

Source: Securities Exchange of Thailand

GOVERNMENT FINANCE
1984-1993

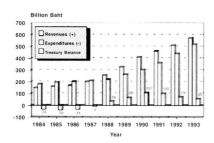

Sources: Comptroller-General's Department
and Bank of Thailand

GOVERNMENT EXPENDITURE BUDGET
Budgetary Appropriation: 715,000 M.Baht
Fiscal Year 1995

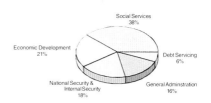

Source: Bureau of the Budget

Other Indicators

TOP 20 EXPORT EARNERS, 1993
and % Growth Rate from Previous Year

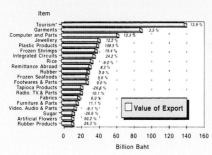

Sources: Bank of Thailand
Dept. of Business Economics
Tourism Authority of Thailand

Preliminary Figures

INTERNATIONAL TOURIST ARRIVALS
1993 Total 5,760,533 Persons

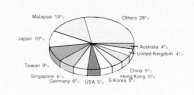

Source: Immigration Division
Police Department

SOURCES OF GROWTH 1992-1994
Percentage Real Growth Rates

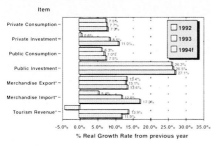

Source: NESDB estimations
Note: * = Current

COMMERCIAL PRIMARY ENERGY
and Net Import/Consumption 1976-93

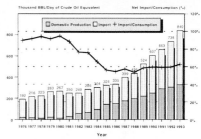

Source: National Energy Policy Office

EXCHANGE RATES, 1980-1994
Simple Average Free Market Rates

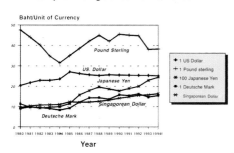

Source: Bank of Thailand

MEGA PROJECTS, 1992-2000
Selected Infrastructural Investments

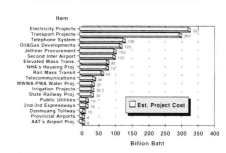

Sources: Bank of Thailand's estimation
and other sources

Bibliography

Arbhaphirama, A. ; *Thailand Natural Resources Profile : Is the Resource Base for Thailand's Development Sustainable?* Bangkok, 1987.

Blanchard, Wendell ; *Thailand : Its People, Its Society, Its Culture.*

Batson, Benjamin A. ; *The End of the Absolute Monarchy in Siam.* Singapore, 1984.

Bowring, Sir John ; *The Kingdom and People of Siam*, two volumes. Oxford University Press, 1977.

Bunnag, Tej ; *The Provincial Administration of Siam 1892-1915.* Kuala Lumpur, 1977.

Chakrabongse, Prince Chula ; *Lords of Life : A History of the Kings of Thailand.* London, 1967.

Chaloemtiarana, Thak ; *Thailand : The Politics of Despotic Paternalism.* Bangkok, 1979.

Chu, Valentin ; *Thailand Today : A Visit to Modern Siam.* New York, 1968.

de la Loubère. Simon ; *A New Historical Relation of the Kingdom of Siam.*

de Young, John E. ; *Village Life in Modern Thailand.* Los Angeles, 1963.

Henderson, John W. ; *Area Handbook for Thailand.*

Hutchinson, E.W. ; *Adventurers in Siam in the Seventeenth Century.* London, 1940.

Indhapanya, Wuttithep and Atikul, Jamlong ; *Economic Significance of Tourism in Thailand.* Bangkok, 1985.

Ishi, Yoneo ; *Thailand : A Rice Growing Society.* Honolulu, 1978.

Jintakannon, Nareewan ; *Tourist Industry Labour Force Survey 1987.* Bangkok 1988.

Kirsh, Thomas A. and Skinner, William G. ; *Change and Perspective in Thai Culture.* Ithica, 1975.

Klausner, William J. ; *Reflection in a Log Pond.* Bangkok, 1974.

Matthews, Eunice S. ; *The Land and People of Thailand.* New York, 1964.

Moermann, Michael ; *Agricultural Change and Peasant Choice in a Thai Village*. Los Angeles, 1968.

Moffat, Abbot Low ; *Mongkut the King of Siam*. New York, 1961.

Mokarapong, Thawatt ; *History of the Thai Revolution*. Bangkok, 1972.

Panayotou, T. ; *Food Policy Analysis in Thailand*. Bangkok 1985.

Phillips, Herbet ; *Thai Peasant Personality*. Los Angeles, 1965.

Pramoj, M.R. Seni and M.R. Kukrit ; *A King of Siam Speaks*. Bangkok, 1987.

Rabibhadana, M.R. Akin ; *The Organization of Thai Society in the Early Bangkok Period, 1782-1873*. New York, 1960.

Rajadhon, Phya Anuman ; *Life and Ritual in Old Siam*. New Haven, 1961.

Rajadhon, Phya Anuman ; *Essays on Thai Folklore*. Bangkok, 1968.

Seidenfaden, Major Erik ; *The Thai Peoples*. Bangkok, 1967.

Sernstein, Larry ; *Thailand, the Environment of Modernization*. Sydney, 1976.

Syamananda, Rong ; *A History of Thailand*. Bangkok, 1973.

Tramot, Montri ; *Thai Games*. Bangkok, 1953.

Vella, Walter F. ; *Chaiyo! King Vajiravudh and the Development of Thai Nationalism*. Honolulu, 1978.

Wyatt, David K. ; *Thailand : A Short History*. London, 1984.

Wales, H.G. Quaritch ; *Ancient Siamese Government and Administration*. London, 1934.

Bank of Thailand ; *Monthly Bulletins*. Bangkok, 1989.

Ministry of Agriculture and Cooperatives ; *Agricultural Statistics of Thailand Crop Year 1988/89*. Bangkok, 1989.

Ministry of Agriculture and Cooperatives; *Agriculture in Thailand*. Bangkok, 1992.

Ministry of Education; *Secondary Education and Special Education in Thailand*. Bangkok, 1993.

Tourism Authority of Thailand ; *Annual Statistical Report on Tourism in Thailand*. Bangkok, 1988.

World Bank ; *Thailand : Country Economic Memorandum*. New York, 1989.

Index

Acknowledgements

The Editorial Board is especially grateful to

General Prem Tinsulanonda, Statesman and Privy Counsellor

Dr. Supote Dechates, Deputy Secretary-General, Office of Agricultural Economics, Ministry of Agriculture and Cooperatives

Mr. Suvidhya Simaskul, Director-General, Department of Informations, Ministry of Foreign Affairs

Dr. Sarin Skulratana, Director, Planning Division, Ministry of Transport and Communications

Dr. Kanchit Malaivongs, Deputy Director, National Electronics and Computer Technology Centre (NECTEC)

Khun Nillawan Pinthong

Royal Thai Air Force

Krung Thai Bank Public Co., Ltd.

Tourism Authority of Thailand

Special Acknowledgements: particular thanks to

> Mr. Chukiat Utakapan
> Mr. Smat Ruangnarong
> Mr. Paisan Wangsai
> Miss Busakorn Noonil
> Miss On-anong Karuna

for their support and contribution to the publication of this book.

Thailand in the 90s (Revised Edition) was produced under the supervision of a subcommittee, chaired by **Prof. Dr. Thienchai Srivichit,** and comprised of the following members:

Dr. Suvit Yodmani
Khunying Kullasap Gesmankit
Mr. Seree Wangpaichitr
Mr. Prapun Naigowit
Mrs. Subhat Sawasdirak
Mrs. Phenkhae Wajanasoontorn
M.L. Panadda Diskul
Miss Orasa Varamisra
Mr. Suchaya Kasjamras

Dr. Yenchai Laohavanich
Khunying Somsri Kantamala
Mr. Somporn Kongsit
Mr. Maytee Leelawat
Mrs. Amara Panananda
Mrs. Choochit Hawkey
Dr. Sumlee Thongthew
Miss Yingprathana Kaoplung
Mr. Poj Hanpol

Mr. Krit Umpote
Mrs. Achaphan Buncharoen
Mrs. Sumalee Ketkaeo
Miss Nipawan Wannasathop

Pictorial Editor

Mr. Seree Wangpaichitr

Photographic Credits

Bureau of the Royal Household
The Office of His Majesty's Principal Private Secretary
Department of Information, Ministry of Foreign Affairs
Department of Public Welfare, Ministry of Labour and Social Welfare
Department of General Education, Ministry of Education
National Energy Policy Office, Office of the Prime Minister
The Armed Forces Information Office, Supreme Command Headquarters
Office of the National Culture Commission, Ministry of Education
The Faculty of Painting, Sculpture and Graphic Arts, Silpakorn University
Ministry of Justice
Ministry of Agriculture and Cooperatives
The National Commission on Women's Affairs, Office of the Prime Minister
Office of the Board of Investment
The Electricity Generating Authority of Thailand
Port Authority of Thailand

Anw... International Public Company Limited
Tourism Authority of Thailand
Shinawatra Satellite Public Company Limited
Eastern & Oriental Express
Komol Keemthong Foundation (*60 Years of Suan Mokkh: Pictorial Journey*)
Mr. Suchaya Kasjamras
Mr. Noppadol Santichart
Mr. Surapol Supavattanakul
Mr. Bancha Chunprapanusorn
Miss Anutra Hongsuwan
Mr. Prayudh Panyasiri
Mr. Kitti Chansong

Design by

Miss Ratchanee Thainirunprasert

Published by

The National Identity Office
Office of the Prime Minister, Bangkok, Thailand, 1995.

Copyright

© 1995 by Office of the Prime Minister, Royal Thai Government
All rights reserved. Published in 1991. Revised Edition 1995.

Printed by

Amarin Printing and Publishing Public Company Limited
Bangkok, Thailand.
Tel. 882-1010

ISBN 974-8363-68-6